Pan-African History

Pan-Africanism, the perception by people of African origins and descent that they have interests in common, has been an important by-product of colonialism and the enslavement of African peoples by Europeans. Though it has taken a variety of forms over the two centuries of its fight for equality and against economic exploitation, commonality has been a unifying theme for many Black people, resulting for example in the Back-to-Africa movement in the United States but also in nationalist beliefs such as an African 'supra-nation'.

Pan-African History brings together Pan-Africanist thinkers and activists from the Anglophone and Francophone worlds of the past two hundred years. Included are well-known figures such as Malcolm X, W.E.B. Du Bois, Frantz Fanon, Kwame Nkrumah, and Martin Delany, and the authors' original research on lesser-known figures such as Constance Cummings-John and Dusé Mohamed Ali reveals exciting new aspects of Pan-Africanism.

Hakim Adi is Senior Lecturer in African and Black British History at Middlesex University, London. He is a founder member and currently Chair of the Black and Asian Studies Association and is the author of *West Africans in Britain 1900–1960: Nationalism, Pan-Africanism and Communism* (1998) and (with M. Sherwood) *The 1945 Manchester Pan-African Congress Revisited* (1995).

Marika Sherwood is a Senior Research Fellow at the Institute of Commonwealth Studies, University of London. She is a founder member and Secretary of the Black and Asian Studies Association; her most recent books are *Claudia Jones: A Life in Exile* (2000) and *Kwame Nkrumah: The Years Abroad 1935–1947* (1996).

Pan-African History

Political figures from Africa and the
Diaspora since 1787

Hakim Adi and Marika Sherwood

Routledge
Taylor & Francis Group

LONDON AND NEW YORK

First published 2003 by
Routledge
11 New Fetter Lane, London EC4P 4EE

Simultaneously published in the USA and Canada by
Routledge
29 West 35th Street, New York, NY 10001

Routledge is an imprint of the Taylor & Francis Group

© Hakim Adi and Marika Sherwood

Typeset in Garamond by
HWA Text and Data Management, Tunbridge Wells
Printed and bound in Great Britain by
The Cromwell Press, Trowbridge, Wiltshire

British Library Cataloguing in Publication Data
A catalogue record for this book is available from the British Library

Library of Congress Cataloging in Publication Data
Sherwood, Marika.
  Pan-African history : political figures from africa and the diaspora since
  1787 / Marika Sherwood and Hakim Adi.
      p. cm.
  Includes index.
    1. Pan-Africanism–History. 2. Black nationalism–History.
  3. Nationalists–Africa–Biography. 4. African Americans–Biography.
  I. Adi, Hakim, II. Title.

  DT30 .S515 2003
  320. 54′9′092396–dc21   2002011566

ISBN 0–415–17352–3 (hbk)
ISBN 0–415–17353–1 (pbk)

Contents

Preface   vii

Dusé Mohamed Ali   1
Ahmed Ben Bella   7
Edward Wilmot Blyden   11
Amilcar Lopes Cabral   16
Aimé Césaire   20
Quobna Ottobah Cugoano   26
Constance Cummings-John   29
Martin Robinson Delany   34
Cheikh Anta Diop   40
Frederick Douglass   44
W.E.B. Du Bois   48
Olaudah Equiano   53
Nathaniel Akinremi Fadipe   57
Frantz Fanon   64
Amy Ashwood Garvey   69
Marcus Garvey   76
Joseph Ephraim Casely Hayford   82
James Africanus Beale Horton   86
W. Alphaeus Hunton   90
C.L.R. James   95
Claudia Jones   100
Martin Luther King Jr   105
Toussaint L'Ouverture   109
Patrice Émery Lumumba   113
Ras T. Makonnen   117
Malcolm X   123
Nelson Rolihlahla Mandela   129
Harold Moody   134
Jamal Abd al-Nasir [Nasser]   138
Francis Nwia Kofi Kwame Nkrumah   143
Julius Kambarage Nyerere   147
George Padmore   152

Paul Leroy Robeson   159
Walter Rodney   163
Léopold Sédar Senghor   169
Ladipo Felix Solanke   174
Sékou Ahmed Touré   177
I.T.A. Wallace-Johnson   181
Eric Williams   185
Henry Sylvester Williams   190

Index   195

Preface

The dawn of the twenty-first century coincided with an upsurge in Pan-African activity, the most obvious example being the creation of the new African Union by Africa's governments, largely as a response to the adverse consequences of globalisation.[1] Fears about globalisation have also led to a renewed interest in diasporas and 'transnational studies' and consequently there is a continuing and increasing interest in the history and significance of the African diaspora, the global dispersal of peoples of African descent, responsible for the emergence of Pan-African ideologies.[2]

However, there has never been one universally accepted definition of what constitutes Pan-Africanism. Most recent writers on the subject are reluctant to provide definitions or provide several, acknowledging that the vagueness of the term reflects the fact that Pan-Africanism has taken different forms at different historical moments and geographical locations. Others, recognising that definition is dependent on time and place, feel forced to provide lengthy historical explanations of the development of the various Pan-African ideas and movements that have emerged since the late eighteenth century.[3]

So what do we mean by major figures from Pan-African history? Our definition includes women and men of African descent whose lives and work have been concerned, in some way, with the social and political emancipation of African peoples and those of the African diaspora. Not surprisingly their perspectives have differed, according to time, location and the nature of the problems they confronted. Some may have focused on just one part of Africa, North America, the Caribbean or Europe, yet their lives and work have achieved symbolic status, or been influential amongst people of African descent and others struggling against oppression and for liberation. What underlies their manifold visions and approaches is the belief in some form of unity or of common purpose among the peoples of Africa and the African diaspora.

Such perspectives might be traced back to ancient times, but modern Pan-African history is principally connected with the dispersal of peoples of African origin brought about by the trans-Atlantic trade taking enslaved Africans to the Americas, at the beginning of the sixteenth century, and the subsequent emergence of global capitalism, European colonial rule and imperialism. Pan-African history therefore includes chronicling a variety of ideas, activities and movements that celebrated Africaness, resisted the exploitation and oppression of those of African descent, and opposed the ideologies of racism.

Our earliest entries are three activists of the eighteenth century who played a significant role in the struggles against slavery and racism: Toussaint L'Ouverture, the leader of the revolution in St Domingue, the only successful slave revolution in history, helped to establish Haiti as a symbol of the possibility of successful liberation and African independence in the Western hemisphere. The two British-based writers and activists, Olaudah Equiano and Ottobah Cugoano, pioneered the writing of the slave narrative and were influential champions of the humanity of Africans and the abolitionist cause.

During the nineteenth century the existence of legal slavery and the trade in enslaved Africans continued in many parts of the Americas and Africa, while in Africa itself, European colonial activity increased throughout the century, culminating in the so-called 'scramble' for Africa and the onset of the era of imperialism. As in previous centuries, the crimes perpetrated against those of African descent were excused and justified by racist ideologies which now sometimes assumed a pseudo-scientific form. For most activists, in this period of Pan-African history, the struggle to 'vindicate the race' and refute notions of African inferiority was a necessity that became one of the dominant themes in their writing and activism. For some in the diaspora, like Martin Delany and Edward Blyden, a physical return to Africa was seen as vital, not least for the 'regeneration' of the continent itself. Others, such as Frederick Douglass, the foremost African American activist of the nineteenth century, took a different view and were determined to struggle to end legal slavery and to gain their rights in the USA, the country of their former enslavement.

In Africa itself, Sierra Leonean James Horton, was just one of those who began to develop the principles of a new political science that concerned itself with the possibilities and principles of African self-government and an embryonic nationalism. The nineteenth-century activists have been seen as significant pioneers in the development of Pan-African thinking. Horton and Edward Blyden laid the foundations for the nationalist movements and ideologies that were later developed by J.E. Casely Hayford and others in West Africa in the early twentieth century. Blyden was the inspiration for the Francophone Négritude movement, while it was Delany who first used the phrase 'Africa for the Africans', later associated with, and popularised by, Marcus Garvey.

The organised Pan-African movement can be said to have begun with the founding of the African Association in London in 1897 and the subsequent convening, in the same city, of the first Pan-African conference three years later.[4] Led by the Trinidadian Henry Sylvester Williams, the early twentieth-century Pan-Africanists were concerned with strengthening the unity of all those of African descent, so as to solve what they saw as 'the problem of the twentieth century ... the problem of the colour line', and to 'secure civil and political rights for Africans and their descendants throughout the world'. The struggle against colonialism and the activities of the imperialist powers in Africa, the Caribbean and elsewhere also became one of the most important issues for Pan-Africanists during the first part of the century. Some, such as Dusé Mohamed Ali, believed that economic considerations must inform their Pan-African vision and maintained that the development of business and trade connections were crucial if 'true independence' was to be achieved. One of the key figures in Pan-African history in the early twentieth century, the Jamaican Marcus Garvey, combined political and economic aims with the advocacy of a physical and psychological return to the African continent.

During the 1930s, Pan-Africanism was strongly influenced by the international communist movement and by socialist, anti-imperialist and internationalist perspectives, such as those developed by the Profintern's International Trade Union Committee of Negro Workers. It was these perspectives that informed the activism and writing of George Padmore and Isaac Wallace-Johnson and the work of Alphaeus Hunton, Paul Robeson and W.E.B. Du Bois in the Council of African Affairs and elsewhere. C.L.R. James was of course for many years one of the leading figures in the international Trotskyist movement, while Marxism and an internationalist perspective were also present in the life and work of Claudia Jones, Frantz Fanon, Aimé Césaire and Walter Rodney.

Before 1945 many of the leading political figures in Pan-African history lived and worked in the diaspora rather than in Africa itself. Indeed for a time Europe might be seen as a centre of the Pan-African world. The influential Négritude movement was originated by Césaire and Senghor while they were studying in Paris and many others from Africa and the Caribbean, including Cheikh Anta Diop, Harold Moody, Nathaniel Fadipe and Ladipo Solanke, first became active during their time as students or workers living in France or Britain, the two leading colonial powers. The series of Pan-African congresses organised by W.E.B. Du Bois were also mostly held in Europe, while the 1945 Pan-African Congress, which some have seen as the apogee of the Pan-African movement, was organised and held in Manchester in Britain. After 1945 however, the focus of Pan-African activity certainly switched to Africa and to a growing concern for a continental unity that could contribute to the liberation of Africa from colonial rule and end the inequalities suffered by all those of African descent around the world. Indeed some of the key figures whose lives and work had begun outside Africa, ended their lives on the continent, for example, George Padmore and W.E.B. Du Bois in Ghana, and Alphaeus Hunton in Zambia.

Pan-Africanism within Africa was greatly stimulated by the career of Kwame Nkrumah and by the end of formal British colonial rule in the Gold Coast in 1957. Independent Ghana became a beacon that drew many from the diaspora to Africa, but it also played an important role in building a new type of Pan-Africanism, centred on the African continent, which, in 1963, culminated in the founding of the Organisation of African Unity. Nkrumah's vision of African unity was also shared by Guinea's Sékou Touré, by the Algerian leader Ahmed Ben Bella and by others including Julius Nyerere of Tanzania. But as in Algeria, political independence came slowly in some parts of Africa and had to be fought for in prolonged wars of national liberation. One of the most influential of the leaders emerging from this period of Africa's history was Amilcar Cabral who, until his assassination in 1973, led the anti-colonial struggle against Portugal in Cape Verde.

The liberation of the African continent from the last vestiges of settler colonialism and racism could not be completed without the ending of apartheid in South Africa. There were many key and heroic figures in that lengthy struggle and we have included the most famous, Nelson Mandela, the twentieth-century's most famous political prisoner and his country's first Black president, eventually became a celebrated figure in South Africa and abroad and a symbol for African liberation throughout the continent and the diaspora.

Choosing our subjects was no easy task: why omit, for example, the nineteenth-century Pan-Africanists Alexander Crummell and Bishop James T. Holly or Mojola Aghebi of Nigeria and the Haitian Benito Sylvain? One reason is that to have included these and many others worthy of inclusion would have required more than one volume. We have tried to include some, but undoubtedly not all, key political figures from Africa, the Caribbean, the United States and Britain and our aim has been to keep some sense of balance between the number of entries from each geographical region. We recognise that there is a distinct Anglophone bias in our choices. We have, for example, not included any figures from South America. In some ways, this could be said to reflect the historical development of modern Pan-African ideas and movements that have mainly been centred in the Anglophone world, and from which such figures as Martin Delany, Henry Sylvester Williams, Isaac Wallace-Johnson, C.L.R. James and Walter Rodney have emerged. However, we have also included several key activists, writers and thinkers from other parts of the world who have an international as well as a Pan-African significance. These include Senghor and Césaire, the principal founders of the Négritude movement, and Patrice Lumumba, Frantz Fanon, Cheikh Anta Diop and Amilcar Cabral. We have also sought to include some 'neglected' figures, who either are not as well known as perhaps they should be, or who hitherto have not been favoured with biographies: the two Nigerians Nathaniel Fadipe and Ladipo Solanke, the Sierra Leonean Constance Cummings-John and the Guyanese activist Ras T. Makonnen would be included in this category.

Is it not possible that there were more key women figures in this Pan-African history, or simply that many have gone unrecognised? It may be that their oppression prevented women from playing as active a role as men in political affairs. Undoubtedly it was not, and still is not, easy to rise to the fore in a 'man's world'. But it can also be argued that scholars have not sufficiently turned their attention to the lives and contributions of women. The general lack of research on the contributions of women in Pan-African history is sadly reflected in this book. Had Constance Cummings-John not written an autobiography she would have remained unknown except to those who admired her around the world. There is no substantial research on the life and work of Amy Ashwood Garvey, who is included here, and none at all on Eslanda Goode Robeson, who is thus, most regrettably, omitted from this work. Claudia Jones, who is included here, is the subject of a recent biography, but that only deals with the last ten years of her life.

Length of entries does not reflect the importance of the individual, but more the availability of other materials to readers. Thus the length of the entry on Nathaniel Fadipe is due to the fact that it reflects wholly original research as there are no biographical entries on him anywhere. On Amy Ashwood Garvey the only available materials are a brief biographical article and a biography based on some of her rescued papers still held privately and not available to researchers. Thus, again much of the research is original. Other entries provided different challenges: for example, although there are articles in print on some aspects of Dusé Mohamed Ali's life, the life itself had to be pieced together from these, a dissertation on him, and again, original research.

Where an individual led a very full life, such as for example, Julius Nyerere and Eric Williams, our text focuses on their Pan-Africanist activities or writings. For literary figures, such as Césaire, or authors whose life and work might be little known, such as Cugoano, we felt it necessary to include at least some quotations from their essays, poems or plays. In 'Further reading' we have only included biographical material; works by the subject of the entry not listed in the text are listed separately under 'Main publications'.

Many of the people we have chosen to write about knew or collaborated with each other. To take just one example, Constance Cummings-John had links with Alphaeus Hunton, Ladipo Solanke, Harold Moody and George Padmore. These links are indicated in the text by the highlighting of the person's name.

The word 'Black' is used to denote Africans or people of African descent.

Notes

1 Perhaps the most significant and historic manifestation of twenty-first century Pan-Africanism occurred in Sirte, Libya in March 2001, when over forty African heads of state and government proclaimed the creation of the African Union, the Pan-African body seen by many as a step towards the 'United States of Africa' envisaged by earlier Pan-Africanists such as Kwame Nkrumah. The African Union, developed to replace the Organisation of African Unity (OAU), will have its own executive assembly, parliament and court and will lead to the creation of a common defence, foreign and communications policy, as well as closer economic ties between all African countries. It was established because many African countries recognised the necessity of combating the adverse consequences of globalisation and the African continent's continued marginalisation in international affairs.

2 The term 'African diaspora' is itself of fairly recent origin, although the concept itself is considerably older. For a discussion of this concept see J.E. Harris, 'The Dynamics of the Global African Diaspora' in A. Jalloh and S.E. Maizlish (eds), *The African Diaspora*, Texas, A&M University Press, 1996 and G. Shepperson, 'African Diaspora: Concept and Context', in J.E. Harris (ed.), *Global Dimensions of the African Diaspora* [2nd edition], Washington, DC, Howard University Press, 1993, pp.41–51.

3 Some recent writers recognising the difficulty of providing a definition have been more interested in 'rethinking Pan-Africanism and re-evaluating its various expressions and manifestations'. See for example, Lemelle and Kelley's 'Introduction – Imagining Home: Pan-Africanism Revisited', in S.J. Lemelle and R.D.G. Kelley (eds), *Imagining Home – Class, Culture and Nationalism in the African Diaspora*, London, Verso, 1994. For other working definitions of Pan-Africanism see George Shepperson, 'Pan-Africanism and "Pan-Africanism": Some Historical Notes', *Phylon*, 23, 1962, pp.353–4, and St Clair Drake, 'Diaspora Studies and Pan-Africanism,' in J.E. Harris (ed.), *Global Dimensions of the African Diaspora* [2nd edition], Washington, DC, Howard University Press, 1993, pp.451–515.

4 See P.O. Esedebe, *Pan-Africanism – The Idea and the Movement 1776–1963*, Washington, DC, Howard University Press, 1982, pp.45–6, for the assertion that the 1893 Chicago Congress on Africa should be seen as the 'beginning of Pan-Africanism as a movement' and the occasion when the term 'pan-African' was first used.

Dusé Mohamed Ali
(1866 – 1945)

An itinerant, well-travelled actor in the first half of his life, Dusé Mohamed Ali spent the second half writing and working against what he called the 'rising tide of aggression, segregation and oppression which threatens to engulf us. Combines [combinations of large European companies] in African raw commodities … threaten to undermine the very fabric of African agriculture and Native endeavour'. He was thus the first modern Pan-Africanist to understand the absolute necessity for an economic approach to the liberation of Africa and Africans.

Mohamed Ali, by his own account, was the son of an Egyptian army officer and his Sudanese wife. At an early age he was sent to England to be educated and as apparently he could return home only infrequently, he lost his native language/s. In 1882 his father and brother were killed in the bombardment of Alexandria which led to the British occupation of Egypt. His mother and sisters, whom he never saw again, fled to the Sudan. It seems that he acquired the name Dusé from a French captain by that (or a similar) name who thought 'Mohamed Ali' made him indistinguishable from all the others bearing that name.

Bereft of family financial and other support, the sixteen-year-old had to leave school. He worked as an actor in Britain and the USA, and wrote some plays, which, though performed, were unsuccessful. He apparently worked his way around the world, visiting India, North, South and Central America, and the Caribbean. In the USA he worked for a while as a 'penny-a-liner' journalist. Returning to Britain, he reverted to the stage and began writing for the British press. From 1909 he was a regular contributor to the liberal weekly *New Age*, criticising various aspects of contemporary society, advocating Egyptian nationalism and castigating the oppression of Black peoples. His writings demonstrated that Ali was a well-read man.

In London from a recent trip to Egypt Theodore Roosevelt, in a public speech, and to considerable applause, urged on Britain the necessity of using 'violence and injustice' in dealing with the 'uncivilized' and 'fanatical' Egyptians, whose attempt at self-government was a 'noxious farce'. Ali was incensed, and immediately took up the *New Age* editor's advice to write not an article but a book refuting Roosevelt. *In the Land of the Pharaohs* was published in 1911 in both London and New York, and won instant acclaim for having been written by a 'real Egyptian' with 'inside knowledge'. That the latter was not true, and that much of the book had been copied from previous publications, did not detract from Ali's new fame, even when the plagiarism was made public. Ali duly apologised. However, his excoriation of British racism and imperialism and his forecasting the end of the British empire, as well as his castigation of Roosevelt as the ex-president of a country which condoned the 'lynching and burning of defenceless Negroes', endeared him to readers in the subjugated world, who must have seen through the book's occasional attempts to placate English readers.

Ali was duly invited to attend the bland Universal Races Congress in 1911, which focused on creating a 'better understanding between races'. He was put in charge of publicity and the entertainments. Among the few Black men at the Congress were W.E.B. Du Bois and the Sierra Leonean entrepreneur John Eldred Taylor.

Taylor proposed financing a newspaper. Already convinced that something had to be done about the lack of contacts between Africans, Asians and their descendants in the diasporas, Ali promptly accepted. However, this relationship broke down and the financing of the *African Times & Orient Review* (*AT&OR*), which had begun to appear in July 1912, passed to a consortium of West African professionals and businessmen, which included J.E. Casely Hayford. After a hiatus during the First World War, the consortium was enlarged and the paper was renamed *The Africa and Orient Review*, but was indistinguishable from its predecessor. The final edition appeared in 1920.

The *AT&OR* intended to 'lay the aims, desires and intentions of the Black, Brown and Yellow races ... at the throne of Caesar' and to present 'the truth about the African and Oriental condition that is rarely stated with precision and accuracy in the columns of the European press'. It was thus following in the footsteps of Henry Sylvester Williams' journal, the *Pan African*. The *AT&OR* exposed abuses in the British colonies, which provided material for questions in parliament by supportive MPs, and carried news and information on and from the African and Asian worlds, and on Islam, of which Ali was a strong supporter. (He was also occasionally anti-Semitic.) The *AT&OR* supported business, and appealed to African Americans to enter into trading relationships with Africans in order to supplant the existing exploitative European/African relationships. Ali also exhorted his readers to unity; as he explained in an editorial:

> Europe stretches out her hands on every side to squeeze the darker races to her advantage, because she knows the people of Africa and the people of Asia to be divided. Her aim has been to promote division. It therefore behoves you, men of Asia, men of Africa, to join yourselves in one common bond of lasting friendship.
>
> (*AT&OR*, November 1912)

The *AT&OR* was distributed widely in the Black and Islamic worlds, whose representatives thronged Ali's offices at 158 Fleet Street. Copies were placed in the saloons of steamships

Among the supporters of the paper was Samuel Coleridge-Taylor, the British composer of African descent, who recommended the paper in its first issue as 'setting out to be the medium for promoting a better understanding between the Orient and the Occident ... It should be welcomed by all thoughtful and unprejudiced people ... [and] heartily supported by the coloured people themselves'. Privately, he promised Ali to 'do my best to secure you subscribers'. Other contributors to this exciting new paper included the nationalists Sundara Raja of India, Muhammad Farid of Egypt and Frank O'Donnell of Ireland; Zaffar Ali Khan and Kamal al-Din of the Woking Mosque, respectively the editors of the *Zamindar* of India and the London-based *Islamic Review*; Josiah Gumede, the future president of the African National Congress; notable African Americans William Ferris and John E. Bruce, who had been impressed by *In the Land of the Pharaohs*, and Booker T. Washington; among the Africans was the Gold Coaster Kobina Sekyi. Another contributor was MARCUS GARVEY, who in 1912–13 worked at the *AT&OR* offices in an unsubstantiated capacity; his article 'The British West Indies in the mirror of civilisation: history making by colonial Negroes' was published in the October 1913 issue. Undoubtedly, Garvey must have derived many of his ideas on African nationalism from Ali, and the many political activists who visited the *AT&OR* office.

The paper and the publication of his book naturally made Ali well-known amongst people in Britain interested in the colonies. This, for example, led to his involvement with a conference convened in 1913 by the African Society and the Anti-Slavery Society, to discuss 'the best way of helping Africans in London'. The conference sent a proposal to the Colonial Office for the establishment of an African Club for students to 'shelter' them from 'harmful influences'. Ali had criticised the proposal, maintaining that such a hostel should not be under government supervision; he also suggested the establishment of universities in Africa as a substitute.

Ali also became involved with – and established – many organisations, Islamic, Ottoman, Egyptian. Perhaps the most important was the African Progress Union (APU) formed in about 1918 by Africans and West Indians resident in London. The APU supported delegations from Africa arriving in Britain; demanded the restoration of German colonies to Africans, and that the 'principle of self-determination', promulgated for small European nations, should also be applied to African colonies. These contacts were added to those Ali had already made through the *AT&OR* when he had become involved in trading enterprises.

It is not known why Ali did not attend either the 1919 or the 1921 Du Boisian Pan-African congresses. This is especially surprising in view of his wide-ranging interests as evidenced, for example, by his being one of the presenters of a scroll to African American singer Roland Hayes in recognition of his work which would 'redound ... to the amelioration and recognition of the undoubted mental capacities and endowments of your brothers of the Negro Race'. Among the signatories were ten West Africans and one Trinidadian.

The British government, which had been keeping Ali under surveillance, concluded that Ali was a 'notorious disseminator of sedition'. It banned the *AT&OR* in India and Africa in 1916, and turned down Ali's 1914 and 1917 requests for a 'safe conduct' to visit West Africa. However, in 1920 a permit was issued. Ali's purpose was to discuss with local businessmen the plans he had proposed to an African American banker to set up branches in West Africa. He argued that a 'native bank' was needed as the European banking monopoly 'strangled native enterprise'. Guaranteed deposits were needed for the scheme to succeed. Though the Lagosians received Ali warmly, the Lagos businessmen were not enthusiastic about the proposal. Those in Ibadan and the Gold Coast were. Ali set up the Inter-Colonial Corporation with six Gold Coasters in September 1920 as a 'co-operative scheme to benefit the small African trader deserving a greater scope than is possible under the present system'. (*West African Mail*, 18 June 1921) The aim was to export produce, bypassing the powerful British export monopolies.

Ali's next step was a trip to the USA, to interest Negro businessmen in the Corporation. He had enlisted the support of John E. Bruce, who had been the major African American distributor and supporter of the *AT&OR* and had previously manifested an interest in such ventures. However, the manipulations of some London-based African business partners caused the collapse of the Corporation. Another disaster was the bankruptcy of the Mechanics Savings Bank of Richmond, Virginia, before the planned West African bank could be set up. Coupled with the commercial failure of the *AT&OR*, Ali was forced to remain in the USA; his wife Beatrice (née Pardoe-Nash) remained in England.

With the aid of Bruce, Ali was able to earn a living as a lecturer and by writing articles for the Negro press. Overcoming his previous criticisms of Garvey, Ali was appointed the 'foreign affairs specialist' for Garvey's *Negro World*, for which he also reviewed books and plays. He served for a while as the United Negro Improvement Association's (UNIA) Foreign Secretary, corresponding with, for example, Kobina Sekyi in the Gold Coast and Dr Moses da Rocha in Nigeria, who had attended the 1900 Pan-African Congress, on behalf of the UNIA. However, Ali's relations with Garvey were clearly never easy as Garvey himself turned down the proposal by the UNIA New York Branch that Ali should be part of the UNIA delegation to the League of Nations. Ali was also critical of some aspects of Garvey's programme and was so distressed by the general ignorance of conditions in Africa among UNIA members, that at their 1922 Convention, 'as a matter of enlightenment', he read out Sekyi's 'Education in West Africa', which he had published in the *AT&OR* in 1917.

Ali had been elected a member of the Negro Society for Historical Research on the basis of his 1911 book, and was also a member of the American Negro Academy, at whose 1922 conference he read a paper on 'The necessity for a chair of Negro History in the universities of the world'. In 1923 he lectured for a week at the Tuskegee Institute on 'African Origins, Civilisation and History'. Ali was also a patron of the Native African Union of America formed *c.*1926, which aimed to uphold the interests of Africans in America. It is not known whether he made contact with Barbados-born Richard B. Moore, then a communist activist in Harlem, who had been a distributor of the *AT&OR* and later in life wrote that he had first learned about Africa from the pages of that newspaper.

Ali also returned to trying to find ways to bypass the huge, monopolistic European combines which controlled all African trade. However, the companies he set up in cooperation with Gold Coasters Alfred Lincoln Cudjoe and then Winifred Tete-Ansa both failed. Ali's final attempt to break British trade monopolies involved selling West African cocoa direct to the New York buyers. To arrange this he had to travel to the Gold Coast; in August 1931 he and his White second wife, Gertrude La Page (a stage name), were refused permission to land: his business plans were obviated. In Lagos friends signed a bond permitting the couple to land. Ali was never to leave; Gertrude returned to the USA in March 1937.

Almost destitute, Ali sought journalistic employment, at first writing for the *Daily Times*, and then becoming editor of the *Nigerian Daily Telegraph*. (Both papers were Nigerian-owned.) By 1933, probably with financial help from Amos Shackleford, a Lagosian West Indian-born businessman, he started his own weekly paper, *The Comet*. As it avoided parochialism and carried more world news than was common in the Nigerian press, the paper immediately attracted contributors of high calibre and political commitment, such as Obafemi Awolowo, who became Prime Minister of Nigeria's Western Region in 1954. Ali wrote a regular front page column on international affairs. The paper became 'a source of inspiration and challenge for the emerging new leaders of Nigeria who had vision of an independent nation', according to Fred I.A. Omu, a historian of the Nigerian press, who also saw *The Comet* as the newspaper that 'most personified the embitterment of the Nigerian' over the invasion of Abyssinia.

This view is corroborated by Anthony Enahoro, who was to become the Western Region's Minister of Home Affairs. In his autobiography Enahoro recalls that *The Comet* was his 'family's favourite newspaper … [Through its reporting of the war in Abyssinia] the fellow-feeling with other Africans was a newly awakened sentiment … The seeds of nationalism were being sown in me … ' (*Fugitive Offender*, 1965, p.45). Chief Enahoro became editor of *The Comet* in 1945, when running a paper had become too onerous for its aging publisher/editor, and it was bought by Nnamdi Azikiwe.

The paper was much more conservative and much more financially successful than the *AT&OR* had been. Its circulation remained at 4,000 per week, until the arrival in 1937 of the populist, radical *West African Pilot* published by Nnamdi Azikiwe. This financial success was probably due not only to *The Comet*'s content, but to the advertising it was able to attract. Ali was no longer alienating the European business community, as he had been in his London publishing days.

Besides writing for and editing the paper, Ali also wrote a historical romance, *A Daughter of the Pharaohs*, and a novel, *Ere Roosevelt Came*, a fictionalised account of Black politics in the USA. Both were published in instalments in *The Comet*.

Ali's political involvements were now more nationalist than Pan-Africanist. For example, in 1938 he was appointed head of the resuscitated Master Printers' Federation; he was involved in the 1941 railway dispute, during which he (and Nnamdi Azikiwe) attended the discussions between the Railway Workers Union and the Railway's General Manager; in 1943 he supported the National Union of Teachers in their dispute with the government. He was a patron of the Young Muslim Society of Lagos and supported other Muslim associations. His life-long contribution was acknowledged when he chaired the meeting on 26 August 1942 at which the National Council of Nigeria and the Cameroons was formed. He remained involved with, but did not become a member of the organisation.

Dusé Mohamed Ali died in Lagos on 25 June 1945.

MS

Further reading

Duffield, Ian, 'The business activities of Dusé Mohamed Ali: an example of the economic dimension of Pan-Africanism, 1912–1945', *Journal of the Historical Society of Nigeria*, (4) no. 4, June 1969.

Duffield, Ian, 'Dusé Mohamed Ali and the development of Pan-Africanism 1866–1945', PhD Thesis, University of Edinburgh, 1971.

Duffield, Ian, 'Dusé Mohamed Ali: his purpose and his public', in A. Niven (ed.), *The Commonwealth Writer Overseas*, Liège, Marcel Didier, 1976 (this contains a list of Ali's writings).

Duffield, Ian, 'Some American influences on Dusé Mohamed Ali', in Robert A. Hill (ed.), *Pan-African Biography*, Los Angeles, African Studies Center, Univ. of California, 1987.

Duffield, Ian, 'Dusé Mohamed Ali, Afro-Asian solidarity and Pan-Africanism in early twentieth-century London', in J. Gundara and I. Duffield, *Essays in the History of Blacks in Britain*, Aldershot, Avebury, 1992.

See also

Clarke, John Henrik, *Marcus Garvey and the Vision of Africa*, New York, Random House, 1974.

Geiss, Imanuel, *The Pan-African Movement*, London, Methuen, 1974.

Martin, Tony, *The Pan-African Connection*, Dover, The Majority Press, 1983.

Martin, Tony, *Literary Garveyism*, Dover, The Majority Press, 1983.

Ahmed Ben Bella
(1916 –)

Ahmed Ben Bella Pan-Africanist, leader of the Algerian national liberation struggle and one of the first to begin the armed struggle against French colonial rule, became the first President of Algeria in 1963 until overthrown by a military coup in 1965.

Ben Bella was born in Marnia in the Oran district of Algeria, on the Moroccan–Algerian border, on 25 December 1916. At the time of his birth Algeria was a French colony with over 1 million French settlers and colonial policies that openly discriminated against Algeria's Muslim population. One of seven children, his father was a peasant farmer and small trader; Ben Bella was the only one of five sons who lived beyond early adulthood. He was educated locally in Marnia and then at a secondary school in Tlemcen, where he was one of the pupils who openly opposed the eurocentric teaching imposed under French colonial rule. Around 1937, Ben Bella became involved with the nationalist and anti-settler movement in Algeria, spearheaded by the Union Nationalist des Musulmans Nord-Africains, which in March of that year became the Parti de Peuple Algérien, an organisation that was savagely persecuted by the French colonial authorities.

When Ben Bella left school without qualifications he did a variety of jobs before being called up for military service by the French government in 1937. He was posted to an Alpine infantry regiment based in Marseilles, which included both French and Algerian conscripts, and was soon made a sergeant. When the Second World War broke out he remained in the army and saw action defending France from German air attacks. He was mentioned in despatches several times and was eventually awarded the Croix de Guerre. In 1940, following France's capitulation, he was demobilised from the army but invited to remain in Marseilles as a professional footballer. But Ben Bella returned to Algeria and took over the running of his father's farm. Recalled to military service in 1943 in an Algerian regiment, he led the opposition to the discrimination against Algerian soldiers practised by the French military authorities and was transferred to a Moroccan regiment. He subsequently fought in Italy, where he became a sergeant-major and took part in the Allied liberation of Rome. He was again mentioned several times in despatches and was awarded the Medaille Militaire by Charles de Gaulle.

In May 1945 Ben Bella heard of the uprising by Algerians at Setif and Guelma and the reprisals by the French colonial authorities that led to tens of thousands of Algerian deaths. He decided to return to Algeria and to contribute to the struggle of the Algerian people.

At the urging of his compatriots Ben Bella became a town councillor in Marnia, responsible for food supplies and rationing and led protests against the electoral system that discriminated against Algerian voters. He became a member of the main nationalist party the Mouvement pour le Triomphe des Liberées Démocratiques (MTLD) and, after losing his farm, he left Marnia for Algiers, changed his name and went underground to work for the MTLD. In 1947 he became the leader of a new grouping within the MTLD, the Organisation Spéciale (OS), which represented a split between those who believed in constitutionalism and those like Ben Bella who were ready to begin the armed struggle for Algerian independence. At the 1949 congress of MTLD Ben Bella was appointed chief political organiser and began to develop the organisation's subversive activities that included raising funds by bank robbery. In 1950 Ben Bella was implicated in a raid on the post office at Oran, arrested and sentenced to eight years imprisonment. In 1952 he escaped and went first to France and then Egypt where with the help of Egyptian supporters the OS was re-established.

In April 1954, Ben Bella was one of nine 'historic leaders' who, meeting in Switzerland, formed the Comité Révolutionnaire d'Unité et d'Action (CRUA). This organisation, based on the OS was determined to begin the armed struggle. On 10 October 1954 it was re-named the Front Libération Nationale (FLN), the Armée de Libération Nationale (ALN) was established and on 1 November 1954 launched the attacks which signalled the start of the uprising and the beginning of Algeria's war of independence. Ben Bella was at this time based in Egypt and involved in securing arms for the ALN in many countries including Libya, Jordan, Morocco, Saudi Arabia and Egypt itself.

In 1956 he survived two attempts by the French security services to assassinate him but in October was arrested in Algiers, when the plane he was travelling in was diverted by the French authorities, who had previously agreed to safe passage after a meeting with the FLN leaders in Rome. Ben Bella was imprisoned in France for six years but continued to involve himself in the Algerian struggle from his cell and on many occasions led hunger strikes demanding rights for Algerian political prisoners. In 1958, while he was still incarcerated, he was appointed vice-chairman of the Gouvernement Provisoire de la République Algérienne (GPRA).

By 1962 it became clear that the French government could not win the war in Algeria and had to agree to self-determination for the Algerian people. Ben Bella at first opposed negotiation with the French and then, according to his own account, reluctantly signed the peace agreement at Evian-les-Bains in March 1962. He then went to Morocco and continued to voice his differences with other GPRA leaders, most openly at the FLN congress in Tripoli in June 1962. Following a referendum in Algeria in July 1962 independence was proclaimed, but sharp disagreements were evident between the FLN leaders. Ben Bella and Boumedienne, the commander of the ALN, gained the upper hand and established a Bureau politique that nominated candidates for the Constituent National Assembly. It was this body that proclaimed the Democratic Peoples Republic of Algeria in September 1962 and approved Ben Bella's new government dominated by representatives of the ALN. Ben Bella himself became Prime Minister.

During the three years of his government Ben Bella declared his intention to develop a socialist Algeria. However, the Algerian Communist Party, the Party of Socialist Revolution and eventually all political parties were prohibited and the FLN was declared 'the one and only party of progress'. The Algerian General Workers' Union was also incorporated within the FLN and after an overwhelming referendum vote a new constitution was enacted and Ben Bella voted President of the Republic in 1963. Ben Bella's government nationalised most of the land that had been in the possession of French settlers as well as some important industrial plants and initiated a programme of 'autogestion' or self-management, while foreign trade was controlled by the state. Many of Ben Bella's domestic policies ended in failure or were severely criticised and on several occasions he had to use the ALN to suppress internal revolts. But in the field of foreign policy he played a significant role in the development of the Organisation of African Unity and in supporting anti-colonial and anti-imperialist struggles throughout Africa and in other parts of the world.

In the course of its struggle against French colonial rule the FLN had made clear that it was for the unity of all those fighting against imperialism and was especially concerned about Pan-African unity. It became a founder member of the Afro-Asian Peoples' Solidarity Organisation in 1957 and in 1958 participated with observer status at the Conference of Independent African States held in Accra. From that time on the organisation became more closely aligned with KWAME NKRUMAH's Ghana, particularly in opposition to the more conservative leadership of several Francophone African countries which tended to openly support or were reluctant to oppose French rule in Algeria. The GPRA attended the 1961 Casablanca Conference and was formally recognised as the legitimate government of Algeria. Henceforth it was regarded as belonging to the more radical Casablanca group of African countries including Ghana, the United Arab Republic and Guinea. Following the Sharpeville massacre, it had been one of the first African organisations to propose an economic boycott of South Africa and to advocate military support to those opposed to the South African government. The FLN also developed friendly relations with Cuba and openly opposed what it referred to as 'Israeli Zionism' in the Middle East. At its Tripoli congress in 1962, the FLN reaffirmed that its foreign policy was anti-imperialist in orientation and also made clear its support for the Non-Aligned Movement, of which it became a leading member.

At his inaugural speech at the UN in 1962, Ben Bella stressed that in Africa 'the credo of Algeria's political and diplomatic action will be the liquidation of colonialism in both its classic and disguised forms'. Based on this principle his government was soon giving military support, training and finance to the African liberation movements fighting against Portuguese colonialism and those waging the anti-apartheid struggle in South Africa. Both the African National Congress and the Pan-Africanist Congress of Azania had offices in Algiers, as did SWAPO (the South West African People's Organisation), MPLA (Movimento Popular de Libertação de Angola), ZANU (Zimbabwe African National Union) and ZAPU (Zimbabwe African People's Union) and several other liberation organisations.

At the founding conference of the Organisation of African Unity (OAU) in 1963, Ben Bella played a prominent role in establishing the African Liberation Committee

(ALC) that was designed to coordinate support for liberation struggles throughout Africa. Indeed he argued that the signing of the OAU Charter would 'remain a dead letter if we do not give unconditional support to Angola, Southern Africa, Mozambique and Portuguese Guinea, unconditional support which these people under colonial rule have the right to expect from us'. He added that 'African unity depends largely on an efficient solidarity with those who are still fighting for freedom'. Algeria became one of the nine members of the ALC and Ben Bella's government immediately donated 100 million Francs to its finances. After the OAU conference, Algeria incorporated the OAU Charter into its constitution and was one of the first countries to implement the OAU's decision to boycott Portuguese and South African goods. Ben Bella's government closed down the Portuguese consulate in Algiers and offered support to those who were fighting against the Portuguese dictatorship.

He came to be seen as one of the leading advocates of the 'Third World' and had a high international profile. He was about to host the second Afro-Asian Conference in 1965 when he was overthrown by a military coup led by Boumedienne.

Ben Bella was kept in detention until 1979 when he was placed under house arrest until 1980. After his release he went into exile in Europe and became an opponent of the FLN government. He only returned to Algeria in 1990 as the founder and leader of the Mouvement pour la Démocratie en Algerie (MDA). He has continued to play a role in Algerian politics and was one of those who tried to persuade the FIS (Front Islamique de Salut) to renounce violence in the bloody conflict that engulfed Algeria from 1992.

HA

Further reading

Uwechue, Raph (ed.) *Makers of Modern Africa: Profiles in History*, third edition, London, Africa Books, 1996.

Edward Wilmot Blyden
(1832 – 1912)

Edward Wilmot Blyden, politician, writer and diplomat, has been seen as one of the key thinkers in the development of Pan-African ideas. Edward Blyden was born the third of seven children in the then Danish colony of St Thomas in the Virgin Islands, at a time when slavery had not yet been abolished. Both of Blyden's parents were free, however; his father was a tailor and his mother a school teacher. Blyden was educated at a local school by his mother and for a time in Venezuela, his family's temporary home from 1842–4. Here he became fluent in Spanish, the first of many languages he was to master.

In 1850 Blyden attempted to enrol at Rutgers' Theological College in the USA, but as a Black student was refused admission there and at two other US colleges. Blyden's experiences of racism and the impact of slavery in the USA led him to embrace many of the ideas of the American Colonization Society that promoted the repatriation of free African Americans to Liberia in West Africa. It was members of the New York Colonization Society who paid Blyden's passage to Liberia in December 1850. The American Colonization Society had been founded in 1817 as an unholy alliance of humanitarians and slave-owners with differing motives for encouraging the migration of African Americans. It was instrumental in the founding of Liberia and that country, although declaring itself independent in 1847, retained strong ties with the USA. The Black colonisation of Liberia was seen by some African Americans as providing an opportunity to prove the capabilities of those of African descent, in opposition to the virulent racism that then existed, and as the means to establish a base in Africa in order to elevate the position of all Africans. It was clearly these possibilities of 'Negro elevation' that appealed to the young Blyden, who arrived in Liberia in January 1851.

Blyden continued his education in Liberia at Alexander High School, where he studied theology, classics, geography and mathematics, while in his spare time he learned Hebrew in order to study biblical passages relating to Africans. He was for a time a lay-preacher and from 1854 a teacher. Then in 1858 he became Principal of Alexander High School and devoted much of his time to improving conditions at the school as well as continuing his own academic studies, which he believed was a necessary preparation for political leadership. In order to further his knowledge he began corresponding with several people in England including, from 1860, W.E. Gladstone, at that time the Chancellor of the Exchequer.

Soon after his arrival Blyden had also become a correspondent of the government-owned *Liberian Herald*, the only newspaper in the country. From 1855–6 he was appointed editor and also began to write articles in support of 'race pride', further emigration to Liberia and the American Colonization Society, then under attack from various critics in the USA, including MARTIN DELANY. Blyden believed that the colonisation of Liberia was 'the only means of delivering the coloured man from oppression and of raising him up to respectability'. 'The object of Liberia', he wrote, 'was the redemption of Africa and the disenthralment and elevation of the African race'. It was because of his beliefs that Blyden was also often critical of those in Liberia more concerned with material wealth. From his early days in Liberia Blyden also delved into history to find evidence to refute charges of African inferiority and to combat existing racist ideologies. He published his first major work on this subject, *A Vindication of the Negro Race*, in 1857. But at the same time Blyden believed that African redemption would be brought about through the 'Christian civilisation' of African American migrants.

In 1861 Blyden and Alexander Crummell were appointed Liberian commissioners to Britain and the USA with a mission to interest British and American philanthropists in financing Liberian education. The following year both men were appointed commissioners to encourage African American migration to Liberia. In 1862 Blyden was appointed Professor of Classics at Liberia College, the first secular, English-speaking institution of higher education in tropical Africa. Blyden was disappointed to find that African Americans were less inclined to migrate to Africa than he had hoped and often berated his audiences for lack of belief in what he called 'African nationality', the ability to determine their own affairs in Liberia or other states in Africa. But Blyden often gave little consideration to the rights of those African peoples already living in Liberia. He had himself participated in military expeditions against Liberia's indigenous population, which he saw as part of the country's 'civilising mission'.

In 1864 Blyden was appointed Liberian Secretary of State, and used his position to encourage migration from the Caribbean as well as to warn African Americans that the victories won during the course of the Civil War were only temporary, and that they too needed a 'home and nationality of their own'. In order to further develop Liberia, Blyden believed that it must aim to incorporate those Muslim African states in its interior. In order to facilitate communication Blyden decided to learn Arabic and in 1866 went to Lebanon to study. On his return he introduced Arabic onto the curriculum at Liberia College. His subsequent writings in defence of Islam were collected together in one of his most famous books, *Christianity, Islam and the Negro Race*, published in 1887.

But Blyden soon found that his entry into Liberian politics brought its own problems. He became involved in several disputes with political rivals over migration from the Caribbean, the extension of Liberia's boundaries into the interior and other matters. Blyden and others came to view these political rivalries as based on colour and claimed that those Liberians of mixed parentage had established a pigmentocracy to work against his goal of establishing Liberia 'as the nucleus of a West African state'. In 1870 Blyden even wrote a short article, 'Mixed Races in Liberia', which although not intended for publication was eventually made public. It contributed to a worsening of the political situation in Liberia, and led to a physical attack on Blyden which forced him to flee to Sierra Leone in 1871. Blyden continued to launch attacks on those he referred to as the 'mulatto' for the rest of his life, even insisting to the American Colonization Society that they should be kept out of Africa.

From Sierra Leone, he travelled to England and encouraged both the Church Missionary Society and the British government to expand their activities into Sierra Leone's hinterland. He believed that the expansion of 'Christian civilisation' throughout the region could create the basis for the emergence of a large and influential West African state. In 1872 Blyden himself went on an expedition on behalf of the British government to contact African rulers in the hinterland of Sierra Leone and to encourage them to come under British 'protection'. In 1873 he was appointed the British Government Agent to the Interior and continued to demand that the British government 'take charge of the Western Soudan'. However, at other times Blyden was just as insistent that the US government 'stretch a chain of colonies of her own citizens through the whole length of the Soudan', and he continued to encourage African Americans to migrate to Liberia and elsewhere in Africa, in order to effect the 'regeneration of the continent' and to solve the problems of the American 'Negro'. In this regard Blyden even welcomed racist legislation and discrimination in the USA in the hope that this would encourage more people to migrate to Africa, and at the same time he actively discouraged African Americans from becoming involved with political issues in the USA.

In 1872 Blyden established *Negro* in Sierra Leone, a newspaper designed to 'serve the race purpose' and one of the first papers specifically aimed at a readership in Africa, the Caribbean and the USA that was published until 1874. He was certainly one of the pioneers in the development of cultural nationalism in West Africa, became a zealous advocate of the need for a West African university to train West Africans for self-government and was connected with the movement for an independent African church.

In 1874 Blyden returned to Liberia and from 1875–7 was Principal of Alexander High School. In 1877 he once again accepted a diplomatic appointment and became Liberia's ambassador to Britain. In 1880 he became President of Liberia College and was at the same time appointed Minister of the Interior and Secretary of Education in Liberia's government. As an educator Blyden held to the contradictory view that Africans must develop an education suited to their own needs, history and culture while at the same time maintaining the need for the study of Latin, Greek and the Bible. He therefore encouraged the study of West African languages and of Arabic. But by 1884 Blyden was involved in yet another dispute at Liberia College and he again sought refuge in Sierra Leone before accepting an invitation to stand as a presidential candidate in the Liberian election of 1885. Blyden was unsuccessful in the election and during the next fifteen years spent much of his life outside Liberia, mainly in Sierra Leone. In 1892 he was again appointed Liberian Ambassador to Britain and between 1896–7 was Agent of Native Affairs for the British colonial government in Lagos.

Blyden began to believe that British imperialism might play a more important civilising role in West Africa than migrants from the USA or the Caribbean, and that by this means a great West African empire might be established. He supported British imperialism not only in West Africa but elsewhere too, welcoming the invasion of

Egypt in 1882. He believed that Britain was the colonial power that would best protect the interests of Africans, but also that the partition of the continent by the European powers was in the interests of 'African regeneration' and 'for the ultimate good of the people'. He was even reluctant to criticise the atrocities carried out by Belgian and American interests in the Congo. Blyden believed that under British rule Africans could be educated for self-government and he was himself particularly interested in training Muslim youths throughout West Africa as agents of British rule. In 1901 Blyden was appointed Director of Mohammedan Education in Sierra Leone, a post he held until 1906. But although he wished to train Muslims 'in Western ideas', he continued to believe that European colonial rule might best be conducted through traditional African institutions. In 1908 his newspaper articles on these subjects were collected together in the book, *African Life and Customs*.

In 1874 he helped to establish the *West African Reporter* and later the *Sierra Leone Weekly News*, and contributed to both papers. His ideas became particularly influential amongst Western-educated West Africans. He believed that Africans had their own unique contributions to make to the world based on their unique 'African personality'. At first concentrating his efforts at building West African unity in Liberia and then in Sierra Leone, Blyden later began to concentrate many of his activities in Lagos, again campaigning for a West African university as the best means to build West African unity.

Through his activities and writings it is clear that Blyden's ideas had a significant influence on the younger generation of those who began to organise on a pan-West African basis or who demanded political reforms throughout the British West African colonies, including John Mensah Sarbah, Majola Agbebi and J.E. Casely Hayford. Blyden, however, was much more concerned with cultural rather than political nationalism and he never provided practical political leadership either in Africa or in the USA or Caribbean. In the USA he exhibited some support for the views of Booker T. Washington, who was also opposed to political activism. His support for Islam and Muslims alienated many Christians, while his advocacy of polygamy was seen by some as simply justification for his unorthodox relationship with Anna Erskine, the mother of five of his children.

But Blyden was one of the key contributors to the ideologies of Pan-Africanism and West African nationalism, and one of the first to articulate a notion of 'African personality' and the uniqueness of the 'African race'. His ideas, encompassing as they do support for European imperialism, the 'civilising mission', the partition of Africa, and various notions of race, are clearly rooted in the nineteenth century and point to Blyden being amongst the most steeped in eurocentric thinking, yet his ideas can be seen as influencing many in the twentieth century from Marcus Garvey to George Padmore and Kwame Nkrumah. During his lifetime his supporters were just as likely to be found amongst the higher echelons of the British government and Colonial Office as they were amongst 'race conscious' youths in West Africa or the USA.

Edward Blyden died in Freetown, Sierra Leone on 7 February 1912 and was buried at the Race Course Cemetery.

HA

Main publications

A Vindication of the African Race: Being a Brief Examination of the Arguments in Favour of African Inferiority, first published Monrovia, 1857, published as *Liberia Offering*, New York, 1862.

Christianity, Islam and the Negro Race, London, 1887 [third edition, University of Edinburgh Press, 1967].

African Life and Customs, London, C.M. Phillips, 1908.

Further reading

Lynch, Hollis R., *Edward Wilmot Blyden – Pan-Negro Patriot 1832–1912*, London, Oxford University Press, 1967.

Amilcar Lopes Cabral
(1924 – 73)

Amilcar Lopes Cabral, one of the founders of the Movimento Popular Libertação de Angola (MPLA) and founder and secretary-general of the Partido Africano para a Independência da Guiné e Cabo-Verde (PAIGC), was born to a Cape Verdean father and Guinean mother on 12 September 1924 in Bafata, at that time in Portuguese Guinea.

He attended school at Sao Vincente, Cape Verde and then in 1945 went to Lisbon to study agronomy and later hydraulic engineering. While in Portugal he helped to establish the Centre for African Studies in Lisbon, dedicated to rejecting the Portuguese policy of assimilation and to establishing a 'return to the sources', a reclaiming of African culture and history. While he was in Portugal, Cabral came into contact with members of the Portuguese Communist Party, and with students from many other African countries formed the Anti-Colonialist Movement.

In 1952 Cabral returned to Portuguese Guinea and worked as an agricultural engineer. Between 1952–4 he was director of a project to carry out the first agricultural census in the Portuguese colonies in Africa. As director of the census team Cabral learned at first hand the problems of the people of Guinea and while still a civil servant he wrote articles analysing the country's agricultural problems. The experience that he gained during this period of his life he would later draw on during the armed liberation struggle against Portuguese colonial rule.

In 1953 he commenced underground anti-colonial activity in the capital of Guinea, Bissau, mainly amongst educated Africans, many of whom had studied overseas and were at that time called *asimilados*. Various organisational means were used but the Portuguese colonial authorities kept a close watch on their activities and even prevented the creation of a sports and recreation association that they feared might be used as a cover for anti-colonial political activity. Eventually Cabral and others mobilised some of the patriotic workers in Bissau and formed the Movement for the National Independence of Guinea. But after their attempts at legal activity failed, in 1956 with his brother Luis, Aristides Pereira, Rafael Barbosa and two others, Cabral founded the PAIGC and began clandestine political activity in some of the main urban areas of Guinea such as Bafata, Bolama and Bissau. Also in 1956 in Angola, Cabral partici-pated alongside Agostinho Neto and others in the founding of the MPLA.

The PAIGC's main aims were to achieve immediate and total independence for Guinea and Cape Verde and for the democratic rights of the peoples, and to achieve rapid cultural, economic and social progress for these countries. The PAIGC also stood for unity between the peoples of Guinea and Cape Verde and for peaceful cooperation with all the peoples of the world.

The PAIGC began its political activity in the urban centres, but after an abortive dock strike in 1959, when many workers were killed, Cabral and some of the other leading members of the PAIGC left the country and travelled to Conakry in the newly independent Republic of Guinea (the former French colony) and began to develop the strategy of a guerrilla war based on mobilising the peasants in the rural areas. Cabral now considered that open political activity in the urban areas had been a mistake, as these were 'the stronghold of colonialism', and the PAIGC began actively recruiting in the rural areas as well as continuing to build an underground organisation in the towns. A special cadre school was established in Conakry which began to train over a thousand fighters drawn from all sections of the population, but mainly from the urban areas, who then returned to work amongst the peasants. Those who volunteered were always given political as well as military education because as Cabral often stressed 'we are armed militants and not militarists'. In later years cadres were also trained in Algeria, the Soviet Union, East Germany and Cuba. Little support was available form Western European countries and none at all from those such as Britain and the USA, members of NATO that supported Portugal. At the same time the PAIGC continued to seek a peaceful resolution to their struggle for independence and Cabral was sent to address the UN and other international bodies. When the Portuguese government continued to ignore resolutions of the UN Security Council and the demands of the people, a campaign of sabotage and then a national liberation war was begun in Portuguese Guinea and Cape Verde in 1963, and by 1966 two-thirds of the former territory was under PAIGC control.

Cabral was also actively engaged in establishing pan-African unity. In 1960 the PAIGC and MPLA established the African Revolutionary Front for the National Independence of the Portuguese colonies, based in Tunisia, and in 1961 participated in the Conference of the Nationalist Organisations of the Portuguese Colonies held in Casablanca and the third All-African Peoples Conference held in Cairo. Cabral explained, 'We are for African unity, on a regional or continental scale, in as far as it is necessary for the progress of the African peoples, and in order to guarantee their security and the guarantee of their progress'. The PAIGC was also an active member of the Council of Solidarity of Afro-Asian Peoples and the Non-Aligned Movement. After 1963 the PAIGC also gained recognition from the Organisation of African Unity. The PAIGC Secretariat, under Cabral's leadership, also played a key role in successfully establishing the Movement for the Liberation of Guinea and the Cape Verde Islands, based at Conakry, which organised amongst émigrés in the neighbouring countries. In 1961 the PAIGC united with organisations within Guinea and Cape Verde and the émigrés to hold a conference in Dakar, Senegal, at which they formed the United Liberation Front of Guinea and the Cape Verde Islands to coordinate a joint struggle against Portuguese colonialism.

Cabral always stressed that the anti-colonial struggle being waged by PAIGC was not directed against the people of Portugal, or even Portugal itself, but against Portuguese colonialism and the fascist government led by Salazar. He explained that they were fighting 'so that our peoples may never be exploited – not only by Europeans, not only by people with white skin, because we do not confuse exploitation or exploiters with the colour of men's skins; we do not want any exploitation in our countries not even by Black people'.

In his speeches Cabral emphasised PAIGC's Pan-African concerns but also its anti-imperialist orientation, its support for the struggle of the Vietnamese people against the invasion of their country by the USA and its solidarity with the people of Cuba and Palestine. Cabral also spoke in support of the socialist countries in the world and of the aid that they provided for the struggle against Portuguese colonialism, which, he said, reinforced the aid received from African countries.

Cabral paid particular attention to questions of ideology and theory both in his speeches and in several important publications. In his famous speech, 'The Weapon of Theory', given at the first Tricontinental Conference of the peoples of Asia, Africa and Latin America, held in Cuba in 1966, he argued that 'nobody has yet made a successful revolution without a revolutionary theory', and he went on to lament the lack of ideological clarity within many national liberation movements. According to Cabral's thinking, national liberation and social revolution 'are not exportable commodities' but were 'essentially formed by the historical reality of each people'. He went on to argue that 'our peoples have their own history regardless of the stage of their economic development' but that the effect of imperialism was to arrest the historical development of peoples, in some cases even leading to retrogression. Cabral concluded that the basis of the national liberation struggles, such as those being waged in Africa, 'is the inalienable right of every people to have its own history and the objective of national liberation is to regain this right usurped by imperialism, that is to say to free the process of development of the national productive forces'. In other words national liberation could not just be concerned with political independence.

In his speech, 'National Liberation and Culture', given at Syracuse University, New York in 1979, Cabral discusses the importance of culture 'as an element of resistance to foreign domination'. According to Cabral, 'A people who free themselves from foreign domination will not be culturally free unless, without underestimating the importance of positive contributions from the oppressor's culture and other cultures, they return to the upward paths of their own culture'. For Cabral then, the national liberation movement should defend, embody and base itself on the most positive aspects of popular culture and develop a new progressive national culture. In this context he believed that the leaders of national liberation struggles, often drawn from the urban population and the intellectuals, had much to learn from the lives, cultures and struggles of the peasants. They had to 'be capable of committing suicide as a class, in order to be reborn as revolutionary workers, completely identified with the deepest aspiration of the people to which they belong'. While through the national liberation struggle itself, the masses of the people gain an awareness of their own capabilities and political role, and become empowered through conscious participation. 'Let people do it for themselves' became one of the most significant slogans of the Guinean struggle.

Cabral and the other leaders of the PAIGC also had to develop the means to develop and sustain the areas they liberated from Portuguese rule, in other words they had to begin to build a post-colonial state. From 1964 the PAIGC maintained a full-time army of between 4,000–6,000 combatants, supported by armed local militias. These forces managed to control 60 per cent of mainland Guinea by 1968 and keep at bay a Portuguese army of 30,000. Of equal importance was the development of a new economy, and social and political systems in the liberated areas. Despite the many difficulties the PAIGC managed to create the conditions to feed the population, and to establish more hospitals and schools than existed in the occupied areas. In all its work the PAIGC and Cabral paid special attention to the political education of the population, those who were combatants as well as those in the liberated and occupied areas. The PAIGC established committees at the village level to organise local affairs, and in particular gave every encouragement to women to empower themselves and play a leading role. One of the great successes of the PAIGC was drawing the peasant population into the national liberation struggle and creating the conditions for their empowerment, so that people began to govern themselves, take control of their own lives and make their own history. The elected village committees took on increasing responsibilities, for law, education, health and other matters, and were the basis for a participatory democracy and for elections in 1972 for the People's National Assembly, which in 1973 proclaimed the independence of Guinea-Bissau.

Throughout the liberation struggle Cabral and the PAIGC always paid attention to the international arena. In 1972 he spoke at the session of the Security Council of the UN and asked for UN observers to visit Cape Verde and Guinea. In the same year he became the first representative of a people involved in armed struggle to be invited to address the General Assembly of the UN as an observer.

It was on the eve of the independence of Guinea-Bissau that the Portuguese colonialists intensified their attempts to eliminate Cabral. In 1970 Guinean exiles and Portuguese forces attacked the PAIGC office in Conakry, but Cabral was not present. But on 23 January 1973 Cabral was assassinated in Conakry by a dissident member of the PAIGC, recruited by the Portuguese secret police, PIDE, with the promise that after the liquidation of Cabral and the PAIGC, Guinea would be granted independence. After his death, and based on his ideas and leadership, the PAIGC was able to lead both Guinea and Cape Verde to independence from Portuguese rule.

HA

Main publications

Revolution in Guinea – An African People's Struggle (translated by Richard Handyside), London, Stage 1, 1969.
Our People Are Our Mountains, London, MAGIC, 1971.
Unity and Struggle (translated by Michael Wolfers), London, Heinemann, 1980.

Further reading

Davidson, Basil, *No Fist is Big Enough to Hide the Sky*, London, Zed, 1981.

Aimé Césaire
(1913 –)

Together with Senegalese LÉOPOLD SENGHOR, Césaire developed one of the most controversial ideologies of the Black world, that of Négritude. While their interpretations
bifurcated over time, the ideology remains in use, and remains as controversial as it
was in the 1930s. Césaire's plays took his ideas and analyses of the colonial situation
and the struggles for independence to audiences in the Caribbean, in Africa, in North
America and in Europe.

Césaire was born in Basse Pointe, Martinique. The island had been a French colony
since 1635; its aboriginal population was totally exterminated by the French. Slavery
was abolished in 1848. Contrary to English practice, by 1870 universal franchise was
introduced in order for the populace to elect two deputies and a senator to the French
National Assembly; all political power lay in Paris. Compulsory elementary education
was also introduced. Whites and 'mulattoes' owned most of the land and class division
based on colour became endemic.

Aimé was one of six siblings. On his father's side his grandfather was the first
qualified Black schoolteacher in Martinique; his father Fernand also qualified to teach,
but moved to more highly paid work such as plantation management and tax inspec-
tion. His mother, Elénore, was a seamstress. His grandmother, very unusually for a
woman of her generation, was not only literate, but taught all the siblings to read at
a very early age. French, not créole, was the language of the Césaire home.

With such a start in life, it is hardly surprising that young Aimé won a scholarship
to the Lycée Schoelcher, the sole high school for all the French Caribbean colonies.
The education offered there was unadulteratedly assimilationist. The French policy
towards colonial subjects was that they were all to be made into Frenchmen: this
included, for example, learning about your Gaul forefathers and speaking exclusively
French, not the patois or creole of the less educated. They would thus be, at least in
theory, on an equal footing to compete in the French system of meritocracy based on
intellect and education.

Gaining prizes in French, Latin, English and history, and being designated the
best overall student, Césaire was granted a scholarship to attend the Ecole Normale
Supérieure in Paris, to train to become a schoolteacher. He arrived in Paris in 1931 to
attend the Lycée Louis-le-Grand, to prepare for the entrance examinations. Césaire
now learned that he was not accepted as an equal by the Parisians, who saw him
either as a Black (simply inferior), or even worse as a 'nigger' (close to a savage). For
a young man raised on assimilationist principles, this was devastating. He also

recognised that Europe was going through a period of political tensions and economic depression; moreover, the First World War had shown Europe to be not the invulnerable purveyor of civilisation but a perpetrator of brutalities against its own, not just against the 'savages' of the colonies deemed to be in need of civilisation. These new perceptions led to a 'better understand[ing of] the reasons for my own malaise', Césaire was later to explain, but also resulted in a nervous breakdown.

However, Césaire began to acquire a new understanding of Africa, which had been described as irredeemably savage by the colonialists, from Senegalese Léopold Senghor, then a 25-year-old student at the Cité Universitaire. 'In meeting Senghor, I met Africa', Césaire said many years later. Senghor and Césaire became very close, learning much from each other. They, and the other colonial students in Paris, were much influenced by the writings of the African Americans of the Harlem Renaissance, and the works of anthropologists such as Leo Frobenius and Maurice Delafosse, both somewhat less hostile and derogatory of African culture than previous European writers. As Césaire recalled in 1976, on the occasion of Senghor's visit to Martinique, they had been 'weighed down by the same problems ... Our youth was marked by the same questions: who am I? For us – it was a question of a life to live, an ethic to create, and communities to save. We tried to answer that question. In the end our answer was Négritude'.

Working with fellow enthusiasts Senghor and Guyanese poet Léon Damas who had been at the Lycée Schoelcher with him, Césaire published a journal, *L'Etudiant Noir*, which managed to last six issues in the period 1935–6. Based on the concept of Négritude, a phrase coined by Césaire, it was intended to aid interaction between the Francophone Africans and Caribbeans in Paris. This was an essential part of their political/philosophical enterprise, as the Caribbeans had been taught to see Africans as 'barbarians', while the Africans had grown to see West Indians as the bureaucrats imposed on them by the colonial regime.

In 1936 Césaire returned home for the university holidays and saw his Antillean home through not only Parisian but Négritude-influenced eyes. This new vision was expressed in a poem – the first step in a long literary career. *Cahier d'un Retour au Pays Natal* is perhaps the first colonial-authored poem to achieve world fame. It was published and in France in 1939, again in 1947 and more influentially in 1956 by *Présence Africaine*; the first translation appeared in Spanish in 1943 in Cuba. Though much akin to surrealist works of the time, whether Césaire was influenced by the surrealist movement remains a matter of dispute. The fifty-five-page, highly emotional poem 'cannot be fully comprehended except in its Caribbean context', according to literary critic and historian F. Abiola Irele. 'The poem becomes the dramatic exteriorisation of a mental rite of passage.' It is about the 'intensification of being ... When [the poet] comes to celebrate his race, it is in terms of a spirituality that draws its energy from a full, organic and intense cosmic participation ... Césaire's négritude is not only a personal but also a collective vision, a vision of the race founded upon a novel apprehension of the meaning of Africa, which serves as the mediating symbol of a new consciousness ... Africa has polemical significance: the contestation of the colonial hierarchy of values implies the glorification of Africa, and the constitution of a counter-myth ... Africa signified for him a means of mental liberation, as well as a symbol of spiritual salvation'.

Césaire himself explained in 1956 at the International Conference of Black Writers and Artists, organised by *Présence Africaine*, that 'the problem of black culture cannot be posed at the present time without simultaneously posing the problem of colonialism' which had disrupted the history of Africa, destroyed African economy, social structure and culture, and brainwashed diaspora Africans into an acceptance of inferiority. 'The elements that structured the cultural life of a colonised people disappear or become debased as a result of the colonial regime', Césaire said. The struggle for a national culture and the struggle for full liberation were one and the same: thus Négritude is both a cultural and a political movement, related to African nationalism and Black liberation. This revolutionary struggle will regenerate the world and create a new humanism, but one totally different from that which had been proclaimed by Europe, 'which had been used to mask European oppression and exploitation'. As Césaire expressed in *Cahier*:

> for it is not true that the work of man is finished
> that we have nothing more to do
> but be parasites in the world
>
> ...
>
> The work of man is only just beginning
> and it remains to conquer
> all the violence entrenched
> in the recesses of his passion.
> No race has a monopoly of beauty, of intelligence, of strength
> and there is a place for all at the rendezvous of victory.

Césaire's erstwhile pupil FRANTZ FANON also spoke at the Conference. The African American writer James Baldwin wrote that what he had learned from the Conference, despite his misgivings and criticisms, related in his *Nobody Knows My Name* (London, 1964), was 'that there *was* something which all black men had in common, something which cut across opposing points of view ... What they held in common was their precarious, their unutterably painful relation to the white world' (p.35).

Thus Négritude – both Césaire's interpretation of it, and that of Senghor, which developed along the less overtly political lines of a definition of the 'African personality' and a 'Negro essence' – became the source, the foundation of discussions going on in the present day. In 1965 at two conferences, the American Festival of Negro Arts and the subsequent one convened by the American Society of American Culture, there were panels to discuss Négritude, whose concepts in fact underlay much of the discussion. In 1967 at the Cultural Congress held in Havana, Césaire defined Négritude as a 'coming to consciousness that is concrete and not abstract ... [In Paris in the 1930s] it was also the affirmation of solidarity'. Almost thirty years after its publication in French, the above segment from *Cahier* is the frontispiece in C.L.R. JAMES's collection of essays published in 1984 which is called *At the Rendezvous of Victory*.

In 1937, while enrolled at the Ecole Normale, Césaire had married a fellow Martiniquan studying in Paris, Suzanne Roussi, who had also worked on *L'Etudiant*

Noir. Their first child was born in 1938. On gaining their qualifications Aimé and Suzanne returned to Martinique; both were employed as teachers at the Lycée Schoelcher. One of Césaire's pupils was Frantz Fanon, who proved to be much influenced by his teacher's conceptualisation of Négritude. Together Césaire and Suzanne edited, wrote for and published a journal, *Tropiques*. This carried articles on African heritage and promulgated the central ideas of Négritude, that is the acceptance, affirmation and pride in 'Blackness'; it also denounced colonialism.

As by now Martinique was under French Vichy rule, and as the Césaires were anti-fascist, they and the journal were much harassed by the authorities. Massive demonstrations in 1943 resulted in the Vichyist governor being replaced by one appointed by the Free French Committee of National Liberation. In 1945, standing as a communist, Césaire was elected both to the Mayorality of the Martinique capital, Fort-de-France, and as a deputy to the National Assembly. Césaire, like so many others, had been attracted to the communist doctrine which preached racial equality and anti-colonialism.

In 1946, in a plebiscite, the Martiniquans following Césaire's advice, voted to become a département of France, which in theory meant that they would receive equal treatment with the continental départements. It also meant that Martinique, more than ever, would be assimilated bureaucratically and politically with the metropolis. It is difficult to reconcile Césaire's advocacy of this move, which seems contrary to all notions of Black pride or self-assertion, unless he was seduced by the promise that was inherent in an Assembly dominated by the French Communist Party. Many years later he explained that he had hoped 'to be in a strong position ... to exercise moral, political and economic leverage' to ensure equal treatment for Martinique (Davis, p.95)

This election meant that from then onwards Césaire spent many months of each year in Paris. This, for example, permitted him to participate in the International Exhibition of Surrealism in Paris in 1947. In the same year he became one of the co-founders of *Présence Africaine*, a journal still in existence today. The co-founders were representative of the notions of Négritude: besides Césaire there were Senghor, Damas, Birago Diop (another Senegalese) and the Malagasy poet Jacques Rabemananjara; the director not only of the journal but the publishing company was Senegalese Alioune Diop. One of its supporters was Harlem Renaissance writer Richard Wright, then resident in Paris, who became a member of its board. It was *Présence Africaine*, whose journal disseminated Black creative writing in both French and English, that published Césaire's *Cahier* in French in 1956. In 1950 Césaire and Wright collaborated in organising an exhibition of works from the Musée de l'Homme entitled 'Revelation of Negro Art'.

Also in 1956, concurrently with the Hungarian Revolution, Césaire resigned from the Communist Party, which had recently supported France's efforts to deal more 'effectively' with the Algerian freedom struggle. As he explained to the Party's secretary:

> I deny neither marxism nor communism ... I wish to see marxism and com-
> munism put at the service of black people, and not black people at the service of

marxism and communism … This Black Africa, the dam of our civilisation and the source of our culture, it is to her I look for the regeneration of the Antilles.

Césaire's resignation was published as *Lettre à Maurice Thorez* (1956) in both French and English and was widely read in the colonies, especially France's West African départements.

This resignation was also a symbol of his disillusionment: becoming a département had not essentially changed the colonial relationship between France and Martinique. These views, and a new perspective on Europe as having dehumanised itself in the process of racist colonisation, were ideas he had been developing since the publication of *Discourse sur le Colonialisme* in 1950 (reprinted 1970).

On his return from Paris, Césaire resigned as deputy and mayor and formed his own Parti Progressiste de Martininquais. He was re-elected to both posts and his party won 82 per cent of the vote. From now on, Césaire campaigned for autonomy for Martinique, but within the French system, as he could not foresee Martinique surviving without French economic support. Césaire retired from politics in 1993, at the age of 80.

At the Second Conference of Black Writers, held in Rome in 1959, perhaps somewhat in contradiction to his own political position, Césaire spoke almost exclusively on the colonial liberation:

> decolonisation … is always the result of struggle … Decolonisations are not of equal value. This is proved by the unequal treatment of liberated countries … [T]rue decolonisation … is the complete breakup of colonial structures. [T]he struggle against colonialism is not terminated as soon as … imperialism has been militarily vanquished … [T]rue decolonisation will be revolutionary, or not at all.
>
> (Frutkin, p.43)

Césaire now abandoned poetry in favour of drama. Perhaps the most famous of his three plays is *La Tragédie du roi Christophe* (1975; 1990). Henri Christophe ruled free Haiti from 1807; his increasingly despotic rule evoked an uprising and ended in his suicide in 1820. In concentrating on King Christophe's building of a vast palace/ fort replete with courtiers, Césaire 'questions the efficacy of any grand policy that ignores or devalues the African foundation of Haitian culture' and grapples with the problems of leadership in post-colonial cultures. He also, through the character of a rebellious soldier, asks how can the revolution, once made, be maintained? The soldier, Metallus, says:

> We were going to found an island nation
> our very own all by ourselves! …
> But in came the power brokers
> dividing the house …

The play was widely performed: in 1963 at the Salzburg Festival and then in Paris where it was revived in 1991; at the Festival of Negro Arts in Dakar, Senegal in 1966, in Montreal in 1967 and some years later in Yugoslavia and Milan. It was not seen in Martinique until the visit of Senghor in 1976, who took with him the production by the Théâtre National du Sénégal.

Written in response to the assassination of PATRICE LUMUMBA in Zaire, *Une Saison au Congo* (1966; 1974) needed the intervention of influential friends for its premiere in Brussels in 1966. The play deals with the transition of Congo from a Belgian colony to an independent nation and the manipulations of Lumumba's opponents, the Belgian govenment and its business allies as well a rival Congolese leaders which result in the murder of the democratically elected leader. In the play Lumumba says: 'I speak and I restore Africa to itself; I speak and I restore Africa to the world. I speak, and by attacking the root causes of oppression and servitude, I make possible … true brotherhood.'

In 1995 a three-part documentary film, *Aimé Césaire: A Voice for History*, was completed by the renowned Martiniquan film-maker Euzham Palcy; it was featured at the 1997 Philadelphia Festival of World Cinema.

In an interview preceding his being honoured at a special ceremony at UNESCO in 1997, Césaire reaffirmed the statement he had made at the World Festival of Black and African Arts in Dakar in 1966:

> the shield of merely political independence, political independence unaccompanied and unsupplemented by cultural independence, would in the long run prove to be the most unreliable of shields and the most untrustworthy of safeguards.

MS

Main publications not mentioned in the text

Les Armes Miraculeuses, Paris, 1946, 1961.
Soleil cou coupé, Paris, 1948.
Ferrements, Paris, 1960.
Cadastre, Paris, 1961, New York 1973.
Toussaint L'Ouverture: la Révolution Française et le problème colonial, Paris, 1960.
Une Tempête, first performed 1969.

Further reading

Arnold, A. James, *Modernism and Négritude*, Cambridge, Harvard University Press, 1981.
Davis, Gregson, *Aimé Césaire*, Cambridge, Cambridge University Press, 1997.
Frutkin, Susan, *Aimé Césaire: Black between Worlds*, Coral Gables, FL, Center for Advanced International Studies, 1973.
Irele, F. Abiola, 'Literature and ideology in Martinique: René Maran, Aimé Césaire, Frantz Fanon', *Research Review* (Legon), 5/3, 1969.
La Guerre, John Gaffar, *Enemies of Empire*, St Augustine, UWI, 1984.

Quobna Ottobah Cugoano
(1757 – ?)

Quobna Ottobah Cugoano, anti-slavery writer and abolitionist, was born in the Fante village of Ajumako in what is today Ghana. His main written work, *Thoughts and Sentiments on the Evil and Wicked Traffic of the Slavery and Commerce of the Human Species, Humbly Submitted to The Inhabitants of Great Britain*, was first published in 1787 and is one of the earliest written challenges by an African to slavery and the trans-Atlantic slave trade. It is also, at the present time the main source for biographical information about its author. Cugoano was 13 years old when he was kidnapped by African raiders, sold to European slave traders and subsequently transported to Grenada in the Caribbean. In 1772, after nearly two years as a slave in the Caribbean, his owner, Alexander Campbell, took him to England. It is possible that this Campbell was the same man who was temporarily the owner of OLAUDAH EQUIANO in Virginia.

The following year, at the age of 16, Cugoano was baptised John Stuart in St James' Church, London, perhaps in an attempt to confirm and guarantee his liberty. It is not yet known how Cugoano obtained his liberty, whether by running away, purchase or as a consequence of the actions of his owner. He does say that his owner sent him to school and it seems likely that he was employed by Campbell after his arrival in England. He had, however, arrived in the country a few months after the famous Mansfield judgement, and at a time when both baptism and marriage were thought of as means to reinforce freedom from slavery. In 1772, in an historic legal judgement, Lord Mansfield, Lord Chief Justice of England, ruled that James Somerset, formerly a slave in Massachusetts who had liberated himself when brought to England, could not be forced to return to the colonies by his owner. This judgement has been widely interpreted. It did not mean the end of slavery in England, Mary Prince was still a slave in London nearly sixty years later in 1831; but it did undermine the institution of slavery in England which was already under attack from the self-liberation of slaves and the activities of the abolitionists.

Whatever the exact circumstances, by the mid-1780s Cugoano had found employment as a servant to the well-known artists Richard and Maria Cosway in London. As a consequence of this employment and Cosway's patronage by the Prince of Wales, Cugoano came into contact with many of the leading personalities of the day including Joshua Reynolds, William Blake and Joseph Nollekens, and appeared in several paintings and literary portraits.

Cugoano's first known anti-slavery activity occurred in 1786 when he and William Green went to the aid of Harry Demane, who had been forced by his owner on board a ship going to the Caribbean. Cugoano and Green went to Granville Sharpe, the well-known abolitionist, who managed to take legal action to rescue Demane. It is not known exactly when Cugoano came into contact with Equiano, but the two worked together throughout the late 1780s alongside others in the Sons of Africa, as the Black abolitionists styled themselves. From 1786 Cugoano's name appears alongside other 'Sons of Africa' in letters that were sent by them to abolitionists, politicians and others connected with the campaign against the slave trade. It is also from this time that there exist personal letters from Cugoano written with a similar purpose or with reference to the publication of his book.

In 1787 Cugoano published his *Thoughts and Sentiments*, which some writers have alleged might have been co-written with Equiano. There were three editions of the book in 1787 and a French translation was published the following year. Then in 1791 Cugoano published a summarised version of the book entitled *Thoughts and Sentiments on the Evil of Slavery; or the Nature of Servitude as Admitted by the Law of God, Compared to the Modern Slavery of the Africans in the West Indies; In an Answer to the Advocates for Slavery and Oppression*. However, there is as yet no information about how these publications were received by their intended audience. It was also probably in 1791 that Cugoano wrote to Granville Sharpe suggesting that he might travel to Nova Scotia to recruit Black settlers for Sierra Leone. Cugoano's letter suggests that he had suffered from problems of racism in Britain and was looking for an opportunity abroad. But it is unclear whether he left Britain at that time. Indeed little more is known about his life or his death. In the 1791 version of his book he states his intention to open a school 'for all such of his Complexion as are desirous of being acquainted with the Knowledge of the Christian Religion and the Laws of Civilization'. Cugoano adds that his sole motive for such an undertaking is that he has found several of his countrymen in England without access to such knowledge. Once again, at the present time, there is no further information as to whether Cugoano was able to raise the necessary finance for this undertaking nor if he succeeded in his aims.

It is therefore only from his writing that we can judge the importance of Cugoano's contribution to the struggle against slavery and the slave trade. He was the first published African critic of the trans-Atlantic slave trade and the first African to publicly demand the abolition of the trade and the freeing of all slaves at a time when few other abolitionists made such demands. In his writing Cugoano demolishes all the principal pro-slavery arguments which questioned the humanity of Africans or preached the benevolence of the trade. The fact that an African did write such works was in itself an important refutation of the plantocracy racism of the period. But Cugoano did much more, stating that enslaved Africans had the duty to emancipate themselves from slavery and declaring that the inhabitants of Britain were all responsible for the slavery of Africans unless they actively campaigned against it. In order to effect the complete abolition of the trade that he demanded, Cugoano suggested establishing an anti-slavery patrol along the West African coast and what came to be called 'legitimate trade' with Africans. These were exactly the proposals being presented by other abolitionists and precisely the course of action pursued by Britain twenty years later.

Cugoano also warned of the possible dire consequences if slavery and the slave trade were not abolished by referring to historical examples of 'severe retaliations, revolutions and dreadful overthrows' that would be the fate of those who had been traffickers in slaves.

Cugoano's *Thoughts and Sentiments* is important for another reason. Whether or not Equiano was the co-author, Cugoano did refer to other African narratives on slavery, including those of John Marrant and James Gronniosaw whose works had previously been published in England and clearly established himself as part of the tradition of those African writers in England who made their contribution to the abolitionist movement.

HA

Main publications

Thoughts and Sentiments on the Evil and Wicked Traffic of the Slavery and Commerce of the Human Species, Humbly Submitted to the Inhabitants of Great Britain, by Ottobah Cugoano, a Native of Africa, London, 1787; facsimile of the first edition, with an introduction and notes by Paul Edwards, London, Dawsons of Pall Mall, 1969.

Thoughts and Sentiments on the Evils of Slavery and Other Writings, edited with an introduction and notes by Vincent Carretta, London, Penguin, 1999.

Further reading

Edwards, Paul and David Dabydeen (eds), *Black Writers in Britain, 1760–1890*, Edinburgh, Edinburgh University Press, 1991.

Fryer, Peter, *Staying Power: The History of Black People in Britain*, London, Pluto Press, 1984.

Shyllon, Folarin, *Black People in Britain 1555–1833*, London, Oxford University Press, 1977.

Constance Cummings-John
(1918 – 2000)

Constance Cummings-John's political activism encompassed her home of Sierra Leone, the United Kingdom and the USA. Active in political groups in all these countries, she and I.T.A. WALLACE-JOHNSON were the only Krio (i.e. elite, settler) Sierra Leone politicians to fight for the inclusion of Protectorate (i.e. native) peoples in the Sierra Leone political process.

Constance was born into the elite Krio Horton (see JAMES HORTON) family of the British colony of Freetown, Sierra Leone. The Krios were the descendants of rebellious Jamaicans, Barbadians and discontented Black Nova Scotians settled in the area by the British in the eighteenth century. Britain offered some support and encouraged the Krio to become anglophiles and to see themselves as much superior to the peoples of the hinterland, also under British domination, and known as the Protectorate. The population proportion was roughly 1:35.

Constance's family were intellectuals, entrepreneurs and professionals; her mother had been educated in England to become a typical Edwardian cultured lady. Raised in a genteel Europhile household, Constance attended the best of the local (missionary) schools, belonged to elite clubs and societies, and visited with members of the family living in other West African colonies. In 1935 she was sent to London to train as a teacher, a qualification she gained in a year, despite involvement in the major Black organisations in London, the West African Students' Union led by LADIPO SOLANKE and the League of Coloured People under the leadership of Dr HAROLD MOODY.

Against the firm advice of the Colonial Office, in September 1937 Constance went for further study to Cornell University in the USA. This involved travel through the southern states and completed her education in racism, which had begun at her London YWCA hostel and on the streets of London. Was it the anger welling up from this part of her education that gave her the courage, though she was only a teenager, to speak out against a missionary regaling the congregation in a church in Ithaca, NY with tales of jungles and cannibals in Freetown? She not only challenged this Christian's perversions of reality, but accused missionaries of destroying Africans' 'egos … the feeling that we are human beings'.

On her return to London in 1936 Constance became involved in the much more radical Black organisation, the International African Service Bureau (IASB), led by GEORGE PADMORE; she married newly qualified (but much older) lawyer Ethnan Cummings-John, and within a year returned to Freetown. Offered a job as inspector of schools by the colonial government, she chose instead to accept the principalship of the Black-led African Methodist Episcopal Girls' Industrial school, which grew rapidly under her guidance and fund-raising abilities.

By February 1938 Constance had set up a branch of the League of Coloured People, but was soon disappointed in the mainly professional/conservative membership, which was not interested in her aim of involving Protectorate peoples in politics. Within a few months she informed the parent-body in London that she wanted the LCP to affiliate with the newly formed West African Youth League (WAYL). She described to the Londoners the various 'divide and rule – the Colony from the Protectorate' policies being promulgated by the government. She also pointed out that an 'English' graduate from a British university entering the Sierra Leone civil service started at a salary of £400 pa, whereas an African graduating from the same university started at £45.

The WAYL was established in April of the same year by the radical activist I.T.A. Wallace-Johnson, who had recently returned from London. Wallace-Johnson, Nnamdi Azikiwe and a number of Ghanaians, including some of Constance's relatives, had set up the WAYL in Accra in 1935; it aimed for the 'social, political and economic emancipation' of West African colonies. As Wallace-Johnson and Constance had been fellow members of the IASB in London, naturally Constance immediately joined the new organisation, and soon became its vice-president. The WAYL proved vastly popular as it set about establishing trade unions and its own branches amongst the Protectorate; Muslims, previously excluded from all political and social activities, were welcome; Protectorate people served on its various committees. Constance was one of four WAYL candidates to win a seat in the 1938 Freetown Municipal elections, in which she gained more votes than any other candidate. She thus became the youngest and only female politician to win an election in the African colonies. Her main concerns as councillor were education, library facilities, market conditions and city sanitation.

The Colonial Office put considerable pressure on Constance to repudiate Wallace-Johnson, considered as a dangerous communist rabble rouser. She refused, but lost her seat in the 1942 elections. By then Wallace-Johnson was languishing in 'preventive detention' and the WAYL was in its death throes. Constance herself barely escaped detention.

The political situation in Sierra Leone became so dire for Constance that with her two sons, and evading the British embargo on travel to the USA, she travelled there in 1946. Though helped by Asadata Dafora, her New York based, well-known dancer brother (né Austin Horton), Constance was unable to obtain work as a teacher, and had to work in hospitals. Soon she was involved with, and then served on the executive committee of, the American Council for African Education (ACAE), set up by Nigerian Nwafor Orizu, which aimed to encourage and enable West African students to study in the USA. The ACAE was a thorn in the flesh of the Colonial Office as was the Council on African Affairs led by PAUL ROBESON, who was soon to be hounded by the anti-communist witch-hunters; Constance served on the CAA's executive. In 1950 the Council, on the recommendation of ALPHAEUS HUNTON, donated $100 'for the cause of free education for girls in Sierra Leone', and noted Constance's 'splendid and untiring efforts during the past two years towards collecting funds for this institution in your home'.

In 1951 Constance returned to Freetown, where, with her husband's support, the profits from the quarrying business she had started during the Second World War and much fund-raising, she built a school, which she intended to be free. This was anathema to the colonial government, which put every conceivable obstacle in her way. Eventually agreement was reached that she would charge a nominal annual fee. Partly emulating the vocational/commercial education espoused by her relative, Adelaide Casely Hayford, who had started a school some decades earlier, by 1953 the school had 611 pupils and the government agreed in 1954 to pay the salaries of the secondary department staff. While building her school, named after Eleanor Roosevelt whom she had met in the USA, Constance studied for and obtained the licentiate from the London College of Preceptors.

On her return home Constance had joined the Protectorate-led Sierra Leone People's Party, formed by Dr (later Sir) Milton Margai, to contest the forthcoming elections. Its motto was 'One Country, One People'. The reforms in 1951 merged Colony and Protectorate politically; the Legislative Council, while allowed to retain the appointed White members, now had a majority of elected Africans, despite a still grossly limited franchise. At the elections held later that year the SLPP gained an overwhelming majority in the reformed Legislative Council. This was much resented by the majority of the Krios.

Much concerned over the position of women, Constance started the Sierra Leone Women's Movement. The SLWM campaigned on a variety of issues, ranging from trading rights to education, and for a farmers' bank. It published a newspaper, established a women traders' cooperative and conducted evening classes. Constance's constant concern was to include Protectorate women in the work of the SLWM and to ensure that Krio concerns did not dominate it. As the SLWM grew, it made international contacts, and in 1960 became a founder member of the Federation of Sierra Leone Women's Organisations.

In 1952 the Governor appointed Constance to a seat on the Freetown Council, where she continued to work for the issues she had raised in 1938, and those raised by the SLWM. Constance also served on the SLPP's executive, and maintained her campaign for the inclusion of Protectorate peoples and women in its policies. In 1957 general elections were held for the new, elected House of Representatives, though the franchise was still restricted to men. Constance decided to stand for election as an SLPP candidate; she again gained the most votes and became one of two women in the new Sierra Leone government. Though the SLPP was returned to power, the Krio-led opposition party succeeded in forcing the women's resignations.

Though deeply shaken by the accusations levelled at her, but uncomfortable with her position as a government nominee, in 1958 Constance again stood for elections to the Municipal Council and topped the polls. Back on the Council, she continued her struggles for municipal (as opposed to denominational) education, and for the market women against new, high 'tolls' for market stalls, and against the decree forcing women to buy staples of rice and palm oil from the large British firms (rather than direct from producers), and for a farmers' bank. She continued to run the Roosevelt School and to head the SLWM, which demanded more and more international travel.

For example, in 1960 she attended the UN Seminar on the Participation of Women In Public Life held in Addis Ababa.

In 1961 Sierra Leone was granted independence; but Protectorate and Colony were still only united in name, not in spirit. Probably to get troublesome Constance out of the way (there were even plots to murder her), the now conservative-led SLPP government appointed Ethnan Cummings-John as Ambassador to Liberia. Constance hated much of the role now forced upon her, and soon returned to Sierra Leonean politics. In January 1966, the country's second Prime Minister (Albert Margai, the brother of Sir Milton, who had died in 1964) appointed her Mayor of Freetown – the first African woman to be in charge of a free African city. Constance used her position to attempt to unite the people of the city and to elevate the position of women. She initiated a sanitation campaign in the city and the markets; street traders were regulated; attempts were made to channel the energies of the growing number of street urchins; a municipal secondary school was set up.

But Constance did not have much time: political upheavals resulted in a commission of enquiry into Freetown's finances and, while she was abroad attending a meeting of the Women's International Democratic Federation, she was charged with a misuse of public funds. The SLPP lost the 1966 general election, but the new All Peoples Congress government was overthrown by a military takeover. Constance was advised not to return and that it was useless to contest the charge.

Thus Constance returned to London after thirty years' absence. Though the city had changed radically and her old political associations no longer existed, she was soon again involved politically. She worked with the local branch of the Labour Party and the Co-Operative Society; she served in many schools as a governor and became involved with a number of 'community' organisations. Very active in the Campaign for Nuclear Disarmament, Constance spoke on CND platforms around the country, and formed the Women for Disarmament group.

Constance tried to re-settle in Freetown in 1974–6, but the conditions were too chaotic. She returned to her London commitments, but maintained her links with both her old party, the SLPP, the women's movement, and her school. In 1996 she went to Nigeria to attend the launch of her autobiography, and then again tried to settle in Freetown. The SLPP had won the elections, and she hoped to help Sierra Leone regain its stability. Her hopes were soon dashed and she returned to London in 1998. Undoubtedly devastated by the continuing tragic events in Sierra Leone, Constance died on 21 February 2000.

MS

Main publications

Cummings-John, Constance A., *Memoirs of a Krio Leader* (introduced by LaRay Denzer), Ibadan, Sam Bookman Educational, 1995.

Further reading

Cromwell, Adelaide, *An African Victorian Feminist: The Life and Times of Adelaide Smith Casely Hayford*, Washington, Noward University Press, 1986.

Denzer, LaRay, 'Constance A. Cummings-John of Sierra Leone: her early political career', *Tarikh*, 7/1, 1981.

Denzer, LaRay, 'The influence of pan-Africanism in the career of Constance A. Cummings-John', in Robert A. Hill (ed.), *Pan-African Biography*, Los Angeles, African Studies Center, University of California, 1987.

Von Eschen, Penny M., *Race Against Empire: Black Americans and Anticolonialism 1937–1957*, Ithaca, Cornell University Press.

Martin Robinson Delany
(1812 – 85)

Delany was a proponent of the equality of men and women, of a common cause between all expatriated Africans, and of a return to Africa of those with skills to raise it to the new technological standards of the Europeans. His analyses and writing foreshadowed those of both FRANTZ FANON and W.E.B. DU BOIS

Martin was born to a free mother and an enslaved father in Virginia, North America. In 1822, to escape prosecution when the authorities discovered that the family could read, Mrs Delany and the children moved to the free state of Pennsylvania. When Delany Sr managed to buy his freedom he joined his family. However, as the family could not afford to pay for a high-school education, Martin migrated again – to Pittsburgh in 1831, where he worked on the waterfront and attended adult education classes at night.

Martin was accepted as an apprentice by a White abolitionist, Dr Andrew McDowell. He could not complete his unpaid apprenticeship, but his master had so much faith in him that he sent him out to do routine work, for which he was paid. By 1837 he was listed in the Pittsburgh *Business Directory* as doing 'cupping, leeching and bleeding' – standard (ineffectual) remedies for many ills.

Having luckily lodged with a member of the Anti-Slavery Society, young Delany was soon involved in Black politics – for example, he attended the 1836 annual Convention of Coloured Men. In 1840 he joined the campaign for Black enfranchisement in Pennsylvania; in 1843 he launched a newspaper, *The Mystery*, which advocated the end of slavery and adequate schooling for both boys and girls.

Also in 1843 he married Catherine Richards; the couple eventually had nine children, of whom six survived into adulthood. All were named after Black heroes and heroines. Catherine was – had to be – a very resourceful woman. Not only did she support the family financially by working as a seamstress when Delany began to go on lecture tours, and when he was a student at Harvard, but she had to raise the children virtually by herself as Martin was often either on the road or living in other cities.

Delany began to lecture both in order to publicise his newspaper and the issues which his paper advocated. When *The Mystery* folded, Delany moved to Rochester to work on FREDERICK DOUGLASS' paper, *The North Star*. He co-edited the paper from 1847 to 1849. The two men did not always agree: by now Delany was a nationalist and Douglass an integrationist. Their different perspectives were summed up by

Douglass: 'thank God for making me a man simply; Delany always thanks him for making him a *Black man*'.

The paper did not prosper and Delany returned to Pittsburgh and resumed his 'medical' business. He also completed his apprenticeship and then tried to get into a medical school to complete his training. All the medical schools refused him except, eventually, Harvard. But he could not complete the two-year course: after protests by his White fellow students, he was asked to leave at the end of the winter semester, 1851. There were no protests by the considerable number of abolitionists in Boston!

Back in Pittsburgh, Delany now practised as a doctor, but only treated Blacks. In 1852 he tried to patent an invention, but this was refused as he was not considered a 'citizen'. He lectured as much as he could, at least partly to dispute the 'findings' of the phrenologists, who had 'proved' that Caucasians were superior to Africans because they had a larger cranium; thus the enslavement of inferior Africans was 'natural'. From the dissections he had had to perform at Harvard, Delany knew that this was all nonsense.

By now Delany was a grossly troubled man. His trip through the South in 1839 had demonstrated the terrible conditions under which Black enslaved people had to live. Probably his experiences at Harvard, as well as the Fugitive Slave Law passed in 1850, which demanded the return of slaves who had escaped to the North and put the onus of proof of free status on the suspected escapees, were a death knell to Delany's hopes of Black peoples ever achieving equality. Though he continued to maintain that the USA had been built by the labour power of Black peoples, and that they had as much right, if not more, to be there, he began to argue for Black emigration.

To put forth his views Delany published *The Condition, Elevation, Emigration and Destiny of the Colored People of the United States* in 1852. The book reveals the conundrum faced by Delany: he maintained that 'America [is] our destination and our home' (p.171) and devoted many chapters to the achievements of Black peoples in the USA. Yet the situation was hopeless: for example, the franchise, even where granted to Black people, was meaningless: all Blacks could do was vote 'somebody into office to help them make laws to degrade us' (p.191). Believing that 'we must not leave this continent', he advocated emigration. 'Fugitives' should go to Canada or Mexico, while free Blacks should emigrate to 'Central and South America [which] are the ultimate destination and future home of the colored race on this continent' (p.177). Yet, by the time he came to write the Appendix, Delany was considering emigration to Africa. Certainly not to Liberia, whose continued dependence on the White-led American Colonization Society meant that Liberians were not 'freemen [but] voluntary slaves' (p.171). What he now advocated was an 'expedition comprised of a physician, a botanist, a chemist, a geologist, a geographer, and a surveyor to the Eastern Coast of Africa' to search for a suitable place of settlement for 'colored adventurers'. Once settled, the vast riches of Africa would provide an 'immense trade'. He envisaged the building of a railway from the East Coast to the Kingdom of Dahomey to enhance this trade. Britain and France, he felt, would support his scheme.

Most interestingly, Delany analysed the condition of 'colored' people in the USA in terms that foreshadowed the work of psychiatrist Frantz Fanon. 'We have been, by our oppressor, despoiled of our purity, and corrupted in our native characteristics, so that we have inherited their vices, and but few of their virtues, leaving us in character, really a *broken people*', Delany wrote (p.209). Black people had to rid themselves of the devastation wrought by years of subservience; they had to equip themselves (by work and study) to be able to 'return to their former national position of self-government and independence ... [N]o people are respected by any nation, until they are presented in a national capacity', he argued (pp.12, 210).

Delany sought to put his plans into practice by speaking at the various emigration conventions and by going on lecture tours. Prior to the Fugitive Slave Law relatively few Black people were interested in emigration, which had only been promoted by the American Colonization Society, in order, they argued, to rid the States of free Blacks. Now the position was changed. There was a convention in Toronto in 1851; Delany himself called the next one, the National Emigration Convention held in Cleveland in 1854, which was attended by almost 1,500 people. There were two notable innovations at this convention: women were not only welcome at the executive sessions, but were allowed to speak and vote; and there was an emphasis on the unity of all in the African diaspora, irrespective of their actual skin colour. In his keynote address, 'The Political Destiny of the Colored Race', Delany emphasised that:

> for 2000 years the determined aim of the white has been to crush the colored races ... The great issue will be a question of black and white ... The Blacks and colored races are four-sixths of all the population of the world: and these people are fast tending to a common cause with each other ... The white race will only acknowledge as equals those who will not submit to their rule.
>
> (Griffith, 26–7; Sterling, 156)

The convention appointed a Foreign Commission, which sent the Revd J. Holly to investigate the possibilities of emigration to Haiti. As not sufficient funds could be raised, Holly travelled at his own expense and the plans for reconnoitering Central America had to be abandoned. Delany attempted to interest the Jamaican politician Edward Jordon in his schemes, but without success.

In 1856 Delany and his family moved to Chatham, Ontario. There Delany partici-pated in agitation against the Fugitive Law, worked on the Underground Railroad (which helped escaping Blacks), practised medicine, lectured, and contributed to the local *Provincial Freeman*. The Supreme Court Dred Scott decision of 1857, which declared that Blacks were not US citizens, further alienated Delany from his homeland.

Delany read the books of European missionaries and explorers, and was especially taken by any that advocated commercial activities. He sought the advice of Sierra Leoneans settled in Yorubaland about the possibility of Black settlement there. Delany persuaded the 1858 Emigration Convention to agree to support (but it did not fund) a scientific expedition to the Niger River. Delany embarked on a fund-raising tour for an expedition whose object was 'the moral, social and political elevation of ourselves and the regeneration of Africa'. He began to seek 'men of African descent, properly qualified and of pure and fixed principles' to accompany him.

While fund-raising he wrote a novel, *Blake*, which was serialised in the *Anglo-African Magazine*. His hero, Blake, is a West Indian who advocates revolution in the USA and later leads an actual slave revolution in Cuba. The book not only presented a wholly non-subservient Black as the hero, but also espoused the unity of Native Americans and expatriated Africans in the necessary struggles against the colonisers.

However, in the face of competition from the White-led American Colonization Society, Delany had to abandon plans for a large-scale expedition. West Indian Robert Campbell, his sole expedition colleague, left before Delany, and consulted British cotton-growers before sailing on to Lagos. On learning this, Delany left immediately for West Africa. After a five-week stay in Liberia during which he changed his mind about the settlers there, he left for Lagos, where, after lengthy discussions with the men of importance and the ruler, he was granted a 330 sq. foot plot of ground. Delany finally caught up with Campbell in Abeokuta in November 1859. The two men had extensive discussions with the Alake Okukenu of Abeokuta, who agreed to admit a limited number of settlers and to grant them equal rights. The settlers had to respect Ebga laws, the Alake specified. They were to bring 'a knowledge of the arts and sciences, agriculture and other mechanic and industrial occupations'. With financial aid mainly from the British Anti-Slavery Society and the Cotton Supply Association of Manchester, the two men then toured other Yoruba cities, and obtained similar agreements. They then travelled to Britain, where they were positively received.

Both men wrote accounts of their journey; Delany's *Official Report of the Niger Valley Exploring Party*, was published in both London and New York in 1861. It is a very respectful account of the peoples whose countries he travelled through, their agriculture, animal husbandry and implements; their industriousness and affability. Towns and markets he found to be 'orderly and well regulated'. Slavery existed he noted, but of a totally different kind to that in European colonies: the enslaved were prisoners-of-war and criminals, and were not too harshly treated and were usually eventually freed. It was 'Protestant kings and Protestant missionaries' on the coast who were the 'most cruel oppressors' (p.50). The Africans, Delany noted, wondered what the use was of the book-learning and 'civilisation' being brought to them by the missionaries, if power can only belong to the White man? 'Africa is our fatherland', Delany wrote, and must be 'regenerated. Her position among the existing nations will depend mainly upon the high standard she may gain compared with them in all her relations … politically and commercially … Africa [is] for the African race …' (pp.54–61).

However, Delany's plans were doomed to failure. Anglican missionaries in Abeokuta, fearful of the presence of educated African Americans, persuaded the Alake (king) that he should deny signing an agreement with Delany. With the outbreak of the American Civil War, the British became fearful of their source of raw cotton drying up, and sought to advance cotton-growing along the Niger. The first step was the deposition of the Docemo (ruler) of Lagos in 1862. As the British now ruled Lagos, the Alake had little option but to bow to their influence. This led Delany to wonder if there was any difference between the British and the Americans: the 'great powers' policy is changed from that of abject slavery to reducing them to political dependents' (Sterling, p.224).

On his return to the USA, Delany, whose family was still in Chatham, undertook another lecture tour, to describe Africa as he had seen it, which was in contrast to the usual picture of a savage, cannibalistic people. This work was interrupted by the Civil War; Delany 'rejoined' the USA, by becoming a recruiter for the Black Regiments. (This also allowed him to continue educating Blacks about Africa.) In 1864, the year Delany proposed to Abraham Lincoln the creation of Black officers to lead an all-Black army, his family returned to the USA. Lincoln agreed and made Delany a major – thus Delany became the first Black officer in the Union army. But the war ended before Delany's plans could be put into practice.

Delany was reassigned to the Freedmen's Bureau. From now on his career took a new turn. Though he tried, unsuccessfully, to obtain the post of ambassador to Liberia, emigration as a solution to the problems of life in the USA was replaced by the hopes entailed in emancipation. Delany accepted various government positions but was unable to use these to ensure equal treatment for the freedmen. In 1874 he decided to stand for election as an Independent Republican in the State elections, but was unsuccessful.

The initial euphoria of freedom was rapidly replaced by fears that Southern Whites were intent on regaining power. The position of Black peoples in the South deteriorated rapidly. Though the fifteenth Amendment of the Constitution had given them the right to vote, various means were used to deny this and other rights to Blacks. A new bout of emigration fever started, and Delany decided to return to Africa. However, he could not go without a job there, and the government refused him a posting. In 1878 he joined the board of the Liberian Exodus Joint-Stock Steamship Company, but probably bad management and ill luck resulted in bankruptcy.

He returned to the practice of medicine, and despite having to catch up with medical advances, found time to write another book. The *Principia of Ethnology: the Origin of Races and Colour* (1879) was a refutation of social Darwinism, and argued that Africans were just as capable as Europeans.

In 1884 Delany went home to his family, who had settled in Wilberforce, Ohio, the previous year. (Some years previously the first family home there, containing all his papers, had been burnt down.) He died a year later, in January 1885, at the age of seventy-two.

MS

Delany's unpublished works

The Condition, Elevation, Emigration and Destiny of the Colored People of the United States (1852), Baltimore, Black Classic Press, 1993.

Blake, or the Huts of America (1859), Boston, Beacon Press, 1970.

Howard H. Bell (ed.), *Search For a Place: M.R. Delany and Robert Campbell*, University of Michigan, Ann Arbor Paperbacks, 1971.

Further reading

Griffith, Cyril E., *The African Dream: Martin Delany and the Emergence of Pan-African Thought*, University Park, Pennsylvania State University Press, 1975.
Sterling, Dorothy, *The Making of an Afro-American*, New York, Doubleday, 1971.
Ullman, Victor, *Martin R. Delany*, Boston, Beacon Press, 1971.

Cheikh Anta Diop
(1923 – 86)

Cheikh Anta Diop, historian and politician, has become an internationally known writer on the history of Africa, most famous for his thesis on the 'African origin of civilisation', the centrality of Ancient Egypt to Africa's history and to the development of 'civilisation' in Europe.

Diop was born the son of Massamba Sassoum Diop and his wife Magatte Diop in the village of Caytou, near Bambey in the region of Diourbel, in west-central Senegal, then a French colony, in December 1923. He was educated locally, receiving both Koranic and Western education, then secondary education at Dakar and St Louis. In 1946 he left Senegal and entered the famous Sorbonne University in Paris where he initially studied philosophy, while at the same time beginning his own studies in linguistics. Diop was in Paris at a time when it was an important centre of anti-colonialism and anti-imperialism and a meeting place for many activists from French colonies in Africa and the Caribbean, where the ideas of Négritude had developed.

From 1946 onwards Diop was a leading student activist in the anti-colonial and Pan-African movements amongst students in France. He was a founding member, and from 1950–3 secretary-general, of the Association des Étudiants du Rassemblement Démocratique Africain (AERDA), the student wing of the Francophone Pan-African anti-colonial movement that had been founded in Bamako in 1946. Diop was also one of the leading figures in many of the other Pan-African student organisations in France, including the Association Générale des Étudiants Africains en Paris (AGEAP), which was founded in 1946 with African independence from France as its primary goal. In July 1951 he helped to organise the first post-war Pan-African student congress in Paris, which included the participation of the London-based West African Students' Union. From 1952–4 Diop was also the political editor, as well as a major contributor, to AERDA's monthly publication *La Voix de L'Afrique Noire*.

It was during the late 1940s in the famous *Présence Africaine*, the influential journal that Diop helped to establish, that he first expounded his Afrocentric ideas on the 'African origin of civilisation' and the significance of Ancient Egypt as a profoundly African civilisation. Diop's ideas had a major influence on the anti-colonial thinking of other Francophone African students, and undermined the racist ideas then prevalent that Africa had no history and the French colonialist theory of assimilation. At the same time Diop also began to propose the need for a federation of African states, 'from the Sahara to the Cape', if Africa's independence was to be established and consolidated. Underpinning this pan-African unity was Diop's belief in African cultural unity and the important role that historical and linguistic research could play in developing this unity.

Diop wrote his doctoral dissertation on the Egyptian origin of African civilisation, but his research was rejected by the academic authorities in France. His thesis was subsequently published in 1955 as *Nations Nègres et Culture* in *Présence Africaine*, and in English as part of *The African Origin of Civilisation: Myth or Reality* (1974). In his early years Diop was strongly influenced by Marxism and the thinking of AIMÉ CÉSAIRE, but with the publication of his research and his attendance at the First and Second Congresses of Black Writers and Artists in 1956 and 1959, he began to establish his own international reputation that grew throughout the rest of his life. In 1960 the Sorbonne finally awarded him a doctoral degree for research work that was subsequently published in English as *Pre-colonial Black Africa* (1987) and *The Cultural Unity of Black Africa* (1963). By 1966 Diop, along with W.E.B. DU BOIS, was already being honoured by the First World Black Festival of Arts and Culture 'as the writer who had exerted the greatest influence on African people in the twentieth century'.

In 1953 Diop married his French wife Louise Marie Maes, the mother of his four children. For a time he taught science subjects in French schools but returned to Senegal in 1960. The following year he was appointed to a research post at the Institut Fondamental d'Afrique Noire (IFAN), where he founded one of the first radiocarbon dating laboratories in Africa and continued his work to establish that Ancient Egypt was the forerunner of modern African and European civilisation. He also continued his involvement in politics and played a leading role in several political organisations including the Front National du Sénégal, and in 1962 was briefly imprisoned for his activities. In 1961 he was one of the founders and the first secretary-general of the Bloc des Masses Sénégalaises (BMS) which opposed the neo-colonial policies of the government of LÉOPOLD SENGHOR. In 1963 Diop and the BMS refused to accept ministerial posts in Senghor's government, a stand that later that year contributed to the banning of the BMS by the Senegalese government. In 1965 all opposition groups were similarly banned. In 1979 Diop was charged with breaking the law for his involvement with the Rassemblement National Démocratique (RND), a new opposition organisation formed in 1976, but subsequently banned and denied legal recognition until 1981. In 1982 the RND won a seat in the National Assembly but Diop declined to enter parliamentary politics. Diop and the RND established a political journal written in Wolof entitled *Taxaw* (meaning *Stand Up*) as a vehicle for their criticism of the Senegalese government. In particular the journal voiced criticism of the government's policy of retaining French as the medium of instruction in educational institutions. Diop favoured the use of African languages and demonstrated their suitability by translating Einstein's theory of relativity and other foreign works into Wolof.

As a consequence of his writing and research, in 1970 Diop was invited to become a member of the UNESCO's international committee established to oversee the writing and publication of the eight-volume *General History of Africa*. In 1974 he took part in the important international symposium held in Cairo on the theme of 'the peopling of Ancient Egypt', an occasion on which he sought to present evidence to support his thesis that the Egyptians were Black Africans, in the face of contrary views presented by other international experts. Diop was subsequently invited to participate in many international conferences and symposia, throughout Africa, Europe and the US.

Diop's main fame and significance rests on his writing on the history of Africa, much of it based on an elaboration of the research he carried out during the 1950s. He sought to prove that Ancient Egypt was a 'black African civilization', central to understanding the development of culture and civilisation throughout the African continent, where Diop detected many common features. According to Diop's thesis 'the history of black Africa will remain suspended in air and cannot be written correctly until African historians dare to connect it with the history of Egypt'. At the same time he also saw Ancient Egypt as an important contributor to the development of early civilisation in Ancient Greece and elsewhere in Europe, and stated that what he termed 'the moral fruit' of Egyptian civilisation 'is to be counted among the assets of the Black world'. According to Diop's view, therefore, the 'Black world', far from being an 'insolvent debtor', is the 'very initiator of the "western" civilisation flaunted before our eyes today'. Diop also made the suggestion, based on his reading of early Arabic and European sources, that Africans may have made sea voyages across the Atlantic in the pre-Columbian period. Although he was not the originator of this idea, Diop drew attention to a possibility that prompted other writers, especially those in the African diaspora, to carry out more research in this area. In his later works, such as *Civilisation or Barbarism: An Authentic Anthropology*, Diop continued to grapple with some of the key questions about Africa's historical past, such as the existence of laws governing evolution and social change in African societies, the characteristics of African states and social structures and the controversy surrounding a peculiarly African mode of production.

Diop's work also stressed the importance of political and economic pan-Africanism and he wrote two major works, *Black Africa: The Economic and Cultural Basis of a Federal State* (1984) and *The Cultural Unity of Black Africa* (1963), to elaborate and substantiate his views. In Diop's view 'the rediscovery of the true past of the African peoples should ... contribute to uniting them, each and all, binding them together from the north to the south of the continent'. His writing was therefore always presented as a contribution to solving political problems, such as undermining the theoretical basis of imperialist ideologies concerning Africa and Africans. Diop believed that 'the negation of the history and intellectual accomplishments of Black Africans' was the 'mental murder' that paved the way for physical genocide in Africa. It then followed that he believed that a scientific understanding of Egyptian culture and its centrality to Africa was the 'necessary condition' to be able to 'construct a body of modern human societies, in order to renovate African culture'. Diop's belief that in antiquity knowledge passed from Africa to Europe also meant that he believed that Africans must draw not only from African sources but from the 'common intellectual property of humanity'. In his later works he always returned to consider the relation of history to contemporary political problems, including his concern with the nature and history of class struggle and revolution in the African continent.

Cheikh Anta Diop died of a heart attack on 7 February 1986 in Dakar.

HA

Main publications

The African Origin of Civilisation: Myth or Reality? Chicago, Lawrence Hill Books, 1974.
Black Africa: The Economic and Cultural Basis of a Federal State, Chicago, Lawrence Hill Books, 1984.
Pre-colonial Black Africa, Chicago, Lawrence Hill Books, 1987.
Civilisation or Barbarism: An Authentic Anthropology, Chicago, Lawrence Hill Books, 1991.

Further reading

Howe, S., *Afrocentrism: Mythical Pasts and Imagined Homes*, London, Verso, 1998.
Van Sertima, I., and L. Williams (eds), *Great African Thinkers. Vol. 1: Cheikh Anta Diop*, New Brunswick, Transaction Publishers, 1986.

Frederick Douglass
(1818 – 95)

Frederick Douglass, African American writer, abolitionist and political activist, was born a slave in Maryland in February 1818 and named Frederick Augustus Washington Bailey. He was one of several children born to Harriet Bailey, who worked as a field slave for her owner Aaron Anthony. It was rumoured that Anthony was Frederick's father. Frederick Douglass spent much of his early life with his grandmother and saw little of his mother before she died when he was seven years old. A year later he was separated from his grandmother and sent to live with the family of his owner's daughter in Baltimore. It was here that he was first taught to read and write and to learn that this knowledge, forbidden to slaves, might provide the road to his freedom from slavery. Henceforth he found ways to teach himself, or to be taught by others, and by the age of thirteen was secretly reading about the abolitionists and sharing his skills with other Black children.

At the age of fifteen, Douglass as the property of others, left Baltimore and was sent to work as a field hand on a plantation. Here he suffered all the abuses of slavery and soon earned a reputation as a slave who was prepared to resist. As a consequence in 1833 he was hired out to a professional slave-breaker. For six months he was flogged every week but then decided to fight back in what he later wrote was the turning point in his life as a slave. Frederick Douglass could have been killed for his resistance but instead he found new confidence and, as he later wrote, let it be known that 'the white man who succeeded in whipping me, must also succeed in killing me'.

Douglass soon began to plan his escape from slavery but one of his fellow conspirators betrayed him and four others. He was at first imprisoned, but his owner promised him freedom when he was 25 and sent him back to Baltimore, where he was hired out as an apprentice ship's caulker. While living in Baltimore Douglass joined a debating society organised by free Blacks and met his future wife, Anna Murray, who worked as a servant. He was now determined to escape from slavery by travelling northwards by train and boat to Philadelphia and then to New York. On 4 September 1838 Frederick Douglass reached New York City and made contact with abolitionists there. He married Anna Murray eleven days later and moved to Massachusetts where he worked as a labourer. In order to avoid recapture in New York he had changed his name to Johnson, in Massachusetts he became known as Frederick Douglass.

Douglass soon became involved with the American Anti-Slavery Society and its newspaper *Liberator*. Some of Douglass' earliest comments in the *Liberator* were in opposition to the various schemes advocating that Black Americans should be sent back to Africa. By 1841 he had begun to speak at public anti-slavery meetings and soon afterwards it was suggested that he should become a travelling lecturer for the Massachusetts Anti-Slavery Society. For the next ten years Douglass toured the northern states of the US as a lecturer and was associated with the views of the leader of the American Anti-Slavery Society, William Lloyd Garrison, who believed in non-violent opposition to slavery.

Douglass became known as one of the most skilful and eloquent of the abolitionist speakers, who spoke with great dramatic effect about his own experiences of slavery and was thereby able to counter all the pro-slavery propaganda then in existence. He also spoke about racism and segregation throughout the USA. But Douglass was such an eloquent speaker that some people doubted that he had ever been a slave. It was to establish the authenticity of his experiences that he began to write his auto-biography, *Narrative of the Life of Frederick Douglass, an American Slave, Written by Himself*, which was first published in 1845. Almost immediately it became a bestseller and was to become perhaps the most famous of all American slave narratives. Douglass amended and updated his autobiography later in his life and in 1855 wrote *My Bondage and My Freedom*, to be followed in 1881 by *The Life and Times of Frederick Douglass*, but neither surpassed the original *Narrative* in popularity.

Douglass found even greater fame as the author of the *Narrative*, but also put himself at greater risk of recapture. To avoid this fate he decided to leave America and spent two years touring England, Scotland and Ireland. Douglass for a time made common cause with the Chartists and other radicals and became a great celebrity throughout the British Isles, where he spoke to large audiences not only on slavery but also in support of self-determination for the people of Ireland. It was while Douglass was in Britain that his freedom was legally purchased by two English friends who paid his owner $710. It is generally believed that Douglass' lectures and presence in Britain were a major factor influencing the allegiance of the masses in Britain to the abolitionist cause during the ensuing American Civil War.

Douglass returned to America a free man with an international reputation. He also had his own ideas about abolition and in 1847 decided to establish his own newspaper *The North Star*, which he initially edited with MARTIN DELANY. *The North Star* became *Frederick Douglass' Paper* in 1851 and appeared on a weekly basis until 1860 when it changed to *Douglass' Monthly* which was published until 1863. These publications gave Douglass the possibility of presenting his abolitionist views through-out the USA and he was the first African American to own a publishing house. In 1870 Douglass also purchased a half share in the *New Era* and thereafter became editor of the renamed *New National Era* until its demise in 1874.

In the pages of his publications Douglass wrote not only in opposition to slavery and racism but also in support of the emancipation of women. Douglass attended the first convention for women's rights in 1848 and continued to support women's struggle for equality throughout his life, urging them, as he urged African Americans, to demand and fight for suffrage. Douglass' publications also reflected the fact that his views on abolition were changing. He began to realise that violence and political reforms, not just moral persuasion, might be necessary to end slavery, and he began to urge the readers of *The North Star* to engage in political activities. Douglass was personally involved in several political organisations through his life including the Liberty and Republican Parties. He also became a friend of the militant abolitionist John Brown, and although he refused to participate in the famous attack on the arsenal at Harpers Ferry, following it he was liable to arrest and in late 1859 had to flee to Canada, before again travelling to Britain.

During the American Civil War (1861–5) Douglass became a zealous advocate for the emancipation of all the slaves in the southern states and demanded the right of Black volunteers to enlist in the Union armies. He argued that Black people must be permitted to join in the battles for their liberation. From 1863 he was one of the principal recruiters for the first Black regiment to be formed and two of his sons were amongst the first to enlist, but Douglass was not uncritical of the discrimination that existed in the Union army and made his views known to US President Lincoln. At one stage Lincoln asked Douglass to take responsibility for the recruitment of Black soldiers, and although Douglass closed down his monthly paper in preparation he was eventually not offered a government post.

Douglass emerged during the war as one of the most far-sighted political activists and an acknowledged spokesperson for the interests of African Americans. He had already begun to turn his sights to the post-war period and to demand the guarantee of political equality and voting rights throughout the country. Although these basic rights were constitutionally guaranteed by 1870, Douglass continued his political activities, through lectures and journalism, amongst the radical wing of the Republican Party and as one of the leaders of the various national 'Coloured Conventions', including the 'Negro Labour' convention of 1871. Douglass continued to believe that the Republican Party was 'the deck' and 'all else is the sea' and that therefore it was the party to represent the interests of African Americans during the post-war period of Reconstruction. By the late 1870s it was increasingly difficult to make the same argument but Douglass received little reward for his loyalty. When he was finally given a public appointment as Marshal of the District of Columbia in 1877, this was viewed by many as political tokenism and as a means to appease political opposition to the end of Reconstruction. Later on in his life in 1881 Douglass was also named Recorder of Deeds for Washington DC, and in 1889 appointed Consul-General to Haiti and Chargé d'Affaires for Santo Domingo.

Douglass has been viewed by historians as not just one of the most prominent African Americans of the nineteenth century but also as one of the most eminent Americans of that period, whose whole life was not just devoted to the political emancipation of his own people but also to the political advancement of the USA as a whole. He delivered over 2,000 speeches for these causes, wrote numerous articles as well as three autobiographies and his novel of 1853, *The Heroic Slave*. He had, in addition to fighting for those causes aforementioned, also been a zealous campaigner for the temperance movement and a supporter of Cuban independence. Douglass shocked many, including those in his own family, when following the death of his first wife in 1884 he controversially married his former secretary, a White woman, Helen Pitts. Yet here too Douglass felt that he followed his convictions and argued 'what business has the world with the colour of my wife?' Even after this marriage and following his resignation as Consul-General to Haiti, Douglass, then in his 70s, re-emerged as one of the leaders of the movement demanding an end to the numerous lynchings of African American men that were taking place throughout the USA. In 1894, it was on this subject that he delivered one of his last great speeches, 'The Lesson of the Hour'.

Frederick Douglass died in February 1895 in Washington DC and was buried in Rochester, NY, in the USA.

HA

Main publications

Narrative of the Life of Frederick Douglass, an American Slave, Written by Himself, London, Penguin, 1995.
The Life and Times of Frederick Douglass: Written by Himself, Ware, Wordsworth, 1996.
My Bondage and My Freedom, New York, Dover, 1969.
Frederick Douglass – Selected Speeches and Articles (edited by Philip S. Foner, abridged and adapted by Yuval Taylor), Chicago, Lawrence Hill, 1999.

Further reading

McFeely, William S., *Frederick Douglass*, New York, W.W. Norton & Co, 1991.
Quarles, B., *Frederick Douglass*, New York, Da Capo, 1997.

W.E.B. Du Bois
(1868 – 1963)

William Edward Burghardt Du Bois, historian, sociologist, writer and political activist, has been called the 'father of Pan-Africanism' and has been seen as the most influential African-American intellectual of the twentieth century.

W.E.B. Du Bois was born on 23 February 1868 to Mary Burghart and Alfred Du Bois in Massachusetts, USA. He was educated locally and began his journalistic career at the age of fourteen. While still a teenager he was a correspondent for the *New York Age*, *New York Globe* and other newspapers. From 1855–8 he attended Fisk University and then was awarded a scholarship to study for two years at the University of Berlin. He then returned to the United States and became, in 1895, the first African-American student to receive a doctoral degree from Harvard University. His thesis was later published as a book entitled *The Suppression of the African Slave Trade to the United States of America, 1638–1870* (1896). In 1896 he married his first wife Nina Gomer, his partner for over fifty years and the mother of his two children.

From 1894–6 Du Bois was professor of Greek and Latin at Wilberforce University. He then taught sociology at the University of Pennsylvania and completed the research for his famous study of African-American life *The Philadelphia Negro: A Social Study* (1899), and from 1897–1910 he was a professor of economics and history. Du Bois' 'Pan-Negroism', his concern with Africa and the diaspora, was already evident in some of his early writing such as 'The Present Outlook for the Dark Races of Mankind' (1900). By the turn of the century he was already becoming more actively involved in political matters. In 1897 he joined with Alexander Crummell and others to form the American Negro Academy, which amongst other things, stressed the need for higher education for African Americans. He voiced his opposition to the Spanish-American war (1898–1901) and was a supporter of the American Anti-Imperialist League. In 1900 he attended the Pan-African Conference held in London and chaired the committee charged with drafting its appeal 'To the Nations of the World'. It was in this appeal that the famous phrase 'The problem of the twentieth century is the problem of the colour line', first appeared. Du Bois was subsequently appointed vice-chair of the US branch of the Pan-African Association, the organisation established after the Conference. He returned to London in 1911 for the Universal Races Congress, where he presented a paper on 'The Negro Race in the USA'.

In 1903 Du Bois published one of his most influential books *The Souls of Black Folk*, which some have called the most important book ever written by an African American. In this book he identified the 'colour line' as the century's key problem and wrote of the 'two warring ideals in one dark body', analysing the contradiction of being both a Black person and an American in a racist society. He also took the important political step of openly opposing the views of Booker T. Washington, 'the Great Accommodator', as he became known. At a time when there was an escalation of racism and racist attacks on the African-American population throughout the US, Washington, in his infamous 'Atlanta Compromise' speech of 1895, had proposed that African Americans should mainly concern themselves with vocational education and gaining employment. Du Bois, on the other hand, began to urge political protests and the need for agitation in order to fight for those social and political rights denied to African Americans. At the same time he developed his theory of the need of what he called the 'talented tenth', those intellectuals who would be the political leaders of the African-American people.

In June 1905, Du Bois put some of his ideas into practice. He was one of the leaders of a group of young African-American intellectuals who met at Niagara Falls, Canada to draw up a 'Declaration of Principles', a new political programme of protest and agitation that demanded political and social rights. The Niagara Movement, as it became known, campaigned for these rights but also began a legal battle to secure them through the courts. In addition, in 1907, Du Bois and two of his associates published *Horizon* to further propagate the Niagara Movement's views. Following the rapid demise of the Niagara Movement, in 1910 Du Bois became one of the leading figures in the formation of the National Association for the Advancement of Coloured People (NAACP), a member of its executive board, Director of Publicity and Research and editor of its publication, *The Crisis*, until his resignation from the organisation in 1934.

Du Bois' main role at the NAACP was as propagandist and it is estimated that at its height *The Crisis* reached 150,000 African-American households. Du Bois published many of the greatest writers of the Harlem Renaissance, as well as his and others' political views. He clearly wielded influence, especially after Washington's death, but he was not diplomatic and quarrelled not only with his NAACP colleagues but also attacked both the Black churches and sections of the press. He backed America's war effort during the First World War and, although following the war he again demanded that the returning African-American soldiers' fight must continue in the USA, he soon began to be criticised by younger more militant leaders for his conservatism. The most vociferous attacks came from MARCUS GARVEY and the Universal Negro Improvement Association (UNIA) who even referred to Du Bois as 'more of a white man then a Negro', and condemned the NAACP as dependent on 'white money'. But their rivalry was also fuelled by Du Bois' role in convening the series of post-war Pan-African Congresses which seemed to rival Garvey's own UNIA.

Du Bois, who was originally sent to France in 1918 by the NAACP to investigate the treatment of African-American soldiers in the US army, organised the first of a series of Pan-African Congresses in Paris in 1919. He had the support of the French Deputy from Senegal, Blaise Diagne and the French President, Clemenceau, and fifty-seven delegates from Africa, the Caribbean and the USA managed to attend the Congress. Du Bois put forward a proposal for the creation of a new state in Africa based on Germany's former colonies. This would be supervised by the major powers, but also take into account the views of 'the civilised Negro world', a phrase which had mainly African Americans in mind. Initially Du Bois proposed a permanent Pan-African secretariat based in Paris and he hoped that the Congress would make the voice of 'the children of Africa' heard at the post-war peace conference then in session in that city. However, the Paris Pan-African Congress had little influence and its most significant resolutions demanded that the rights of Africans and those of African descent in the colonies and elsewhere should be protected by the League of Nations.

Du Bois then took the initiative to hold a subsequent congress in 1921, located in Paris, London and Brussels, a third in London and Lisbon in 1923 and a fourth, originally scheduled to be held in the Caribbean, was ultimately held in New York in 1927. In 1929 Du Bois made plans to hold a fifth congress in Tunis in North Africa, but was denied permission by the French government. The four congresses established the idea of Pan-Africanism and drew together activists and delegates from the US, Ethiopia, Liberia, Haiti and the colonies as well as those from Africa and the Caribbean resident in Europe. They opposed racism and began to raise the demand for self-determination in the colonies, but few anti-colonial activists from the African continent itself were represented, there was little support from African-American organisations and no permanent organisation or organising centre was established.

Du Bois did visit Africa in 1923, when he was sent to the inauguration of President King of Liberia as the Special Ambassador of the US government. It was also during the 1920s that he first visited the Soviet Union and increasingly he became more interested in Marxism and more radical solutions to the social, economic and political problems facing African Americans, Africa and the diaspora. During the great Depression he also came to understand the problems and exploitation facing all working people in the USA. However, as Du Bois himself admitted, for many years he fought against both legal and social segregation and advocated economic segregation – 'such segregation as would prepare my people for the struggle they were making'. Such apparently contradictory views and differences over the orientation of *The Crisis* brought him into conflict with the NAACP and he resigned from the organisation in 1934.

In 1934 Du Bois was invited to become the head of the Department of Sociology at Atlanta University and remained at the University until he was forced to retire in 1944. During this period he wrote some of his most influential books including *Black Reconstruction in America* (1935); *Black Folk: Then and Now* (1939); and *Dusk of Dawn: An Autobiography of a Concept of Race* (1940). In 1939 he founded the influential journal *Phylon* in order 'to record the situation of the colored world and guide its course of development'.

Du Bois was forced to retire from his position at Atlanta University but in 1944 he rejoined the NAACP as Director of Special Research. In 1945 he attended the founding of the UN at San Francisco and was one of the few African Americans invited to participate in the Fifth Pan-African Congress held in Manchester, England, where he was made International President and Permanent Chairman of the Congress. In the same year he published *Color and Democracy: Colonies and Peace* and in 1947 *The World and Africa*. He became increasingly radical in his writing and speeches. In

1947 he had written the introduction to the NAACP's *An Appeal to the World: A Statement on the Denial of Human Rights to Minorities in the Case of the Citizens of the United States of America*, presented to the Commission on Human Rights of the Economic and Social Council and the General Assembly of the United Nations. As well as criticising the domestic policy of the US government, Du Bois criticised US foreign policy too. He became involved with the presidential campaign of Henry Wallace, the candidate of the Progressive Party, and in 1948 became vice-chairman of the Council on African Affairs, one of the leading anti-colonial organisations in the USA. However, his outspoken political comments were frowned upon by some members of the NAACP, and he was dismissed from his post in 1948 at the age of eighty.

However, even in his old age Du Bois continued his political activity, especially in the international peace movement. In 1949 he took part in several international peace conferences, including the World Peace Congress in Paris and the All-Soviet Peace Congress in Moscow. In 1950 he became the chairman of the New York-based Peace Information Center (PIC), which distributed information about the international movement for disarmament and campaigned to ban the atomic bomb. In the same year Du Bois agreed to stand for election to the US Senate as a candidate for the American Labour Party. Although he was unsuccessful in the election, his activities and those of the PIC brought him into conflict with the US government. He and his colleagues were brought before the courts, accused of being in the employ of a foreign power and the organisation was forced to close down. Du Bois was subsequently acquitted of the charges brought against him, but in 1952 at the height of McCarthyism in the USA, the US State Department refused to issue him with a passport and he was effectively banned from foreign travel until 1958. When his passport was restored Du Bois and his second wife, Shirley Graham, travelled widely, visiting both Eastern and Western Europe as well as China and the Soviet Union. In May 1959 he was awarded the Lenin Peace Prize in Moscow, and as he increasingly began to believe that 'Communism is the only way of human life', he joined the Communist Party of the USA in October 1961.

In 1960, Du Bois was invited by KWAME NKRUMAH to his inauguration as the first President of Ghana. The following year he accepted Nkrumah's invitation to move to Ghana and subsequently became a Ghanaian citizen. He was invited to become Director of the Encyclopaedia Africana project, but his death prevented him from completing this work. W.E.B. Du Bois died in Ghana in August 1963, at the age of ninety-four, and after a state funeral was buried in that country's capital city Accra.

HA

Main publications

The Autobiography of W.E.B. Du Bois, New York, International Publishers, 1968.
Black Reconstruction in America (1935), New York, Atheneum, 1968.
Dusk of Dawn (1940), New York, Library of America, 1986.
The Souls of Black Folk (1903), New York, Bantam, 1989.

Further reading

Levering, Lewis D., *W.E.B. Du Bois: Biography of a Race 1868–1919*, New York, Henry Holt, 1993.

Levering, Lewis D., *The Fight for Equality and the American Century 1919–63*, New York, Henry Holt, 2000.

Marable, M., *W.E.B. Du Bois, Black Radical Democrat*, Boston, G.K. Hall, 1986.

Olaudah Equiano
(1745 – 97)

Olaudah Equiano, abolitionist, political activist and writer, was, according to his own account, born in the kingdom of Benin in the Igbo village of Essaka, thought to be the modern Iseke in Nigeria. He was the youngest son of an embrenche, or leading elder, who had seven children. Little more is known of Equiano's family, other than the fact that his only sister was kidnapped with him by slave raiders when he was about eleven years old. Some modern historians have questioned the veracity of Equiano's account of his early life, and suggest that there is some evidence which points to his birthplace having been in South Carolina, in America, rather than in West Africa.

Equiano's life was recorded in his autobiography, *The Interesting Narrative of the Life of Olaudah Equiano, or Gustavus Vassa, the African,* first published in London in 1789. The autobiography was a bestseller during Equiano's lifetime. It was published in eight English editions and one American edition, and after his death there were ten more editions including translations in Dutch, German and Russian. It is now considered one of the most important examples of early African writing in English. Equiano is recognised as one of the founders of the slave narrative genre, and a major influence on other authors of slave narratives, including the great nineteenth-century African American FREDERICK DOUGLASS.

Equiano's autobiography recounts his early life in Essaka, his kidnapping and the fact that he was passed from one African owner to another before arriving at the coast and being sold to slave traders heading for the Caribbean. He graphically describes the slave ship and Middle Passage and his initial experiences as a slave in Barbados. He was then sent to Virginia and worked on the plantation of a man called Campbell. After a few weeks Equiano was bought by Captain Pascal, an officer in the Royal Navy, who named him Gustavus Vassa after the Swedish monarch of that name. Equiano had previously been given the slave names Michael and Jacob. Pascal brought him to England in 1757 and he then spent two years at sea with his owner on board HMS Roebuck. He was then sent as a servant to two sisters, who began to educate him and persuaded Pascal to allow his baptism in 1759. Equiano returned to sea during the Seven Years War. He served as captain's steward and was also able to further his education, acquiring literacy and numeracy and learning hairdressing. He returned to England in 1760, but was again at sea during 1761. Equiano had been paid during his time on board ship but his owner had confiscated his wages and reneged on his promise to free him. Then in 1763 Equiano was sold to another owner, Captain

James Doran, and taken to the Caribbean island of Montserrat where he was resold to Robert King, a Quaker shipowner and merchant. For the next three years Equiano worked on his owner's ships and then in 1766 he was able to buy his freedom and returned to England.

As a free man, Equiano continued his education and learned to play the French horn. He worked as a hairdresser, sailor and as an assistant to the scientist Charles Irving. In 1773 he went on an expedition to the Arctic and regularly travelled to America and the Caribbean as well as to Europe. It was at this time that Equiano became converted to Methodism. In 1774 he began his anti-slavery activities when his friend John Annis, a former slave, was kidnapped by his former owner and taken to St Kitts where he was subsequently killed. Equiano did everything he could to effect the release of Annis and when he was unsuccessful, he brought he whole matter to the attention of the abolitionist Granville Sharpe. However, from 1775–6 he was again employed by Charles Irving and journeyed to the Caribbean and Central America to act as a buyer and overseer of slaves on Irving's plantation. In his *Narrative*, Equiano does not appear to have any reservations regarding purchasing slaves and even writes that he 'chose them all of my own countrymen'. But he soon found that his own freedom was far from secure in the Caribbean and returned to England in 1777.

In 1779 Equiano made attempts to be sent to Africa as a missionary. These attempts were unsuccessful and Equiano continued with his abolitionist activities, but he did make other efforts to return to Africa, once volunteering to go as an explorer. In 1783 Equiano reported the details of the infamous *Zong* case to Granville Sharpe, when 132 Africans were thrown overboard from the slave ship of that name, in order that the owners might claim insurance money. Although Sharpe was unable to bring a criminal case against the ship's owners, Equiano's efforts did bring the mass murder to public notice and contributed to the growing abolitionist movement in Britain.

Equiano subsequently became one of the leaders of the Black abolitionists in London, who began to style themselves the Sons of Africa. In 1785, accompanied by other Africans he delivered an address to the Quakers in London, thanking them for their abolitionist activities. Equiano and the other Sons of Africa were in close contact with the leading British abolitionists, including Sharpe, James Ramsay, Thomas Clarkson, Peter Peckard the Vice-Chancellor of Cambridge University and Sir William Dolben, whose Bill to regulate the slave trade became law in 1788. Equiano regularly consulted with Dolben and led several delegations of the Sons of Africa to the Houses of Parliament. Equiano himself met with several Members of Parliament, including the Speaker of the House of Commons and the Prime Minister. His activities led to a proposal by the abolitionist James Ramsay that he should confront Members of Parliament and hand them copies of an address condemning the slave trade.

He also began the practice of writing open letters to government ministers and others, including the Queen, through the press. In these letters and articles he attacked the racist and pro-slavery arguments of the day and vigorously supported the demand for an abolition of the slave trade and even slavery itself, arguing that instead a trade in legitimate commerce should be established between Africa and Europe.

In November 1786, Equiano was appointed 'Commissary on the part of Government', responsible for provisions and stores for the 'black poor', who were being sent to Sierra Leone in West Africa. The idea of re-settling some of London's Black population, some of whom were recently arrived 'loyalists' who had served Britain in the American War of Independence, was a private initiative, but it soon had enthusiastic government support. Granville Sharpe was associated with the scheme and it is possible that it was he who suggested Equiano for the post. Equiano thus became the first African to receive a government appointment. But many of the settlers had doubts about the aims of the scheme and in a short time Equiano was alleging embezzlement by the government's appointed agent and ill-treatment of some of the Black settlers. When he made his fears about the organisation of the scheme public through the press, he was accused of insubordination and subsequently dismissed from the post.

It was after his dismissal that Equiano completed his *Narrative* and began touring the British Isles, giving lectures and selling copies of the book. His efforts were very successful but the publication of his *Narrative* led to accusations that he was not the author and that he had been born not in Africa, but in the Danish colony of Santa Cruz in the Caribbean. Equiano was easily able to disprove such allegations and highlighted the fact that they were made by those intimately connected with the continuation of the trade in slaves. Equiano's abolitionist activities were particularly directed towards the British parliament and government. He continually appealed to these circles to end slavery and the slave trade, for freedom to be granted not taken. He was also careful to add practical commercial considerations to his hopes and aspirations by arguing that what would later be called 'legitimate commerce' with Africa would more than compensate British manufacturers for any loss occasioned by the end of the slave trade. Indeed he called upon the manufacturers to expedite the abolition of the slave trade.

It is possible that later on in his life Equiano adopted more radical beliefs in addition to his Methodism and reformist abolitionism. A letter seized by the government during the arrest of Thomas Hardy, shows that Equiano was a friend and supporter of Hardy, the secretary of the London Corresponding Society. The London Corresponding Society was banned by the government and Hardy arrested for high treason. Equiano had joined the society in the early 1790s and had stayed in London with Hardy and his wife. He certainly passed on the names of abolitionists to Hardy and the London Corresponding Society, but nothing more is known of these activities.

In 1792 Equiano married Susanna Cullen and the couple had two daughters. The elder, Ann Maria was born the following year, and the younger, Joanna in 1795. The first child only lived until she was four years old and died in July 1797. Equiano's wife died at the age of thirty-four in 1796. The younger daughter lived long enough to inherit from her father's estate. In 1816 at the age of twenty-one she received £900 from Equiano's will, a sum equivalent to nearly £100,000 today. Equiano therefore died in 1797 a wealthy man but without witnessing the success of the movement to which he devoted so much of his life. The British parliament finally abolished the slave trade in 1807 and abolished slavery itself only in 1833.

HA

Main publications

The Interesting Narrative of the Life of Olaudah Equiano or Gustavus Vassa, the African. Written by Himself, 2 vols, London, 1789; facsimile of the first edition, with an introduction and notes by Paul Edwards, London, Dawsons of Pall Mall, 1969.

The Interesting Narrative and Other Writings, edited with an introduction and notes by Vincent Carretta, London, Penguin, 1999.

Further reading

Braidwood, Stephen, *Black Poor and White Philanthropists: London's Blacks and the Foundation of the Sierra Leone Settlement 1786–1791,* Liverpool, Liverpool University Press, 1994.

Fryer, Peter, *Staying Power – the History of Black People in Britain,* London, Pluto, 1984.

Shyllon, Folarin, *Black People in Britain 1555–1833,* London, Oxford University Press, 1977.

Nathaniel Akinremi Fadipe
(1893 – 1944)

Nathaniel Fadipe believed that it was 'unpardonable' that when all sorts of economic and other schemes were being drawn up by the British government for Africans, Africans themselves were never consulted. He devoted his life to researching and writing on these issues. As his Barbadian-born physician/memorialist said of him, Fadipe 'looked at Africa as an entity ... [He] brought to every subject a stimulating African viewpoint'.

The son of the Revd L.O. Fadipe of the Baptist Mission at Abeokuta, Nigeria, whose wife was a successful market trader, Nathaniel Fadipe attended the Church Missionary Schools at Abeokuta and Lagos. On graduating from the CMS Grammar School in Lagos he was appointed a clerk in the Government Secretariat. From this poorly paid job he moved on to become the personal secretary to the manager of Barclay's Bank in Lagos.

In order to further his education, Fadipe had to go to Britain as there were no tertiary institutions in Nigeria. He enrolled at the London School of Economics in 1925, where his fees were paid by his mother. On graduating in 1929 he was granted a fellowship for two terms at Woodbrooke, an international Quaker residential college in Birmingham, England. He was awarded a *testamur* certificate *cum laude*, having gained marks ranging from an A to a triple A in examinations in history and internationalism. The December 1930 issue of *The Woodbrooke International Journal* published 'Indirect rule in Africa', a paper Fadipe had read at the International Discussion Circle. This was probably Fadipe's first published work; it begins by defining 'detribalisation' as a 'sort of malady ... Old customs which have previously proved quite effective in governing all sorts of social relations within the community are discarded in favour of those which are identified with the white man ... The result is social and moral chaos'. According to the colonialists' philosophy, 'natives', for example those in South Africa working for Europeans, become detribalised and start demanding greater freedoms and rights. In order to ensure the illegality of such demands, the power of the 'natural rulers' is reinforced by the colony's rulers so as to enforce customary rule. Indirect Rule is the system devised to achieve this. Under this system, the 'natural rulers' administer 'native laws and customs' under the guiding hand of a 'political officer', a 'mere suggestion of whose is as good as an order'. Dissent is not permitted. Taking Nigeria and South Africa as examples, Fadipe argues that Indirect Rule is simply 'machinery for control' and a way of imposing preferred 'lines of development'.

In 1930, on a two-year fellowship from the Phelps Stokes Fund, Fadipe travelled to the USA. He spent July at the Hampton Institute, one of the premier Black colleges, before enrolling at Columbia University, New York, where he gained his Master's degree in one year. His dissertation, 'A Yoruba town: a sociological study of Abeokuta', is partly a historical survey, partly a report based on his own experience, as well as government and other reports. It was the first academic study of a Nigerian city by an African.

On completion of his thesis Fadipe was supposed to travel around the USA visiting Black educational institutions, but the offer of a teaching post at Achimota College, Legon, Gold Coast, drew him back to West Africa. The Phelps Stokes Fund, displeased by Fadipe's premature return to West Africa, demanded that he repay part of the grant he had received, which was to have covered a two-year sojourn in the USA. Fadipe clearly had little patience with the paternalism of the Fund, as its director noted that Fadipe 'gave the impression that gifts promised him were his right'.

Achimota, opened in 1926, was the first government-funded educational establishment to offer co-education from kindergarten to lower-level university, including teacher training qualifications, in the British colony of the Gold Coast. As in most British colonies, education had been dominated by denominational establishments; even Achimota received some religious (Quaker) support and was not entirely free of missionary zeal as its first principal, the Revd A.G. Fraser, had been a missionary in East Africa and Ceylon. He was also much influenced by the Phelps Stokes Fund's advocacy of African education focusing on industrial training. Fadipe, who had met Fraser at Woodbrooke, was the only African member of staff during his tenure from 1931 until 1934. His duties at Achimota were as a 'sort of extension lecturer ... to enlighten people on economic matters ... We want farmers to diversify ... part of my task is to study all the possibilities of improving the present position of the people of the Gold Coast who have been badly hit by the low cocoa prices'.

Nnamdi Azikiwe, who had worked as a journalist in Accra, described Fadipe as 'going through hell at Achimota. They accused him of a thousand and one shortcomings, all due to professional jealousy ... How many of us would be unscathed after rubbing shoulders with some snobs at Achimota ... '. It has not been possible to discover more about the situation between Fadipe and his fellow teachers (mainly British) and Revd Fraser, who decided not to renew his contract after its expiration in August 1934. Fadipe's name is omitted from the histories of Achimota.

Though he intended returning to Abeokuta during all the long vacations to gather material for a doctoral dissertation, on learning that his contract would not be renewed, Fadipe spent the summer of 1933 in Europe, attending a Woodbrooke international reunion in Roudnice, Czechoslovakia, after which he spent some time in Prague. A report of the gathering, partly authored by Fadipe, noted that 'our good friend Nat Fadipe left an abiding impression on the inhabitants of Roudnice'. He had given 'a very interesting account of certain developments at Achimota ... where a quiet meeting for worship is held, which is attended by "pukka" Quakers, proselytes and thresholders'.

It was Horace Alexander, who had spoken on Gandhi at Roudnice, that Fadipe had informed of his travel plans. Alexander had lectured on International Relations in Woodbrooke. In 1933 he had written to Fadipe of his plans to set up a Centre for

Political Action in the Service of Peace and Justice. This aimed, *inter alia*, to examine the progress made by the League of Nations and the International Labour Organizations regarding race problems and economic exploitation. Academic enquiry, it was planned, would result in concrete, practical results. Fadipe was immediately interested. The plan confirmed his decision to return to London.

However, events – that is, the foundation of the Peace Pledge Union – overtook the plans for the Centre, which devolved into an irregularly meeting Peacemakers' Group. Alexander became the chairperson of the Friends' Peace Committee. Whether Fadipe was involved in any of these organisations has proved impossible to determine.

Returning to London in 1934, Fadipe enrolled at the London School of Economics (LSE) for his doctoral degree under Professors Bronislaw Malinowski and Morris Ginsberg. How he supported himself, except from payment for occasional journalism, is not clear. He was not in receipt of any fellowships until his final year, when he received some support from the International Institute of African Languages and Cultures; the LSE helped by granting him concessionary fees. His subsidiary aim in writing a dissertation, he wrote, was to inform 'the British public of the African viewpoint re the industrial, political and economic disputes and labour conditions in Africa'. Professor Morris congratulated him on the eventual conferment of the PhD, saying his work was 'a real contribution to sociology'. Though the first sociological study by an African, *The Sociology of the Yoruba* was not published until 1970, despite the Egba Omu Odudowa (an Egba fraternal/political organisation) in Nigeria having received permission for its publication in 1950. Eventually the US fraternity, Alpha Phi Alpha, supported its publication at Ibadan.

Probably dating from the mid–late 1930s are the drafts of two papers by Fadipe found in the Ladipo Solanke/West African Students' Union (WASU) collection in Lagos University Archives. Both deal with Abyssinia: one is 'The diplomats and white man's prestige', the other 'Justice to Abyssinia is justice to Africa'. In the latter he argues that:

> the principle of the White man's prestige and the related one that no hesitation
> need be felt in making the interests of the black peoples subserve those of the
> whites – are the two sides of a medallion which the Governments of Britain and
> France have brought into play during the whole history of the Italo-Abyssinia
> conflict ... These principles explain the shelving of appeal after appeal by Abyssinia
> to the League of Nations ... We Africans surely have a right to accuse our rulers
> of corrupting our morals by the deliberate introduction of the double standard
> of justice.

Where these articles were published is not known.

As he felt that the 'British public [was] most inadequately informed of Africa ... [and] of the unjust conditions the Natives laboured under in many parts of Africa', Fadipe contributed letters and articles to the weekly journal *West Africa* and to other papers and journals. *West Africa* was read by those interested in Africa in Britain as well as in Africa. Some of these articles, such as 'What Kingship Means to an African' in the 15 May 1937 issue, were purely explanatory. During September and October

1936 *West Africa* published a six-part series by Fadipe. These returned to the theme of detribalisation: the new, European-style education aimed to accomplish the same aims as traditional education, that is, 'preparing boys to face the various situations they are likely to meet during their lifetime'. But the adoption of foreign customs should not be taken to extremes; only those that can be put to 'rational use' should be adopted. Africans should also learn and borrow from each other. All forms of art should be encouraged and the young should fill the leisure hours provided by the Western school system usefully, for example, by learning other African languages.

In one of his published letters (18 September 1943) Fadipe suggested that copies of *Hansard* (House of Commons transcripts) should be on sale in each colony; copies of the report of the Commission on Higher Education in East Africa should be made available in West Africa to aid Africans to submit their views to the forthcoming commission on higher education there. The editor of *West Africa* commented that Fadipe, 'this finely equipped Nigerian still in Britain', should be added to the West African Education Commission. The government did not take up the suggestion.

There are numerous unsigned articles in the *West African Review* which could have been written by Fadipe, for example that by an 'African contributor' in the September 1943 issue, on the demand by Africans for a living wage. Two articles concerned with education appeared under Fadipe's name in the April and July 1938 issues. In these he argued that higher education was an absolute necessity, in both East and West Africa. However, even if the standard was raised in the few existing local colleges, funding would still be required for overseas scholarships for the higher levels of undergraduate and postgraduate education. The levels of secondary schools also needed to be raised in order to graduate sufficient numbers to feed into the tertiary colleges. This would necessitate the training of secondary school teachers. He criticised the Commission for Higher Education for advocating lower pay for qualified African teachers than for Europeans.

Other known writings of Fadipe which have not been found are a critique of J.H. Driberg's *The East African Problem* (which suggested that 'social segregation' as practised in Kenya, should be replaced by territorial segregation), and a series on South Africa, which he claimed had been 'syndicated in provincial and local London papers'. It has been suggested that he is also the author of an article in the London *Times* (23 June 1942), 'A colonial view of colonial aspirations', by 'a West African Correspondent'. This article argues for 'the recognition that West Africa is one country', and that 'the Atlantic Charter does apply to us'. (The Charter, promulgated by Roosevelt and Churchill in 1941, promised to restore freedom to all those nations that had lost theirs; Churchill was adamant that it did not apply to colonised peoples.)

An unpublished work is one on the situation in Kenya, commissioned by the Fabian Colonial Bureau. In this Fadipe investigated the ongoing industrial and fiscal exploitation of Kenyan Africans, and other economic issues. He argued that new techniques had been used since 1928 to continue the pro-European land-holding policies, which had been barred then by Government Commissions. However, without giving his reasons – at least in public – Fadipe withdrew the manuscript from the publishers. A manuscript copy of at least one chapter is at the University of Lagos.

Fadipe was involved in pan-African politics in London. According to RAS T. MAKONNEN, Fadipe was close friends with Jomo Kenyatta; both men were involved with the various PADMORE organisations, as well as the League of Coloured People. At least in the beginning, he also supported Aggrey House, the government-sponsored social club/hostel for colonial students, by serving on its first House Committee. Fadipe became involved in the anti-imperialist and pan-Africanist discussions and activism at the West African Students' Union, though he appears never to have become a member. He worked closely with LADIPO SOLANKE, the Union's Warden, and played an important role in WASU's political activities. In 1938 he contributed to the discussion on the ongoing 'cocoa holdup', which Gold Coast farmers were using to attempt to force an increase in the price of their exports. Fadipe chaired sessions at the 1941 and 1942 WASU conferences where his concerns were with economic development; for example, he raised the issue of the possibility of political influences hindering industrialisation. He was also part of the study group formed in 1940 to discuss a demand for self-government within five years. However, based on his work on a paper on the 'needed economic development in West Africa', of which no copy exists, he strongly disagreed with a 1943 WASU proposal for immediate independence. He suggested to Solanke that WASU should consult others, such as the Labour Party's Marxist-leaning Harold Laski, and the Gold Coasters Robert Gardiner and de Graft Johnson about the wisdom of this demand. In May 1943 he gave a talk to the WASU Study Group on 'West African Export Trade', but no documentation survives.

When the British government decided to prepare a report on land and agricultural problems in West Africa, the Union instructed Solanke and Fadipe to research and write their own report on Nigerian Land Tenure. This was forwarded to the members of the unofficial parliamentary committee on West African economic conditions. In 1940 Fadipe also prepared a thirty-six page memorandum, 'Price Control and Living Standards in West Africa' for WASU, recommending an increase in the prices paid for West African produce, such as cocoa and groundnuts. Fadipe argued, as did many in West Africa, that the British Government was deliberately suppressing prices. The matter was urgent as during the war there were huge price increases in West Africa, further lowering the standard of living of all commodity producers and their workers. Naturally the British government disagreed and Fadipe prepared the 'counter-case' for WASU. The 120 printed copies were widely disseminated; the Colonial Office even despatched copies to the colonial governors! It was also sent to White organisations such as the the the Independent Labour Party (which used it for its correspondence course on 'Colonial Problems'), the Fabian Colonial Bureau and the communist-led Labour Research Department. The Anti-Slavery Society promised to send copies to members who asked for it; unused copies were returned in March 1941. The Society's letter accompanying the unsold copies also informed Fadipe that his application for the post of Secretary, vacated by the death of John Harris, had been unsuccessful. The successful candidate was C.W.W. Greenidge – a much 'safer' bet from the Society's perspective.

Fadipe also worked with the National Council for Civil Liberties, and contributed to the session on West Africa at its conference on Civil Liberty in the Colonial Empire held in 1941. Fadipe argued that while under Indirect Rule the violation of civil liberties was relatively subtle, even that could lead to the complete disruption of 'native institutions'. More recent legislation was outright repressive: for example, the Ordinances in Sierra Leone on Sedition and Undesirable Literature. Newspapers were closely watched and could be (and were being) suppressed and their editors imprisoned. The state was the main employer of local labour, but it was hostile to trade unions, whose leaders, such as I.T.A. WALLACE-JOHNSON of Sierra Leone, could be placed in preventive detention.

Fadipe was also in contact with that very early champion of African rights, Dr Norman Leys, whose 1928 book on Kenya, he claims, had heavily influenced him. While in the USA, he had sent a long memorandum to Leys regarding the 'future educational and political developments of Africa'. This resulted in his 'being asked to be [Leys'] consultant on African problems'. Whether he had made any contributions, for example, to Leys' pamphlet on African land matters, published by the Fabian Colonial Bureau in 1942, or to *The Colour Bar in East Africa*, published in 1941, is not known.

It appears from sketchy data that Fadipe also worked with George Padmore, at least on a pamphlet somehow related to the 1944 Empire Prime Ministers' conference. At about the same time he was also working on a paper on land settlement probably in response to the government's intention of fostering post-war emigration to East and Central Africa and of settling Jewish refugees in Northern Nigeria. In 'Africa and White Settlement' (a draft of this paper is in the WASU collection) Fadipe deals with the already existing confiscation of land by British settlers, the crowding of Africans into 'reserves', and with the inequalities in the taxation system. However, Fadipe saw no problems with the settlement of Europeans prepared to work their own farms if first the needs of natives for land were satisfied, and as long as 'the interests of the black peoples [were] given the same weight as those of the whites'.

Fadipe was also friendly with the League of Coloured People, an organisation based on the US' NAACP. Through WASU, the LCP and Padmore he met visiting African Americans, for example Ralph Bunche, who was in London in 1937 en route to East Africa. It is not certain whether it was his early contact with Bunche that resulted in Fadipe being nominated as a possible representative for West Africa at an International Conference on Africa being planned in Washington for early 1943; unfortunately the war forced the conference to be held with delegates (including Africans) from the USA only.

Fadipe also knew Nnamdi Azikiwe, by 1937 the contumacious founder/editor of the *West African Pilot* published in Lagos, and in 1944 co-founder of the nationalist National Council of Nigeria and the Cameroons. The two men had met in the USA; in 1943, during a visit to London, Zik and Fadipe discussed Zik's plan to publish a paper in the UK for distribution in Britain and through all of West Africa. Fadipe offered to become the paper's first editor. Nothing came of these plans.

Fadipe, when sufficiently incensed, also attempted to challenge the government regarding racial discrimination in London. A letter of his reached the Colonial Office in February 1941 and led to a mild level of intervention by the government. Fadipe had written regarding the discrimination faced by Black men looking for work, who at the beginning of the war had even been turned down by the Air Raid Precautions service; yet simultaneously the police were scouring air raid shelters looking for Africans of military age in order to 'impress them into the army'! The government made some enquiries. As far as is known Fadipe never publicly expressed his anger over 'Africans not [being] consulted when Whites draw up schemes for social and economic welfare and for the government' of African countries.

As there were no university research or teaching posts for which an African applicant would have received serious consideration, after gaining his PhD Fadipe was forced to earn his living as an examiner of students of the Yoruba language, as a marker of school examination papers, as a translator for the Ministry of Information, and as a clerk at Unilever's. He continued his academic work on linguistics at London University's School of Oriental and African Studies, but it has not proved possible to determine the exact nature of this.

Nathaniel Fadipe was killed by overwork and perhaps by frustration: he had to combine earning a minimal living at menial tasks with total devotion to the cause of Africa. Seldom managing to get more than four or five hours' sleep, he suffered a brain haemorrhage brought on by high blood pressure. Despite medical attention from one of the best Black physicians in London, Fadipe died at the comparatively early age of fifty-one. As the editor of the journal *West Africa* (10/6 and 26/8 1944) noted, Fadipe, 'one of the ablest and most balanced thinkers Nigeria has produced', was held in:

> great admiration for his intellectual powers and the fairness and justice of his opinions ... [H]is true place was a responsible one in the administration of his country ... [but] it is not really an inveterate habit of the Colonial Governments to seek out and prefer men of his independent, critical cast of mind.

His funeral was attended by all the luminaries of the African diaspora and visiting Africans. In Lagos Nnamdi Azikiwe published an obituary spread over four issues of the *West African Pilot.*

MS

Further reading

Adi, Hakim, *West Africans in Britain 1900–1960*, London, Lawrence and Wishart, 1998.

Frantz Fanon
(1925 – 61)

Frantz Fanon, a psychiatrist, a writer, a freedom fighter and a journalist, spent his brief life explaining the effects of colonialism on people and nations. At first he diagnosed and then, writing from his own experience in the Algerian struggle for independence, he sought solutions, promoted violent struggle, and extolled the necessity for African unity.

Born in Fort-de-France, the capital of the French colony of Martinique, Frantz was the youngest of three sons of a customs officer and a shopkeeper. As a member of the indigenous middle-class, he (and his seven siblings) attended the fee-charging local (and only) *lycée*, where one of his teachers was AIMÉ CÉSAIRE, the recently returned-from-France revolutionary poet espousing *négritude*. This was a philosophy developed by French Afro-Caribbeans and Francophone Senegalese living in exile in Paris: it celebrated and embraced African cultural values, and a Negro 'cultural essence'. Césaire's espousal of his African inheritance caused a scandal in the colony and influenced at least some of his students. Fanon obtained Part I of the baccalaureate in 1943, and promptly left for France to join the Free French Forces. He was sent to officers' training school in Algeria, where his francophile indoctrination was seriously undermined by the racial discrimination he encountered and witnessed. Nevertheless, he appears to have fought with valour, being awarded a decoration for bravery while serving in Europe.

At the end of the war he returned to Martinique, completed the baccalaureate and won a scholarship to France. Before leaving for Europe he campaigned for Césaire, who was standing as a communist candidate for election to the National Assembly in Paris. Settling at first in Paris Fanon moved to Lyons in 1948 to study medicine and then psychiatry. In 1952 he married a socialist French woman, Josie Dublé, who helped with the production of his literary works. A study he conducted of the living conditions of North African immigrants in Lyons was published as an article in *Espirit* in 1952.

The same year saw the publication of his first book *Black Skins White Masks* (1952; in English 1968). It was based on the sociological analysis later also published as an essay ('West Indians and Africans', 1955) and on his training in psychiatry. Fanon delineates the hierarchies existing in Martinique: class over-ruled race, but those of African descent of all classes suffered racial stereotyping and denigration. Martiniquans were taught that all West Indians were superior to Africans; they were also superior to the African-descended inhabitants of the neighbouring French colony of Guadeloupe. However, Frenchmen were naturally superior to all.

In 1953 Fanon was appointed head of the French colonial government's Psychiatric Department at the hospital at Blida-Joinville in Algeria. Algeria had been a French colony since 1830; one million expatriate French had settled there and totally sub-jugated the Algerians. Sporadic fighting against the French overlords escalated into a full-scale war of independence by 1954; a war which grew more and more vicious as it dragged on. France, unable to envisage defeat at the hands of inferior 'natives', resorted to mass bombings and machine gunning; about one million Algerians were killed in the struggle. Many were tortured, supposedly in order to extract information, but also, Fanon came to believe, as an act of sadistic racist fury. Fanon worked with those officially admitted to the hospital in the daytime, and with the independence fighters after hours: he trained nurses, and freedom fighters in how to control their fears and reactions; he supplied medicinal drugs, and housed injured members of the FLN (National Liberation Front) in his own home. Attempting to establish a close link between psychotherapy and political education, he came to realise the importance of culture to the efficacy of therapy.

By 1956 as the strain of his dual life had grown too great, Fanon composed his letter of resignation. But before this could be presented, the 'underground' activities at the hospital were discovered by the French authorities; some workers were jailed, others deported. Fanon, who had just been lauded at the Congress of Black Writers, was deported.

At the Congress Fanon had met fellow writers and thinkers from around the world – and was confronted by the many differences between Africans, Afro-Caribbeans and African Americans. As political papers were prohibited, Fanon talked on 'Racism and Culture'. Racism, he argued, was the most visible element of a total hierarchical relationship established by the colonisers, who had to destory the cultural system of the colonised in order to consolidate their control. By destroying the cultural values of the colonised, they could be manipulated almost as objects, and assimilated into this new order. The indigenous culture becomes ossified into traditionalism, apathy, inertia, guilt and an inferiority complex. 'Racism', Fanon argued in words as true today as 44 years ago, 'is a necessary ideological weapon which accompanies domi-nation ... Since the weapon must be fexible in order to retain its effectiveness, it undergoes many metamorphoses'.

In the letter of resignation he had drafted, Fanon wrote that he could not 'continue in the face of a tissue of lies, cowardice, contempt for man'. France, he alleged, was practising:

> systematic dehumanisation ... [making] the Arab permanently an alien in his own country [who] lives in a state of absolute depersonalisation. The function of a social structure is to set up institutions to serve man's needs. A society that drives its members to desperate solutions is a non-viable society, a society to be replaced.

Fanon now moved physically to Tunis and intellectually began to move away from psychiatry and to concentrate on sociological analysis and political philosophy in his writings. Colonialism he now saw as a form of violence; independence would require a total change of the existing social order. Liberation had to be personal and national. Nevertheless, he continued working as a psychiatrist and lectured at the University of Tunis. He also worked in the editorial office of the Résistance Algerienne as one of the editors of the FLN's paper, *El Moudjahid*. While writing mainly for Algerians, Fanon linked the fate of Algeria to the fate of the whole of Africa and emphasised the necessity for the unity of Africa. He reiterated again and again, both in the paper and in the collection of his essays published posthumously as *Toward the African Revolution* (1964) that 'we have to build Africa', and excoriated the men with black skins and white masks – the colonial parliamentarians and others in positions of power.

Fanon led the Algerian delegation to the Congress of African Peoples organised by GEORGE PADMORE for KWAME NKRUMAH in Accra in 1958. He was put on the Congress' Steering Committee, and rejoiced in the decisive influence of Algeria among the delegates: the struggle in Algeria convinced delegates, he felt, that the 'colonisers can't win'. Kwame Nkrumah pledged Ghana's support of the stuggle, and recognised the provisional government of the Republic of Algeria. Fanon must have felt very comfortable in the Congress discussions, which espoused African unity and solidarity and the determination to banish colonialism. He was one of those at the Congress to demand that African peoples 'pledge themselves to create a militia whose duty is to support the African peoples fighting for their independence'. On his way back to Algeria he was almost killed by a land-mine; while in Rome for treatment, two attempts were made to assassinate him.

When Fanon took up his position as the representative of the Provisional Algerian Government in Accra in 1960, he grew increasingly uneasy about the level of corruption he saw around him. 'The greatest danger that threatens Africa is the absence of ideology', he wrote in that year. He analysed the new governing class – the bourgeoisie – which

> after a few hesitant steps in the international arena, no longer feeling the threat of the traditional colonial power, suddenly develop great appetites. And as they do not yet have any political experience they think they can conduct political affairs like their business. Perquisites, threats, even despoiling of the vicitms ... The discontented workers undergo a repression as pitiless as that of the colonial periods. Trade unions and opposition political parties are confined to a quasi-clandestine state.

1960 was also the year France granted independence to all her colonies. Fanon saw this as fake, as the nationalist leaders who took over he believed were all France's 'clients'. He attended the many conferences held that year to foster African independence: for example, he attended the Second Conference of African Peoples in Tunis, the Afro-Asian Conference in Conakry and the Third Independent African States Conference in Addis Ababa.

Though already ill Fanon travelled to northern Mali to establish southern supply bases for the Algerian Liberation Army. It was probably while he was on this arduous trip that he heard of the assassination of his friend and comrade PATRICE LUMUMBA, the socialist Prime Minister of newly independent (from Belgium) Congo. Lumumba had sought the help of the United Nations with the military unrest and ethnic conflict being engendered by the Belgians and the CIA in the interest of retaining or obtaining control of Congo's rich copper mines. Fanon, in his reflection on Lumumba's death, believed that his friend had not recognised that:

> in reality the UN is the legal card used by the imperialist interests when the card of brute force has failed … The partitions, the controlled joint commissions, the trusteeship arrangements are international legal means of torturing, of crushing the will to independence of people, of cultivating anarchy, banditry, wretchedness … He forgot that the UN in its present state is only a reserve assembly, set up by the Great, to continue between two armed conflicts the 'peaceful struggle' for the division of the world.

Observing the divisions which had been fostered in the country Lumumba had striven to unify, Fanon wrote, 'Africa must advance in totality, there [cannot] be one Africa that fights against colonialism and another that attempts to make arrangements with colonialism'. As he could not be bought, 'the imperialists decided to do away with Lumumba'.

Fanon now began to define what he meant by 'unity', which could take many forms – for example, the economic cooperation being attempted by Nigeria and Liberia, or political co-operation as between Guinea, Ghana and Mali. His last book, *The Wretched of the Earth* (1961, in English 1965) was published just before he lost his battle with leukemia. In this he argued that Europe owed the 'third world' a huge debt as its wealth had derived from slavery and the robbery of the 'fruit of natives' toil'. As Germany was paying reparations to Israel, why not reparations to the 'third world'? (Fanon does not mention Asia – thus his definition of the 'third world' is very partial.) He again criticised the bourgeoisie, which he maintained was growing totally parasitical. National political parties had become agencies for passing power from White hands to Black.

Contrary to accepted communist analysis, the Western proletariat did *not* support colonial struggles, Fanon argued. (While interested in theoretical Marxism, Fanon was never a communist – if for no other reason than that the French Communist Party had not supported the Algerian independence struggle.) Neither did the colonial proletariat, which he saw as having profited from colonialism. It was only the peasantry that was truly revolutionary.

Fanon also argued against Gandhian non-violence. Violence was necessary to cure the colonies from their 'colonial neurosis'. Violence was 'a cleansing force, freeing the native from his inferiority complex and from his despair and inaction; it makes him fearless and restores his self-respect'.

Fanon has been criticised by many for homogenising people – Africans, classes, peasantries as well as the colonial situations which also differed from each other. While this is true, one has to bear in mind that Fanon wrote under great pressure, while involved in other work, and that he was very young. Had he lived longer, had he had more free time to grapple with all that he had assimilated in his brief life, he would undoubtedly have refined his theories.

Too ill to return to Ghana from Mali, Fanon returned to Tunis. Colleagues diagnosed leukemia. He was flown to Moscow where the diagnosis was confirmed. The specialists there recommended treatment in the USA, but Fanon was reluctant to go to the 'country of lynchers'. Instead, he resumed as active a political life as possible in Tunis, including the training of FLN cadres. By April, his health visibly deteriorating, Fanon went to Italy for treatment for rheumatism. He stopped in Rome to see Simone de Beauvoir and Jean-Paul Sartre who were holidaying there. Sartre, who had published Fanon's articles in *Les Temps Modernes*, had just agreed to write the preface to *The Wretched of the Earth*: during a visit to Cuba, he had been converted to the notion that it was only through violence that the oppressed can attain their human status.

Finally, despite his fears of mistreatment because of his colour, Fanon flew to Washington for treatment. His fears were justified: his wife and six-year-old son Olivier flew to join him and demand proper medical attention. African representatives to the United Nations came to visit him. It was to no avail. Fanon died on 6 December. The Algerians sent a plane for his body and gave him a national funeral. He was buried in one of the FLN's cemeteries, where Colonel Boumedienne gave the commemorative address.

Shortly before his death Fanon had written to a friend that 'what matters is not death, but to know ... whether we have achieved the maximum for the ideas we have made our own ... The cause of the peoples, the cause of justice and liberty' (Zahar, p.xx).

Algeria's independence was recognised by France some eight months later.

MS

Main publication not listed in the text

A Dying Colonialism, New York, Monthly Review Press, 1965.

Further reading

de Beauvoir, Simone, *Force of Circumstance* (1963), London, Andre Deutsch, 1965.
Caute, David, *Fanon*, London, Fontana, 1970.
Grohs, G.K., 'Frantz Fanon and the African Revolution', *Journal of Modern African Studies*, 6, 4 (1968).
Jinadu, L. Adele, *Fanon: in Search of the African Revolution*, London, KPI Ltd, 1986.
La Guerre, John G., *Enemies of Empire*, St Augustine, Trinidad, University of the West Indies, 1984.
Memmi, Albert, 'The impossible life of Frantz Fanon', *Massachusetts Review*, Winter, 1973.
Zahar, Renate, *Frantz Fanon: Colonialism and Alienation*, New York, Monthly Review Press, 1974.

Amy Ashwood Garvey
(1897 – 1969)

If ever there was a life of lived Pan-Africanism, it was that of Amy Ashwood Garvey. She not only lived in many parts of the Black world, but participated in the major events – from the founding of Garvey's UNIA to the Pan-African Conference of 1945 and the independence of Ghana in 1957. The loss of her manuscripts mean that we shall never know the full extent of her work for and with Black women.

Amy Ashwood was born in Port Antonio, Jamaica, but with her mother soon moved to Panama, where her father had established a bakery and café. (Because of the dire economic situation in the colony, many Jamaicans sought to earn a living on the American mainland.) In 1904 Amy, her brother and mother returned to Jamaica to enable Amy to further her education. In about 1909 Amy became a boarder at the Baptist Westwood High School for Girls, which offered a thorough academic education as well as music, 'domestic training' and shorthand/typing. Amy also learned of her African origins from her grandmother, whose Asante name was 'Boahimaa Dabas'; she had been kidnapped and sold into slavery.

When only 17 years old she met the recently returned firebrand MARCUS GARVEY at a meeting of the Kingston Literary and Debating Society, where she had spoken in a debate on 'Morality does not increase with civilization'. It is hardly surprising that Garvey was struck by this well-educated, articulate, politicised young woman.

Mr Ashwood hastened to Jamaica as Garvey, then earning a living by selling greeting cards and tombstones, was not considered a suitable *beau* for Amy. She was forbidden to see Garvey, but she disobeyed. Inflamed by a 'joint love for Africa and our concern for the welfare of our race' the pair set up the Universal Negro Improvement Assocation (UNIA) in a building rented by Amy, using her father's business credit. Amy became the secretary of the ladies' division, participated in the debates sponsored by the UNIA and accompanied Garvey on his organisational lectures. Maybe because the UNIA only managed to attract a hundred or so members, making Garvey's prospects appear bleaker than ever, the Ashwoods intervened in 1916 by returning to Panama. At the same time Garvey left for the USA.

By 1918 or early 1919 Amy had joined Garvey in the USA, and the two worked together in re-establishing the UNIA in the USA. Amy once again became the UNIA's secretary, accompanied Garvey to meetings, served on the board of the Black Star Line and 'helped in myriad ways to build the organisation' (Martin, p.33). She and Garvey were married in December 1919, but had separated by mid-1920. The clash of two strong wills, and Amy's refusal to accept subordination to Marcus were the most likely factors in their separation. During his indictment by the federal authorities in the USA, Garvey even claimed that Amy had been part of a conspiracy to destroy him. Whether Garvey's divorce action against his wife was legal remained a contentious issue for many years; nevertheless, Garvey immediately remarried, taking Jamaican-born Amy Jacques, who had replaced Amy Ashwood as UNIA secretary, as his second wife in 1922.

Though Amy wrote that at least one of her reasons for leaving Garvey had been her desire 'to help Afro-American women to find themselves and rise in life', in fact she left for London and a tour of Europe in 1922 (Yard, p.58). In London she read some articles protesting against the way in which Africans were being depicted in the Empire Exhibition then being held at Wembley. She contacted their author, the young Nigerian law student LADIPO SOLANKE. Using Amy's experience with the UNIA, the two founded the Nigerian Progress Union (NPU) in July 1924. The Union hoped to 'solve the social, industrial, economic and commercial problems of Nigeria from the platform of education of the masses of the Nigerian peoples'. The founders were concerned that the Nigerian 'had been taught to hate all his national institutions and customs'. More specifically, it aimed to set up a hostel in London, to send Nigerians to be trained in the 'necessary professions' in various universities, and to promote African literatures, institutions, self-knowledge, welfare and a sense of duty to 'our country and race'. The members, present and past university students, gave Amy the title of 'Iyalode' ('mother has arrived') 'in appreciation of her love, interest and services for the Union as its organiser'. It is not known whether the students approved of her statement to the *Jamaican Gleaner* (25 September 1924) that Nigerians wanted 'education – not politics ... The Negro race is not yet ripe for political emancipation. You must educate him before he will be able to understand anything about politics'. Amy introduced Solanke to the editor of the US journal *The Spokesman*, which from 1925 carried news from the NPU.

Back in New York in late 1924, Amy turned to play-writing and theatre production with the help of Trinidadian calypsonian, composer and actor Sam Manning, who had probably arranged a benefit concert for the UNIA in 1924. Three of her musical shows, which all starred Manning, *Hey, Hey!*, *Brown Sugar* and *Black Magic* were performed at the Lafayette Theatre in Harlem; the shows then toured US cities. In 1929 their company went abroad, touring the Caribbean area. For undisclosed reasons, in Trinidad Amy did not show up at a meeting where it had been announced she would speak on 'The need for West Indian Federation'. In an interview with the *Trinidad Guardian* (14 July 1929) which called her a 'West Indian sociologist', she castigated the 'Negroes there [who are] practically, if not entirely, devoid of race consciousness'.

In the early to mid-1930s Amy was back in Britain. She is reported as having been hospitalised in 1934. On her recovery, she told interviewers that she was researching the possibility of taking a company of artists of African descent to the West Coast of Africa, which she intended visiting later that year. What Amy's exact involvement was with the British theatrical world is not known, but she is reputed to have helped recruit the Black cast for *Stevedore*, a play about racial and trade union conflict in which PAUL ROBESON had the lead role. The plans for West Africa did not materialise:

about a year later, with Sam Manning she opened the Florence Mills Social Parlour in Carnaby Street, in London's West End. It became the haunt of the many Black peoples in London, including such political figures such as GEORGE PADMORE, C.L.R. JAMES and RAS T. MAKONNEN, who recalled that 'you could get a lovely meal, dance and enjoy yourself'.

Amy must have impressed these men: she became one of the founder members and the treasurer of the International African Friends of Abyssinia, formed in 1935 to protest against Italy's invasion of Abyssinia. Described by Makonnen as 'quite a spellbinder', Amy chaired or spoke at some of the nationwide meetings organised by IAFA. For example, she and Padmore addressed a meeting attended by 'several hundred of the African community' in Liverpool. The resolutions passed at the meeting called on the British government and other members of the League of Nations to apply sanctions against Italy and to close the Suez Canal 'as the only effective way of stopping the war in East Africa'. The British government was also asked to lift the embargo on arms shipments to Ethiopia and to permit 'Africans and people of African descent to volunteer to fight in defence of Abyssinia's independence'. Similar resolutions were passed at all the meetings.

Among the people she shared a platform with at IAFA meetings was Samuel R. Wood, of the Gold Coast, who had been general secretary of the National Congress of British West Africa. Now representing the Aborigines' Rights Protection Society (ARPS), he was in London campaigning against proposed new legislation which would affect Africans' land rights and tax them inordinately. A measure of Amy's standing was that on his return to the Gold Coast the ARPS sent a copy of its petition to the British government to Amy, seeking her support.

Amy also renewed her acquaintance with Ladipo Solanke, now heading the West African Students' Union, the successor to the Nigerian Progress Union. In late 1935 she is reported as speaking at the Union on the need to establish an Ethiopian Defence Fund, which was duly set up with £10 collected from the students.

In 1937, when the IAFA was transformed into the International African Service Bureau, Amy and Jomo Kenyatta were named as vice-presidents. With 'active member-ship' open only to Africans and those of African descent, the Bureau aimed to 'support the demands of Africans and other colonial peoples for democratic rights, civil liberties and self-determination', and to 'enlighten' Britons regarding colonial issues.

Little is known at present of Amy Ashwood's life in Jamaica, where she spent the war years. She founded a School of Domestic Science, and a political party named after a well-known figure, the Jag. Smith Party. But both ventures were apparently of little consequence.

In 1944 Amy returned to the USA, ostensibly for medical treatment; the guarantor on her visa application was her brother Claude, then living in Harlem. On arrival she immediately became involved in the Harlem campaign of Adam Clayton Powell for election to the House of Representatives. Probably through her previous acquaintance with Robeson, Amy must have joined the Council on African Affairs, as she is reported as being on the committee that compiled the fifty-five-page report on its 1944 conference, 'Africa – New Perspectives'. At the conference, one of her fellow speakers was FRANCIS (later KWAME) NKRUMAH, then a student in the USA. Amy spoke on the need to support the liberation of the colonies. 'I see no ill in finding white allies', she said. 'But the Negro himself must take the initiative ... [W]e ourselves must feel the prime responsibility for striking the blow in the interests of our posterity and ourselves.' The Conference called on the US government to ensure that 'the fruits of victory shall be shared equally by all peoples' and that 'effective international machinery' should secure 'the social, economic and political advancement of the African and other colonial peoples'. In April 1945 she attended the Colonial Conference called by W.E.B. Du Bois, which called for an international commission 'to oversee and facilitate the transition from colonial status to autonomy'.

In March/April 1944 the US government proved unsympathetic to Amy's plans, even wondering if Amy's 'leftist friends' were behind her proposed scheme to obtain work permits and placements for Jamaican women and girls to 'help in the war effort'. (Some tens of thousands of West Indian men had been recruited to work temporarily in US manufacturing and agriculture during the war.) Amy and the Jamaican Labour Advisor succeeded in obtaining an interview with Eleanor Roosevelt, to solicit her support. It seems the US First Lady could not influence a reluctant government: the available immigration data does not indicate an increase in the arrival of women from Jamaica. Amy also planned to publish an international women's magazine, in order to:

> bring together the women, especially those of the darker races, so that they may work for the betterment of all ... There must be a revolution among women. They must realise their importance in the post-war world ... Women of the world must unite.
>
> (New York Amsterdam News, 1 April 1944)

Sadly, the idea for the magazine was still-born.

Amy also resuscitated what must have been old contacts among the West Indian political activists in New York. She spoke about her plans for women at a meeting called by the West Indies National Council (WINC) on 2 April on 'The Role of the West Indian Peoples in the War – the Post War World'; she shared the platform with Adam Clayton Powell, and WINC activists such as Herman Osborne and Hope Stevens. Amy advocated the formation of a West Indian federation and emphasised that the new constitution granted by the UK 'gave Jamaica nothing'. The WINC had designated 1 August 1944 as 'a national demonstration for West Indian liberation' as it was the 110th Anniversary of West Indian Emancipation. Amy was one of the speakers at the meeting held in Harlem on 27 August. The resolutions adopted and sent to the British government demanded the 'right of self-determination and of self-government for the peoples of Africa' and the release of all political prisoners in the Caribbean.

During her stay in the USA, the FBI had Amy under surveillance, suspecting her of communist involvement, but could find no proof. Given her interests, some of her associates were, of course, communists, as their philosophy was the only one espousing freedom, equality and independence at that time. She spoke at the Council of African Affairs (CAA) Freedom Rally in Madison Square Gardens in New York on 27 June

1944, mistakenly explaining to the tens of thousands in the audience that the British had established a caste system in India and might try to do something similar in the Caribbean; she urged her listeners to register to vote and to re-elect President Franklin Delano Roosevelt. She was friendly with two communists, Doxey Wilkerson and ALPHAEUS HUNTON, the former close to and the latter an official of the CAA. As Benjamin Davis, a communist New York City councillor, was among the many prominent African Americans and West Indians (some also communists) at her farewell party in New York in August 1945, one can see how the US (and later the UK) government spooks jumped to that conclusion.

Was it both pressure from the FBI and reports of the forthcoming Pan-African Congress that drew Amy back to London? She told the *Chicago Defender* (15 September 1945) that she would also be going to Africa, where she 'hoped to work for the education of native women in Liberia'. She felt that the 'mass [of Negro youth] is more solid and is the heat, light and power of any self-determination movement'.

Amy's hopes were at least temporarily transmuted into chairing the opening day of the Pan-African Congress, held in Manchester in October 1945. Its main organisers were old colleagues and acquaintances: George Padmore, assisted by Ras T. Makonnen and Kwame Nkrumah, whom she had met in New York. She addressed the Congress on 19 October, outlining the position of the 'black woman [who] has been shunted into the back-ground to be a child-bearer' by those writing about the Negro. In Jamaica, she reported that the:

> women in the civil service ... take no active part whatever in the political develop-
> ment of the country ... It is among the women teachers that we find a progressive
> movement ... The labouring class of women who work in the fields, take goods
> to the market, and so on, receive much less pay for the same work than the men
> do ... [T]he Negro men of Jamaica are largely responsible for this, as they do
> little to help the women to get improved wages.

From Manchester Amy wrote to another old friend, LADIPO SOLANKE at the West African Students' Union, asking for accommodation prior to her departure for West Africa. Transport being difficult to obtain in these immediate post-war years, it was only with the help of the Liberian consul that she was able to leave for Monrovia, where she arrived in May 1946. There she was fêted, travelled around the country speaking to schoolchildren and women, and gathered material for a book, which, though apparently completed, was never published. She is also said to have adopted two girls, Eva Morris and Lizzie Wilson, with whom she maintained contact for many years.

Amy now hastened to Kumasi in Ghana where she stayed for two years as a guest of the Asantehene. Asante historians confirmed her claim to Asante descent. In Kumasi her plans to raise money locally and abroad to found a school for girls foundered. In 1949 Amy left for Nigeria, where she apparently continued her historical/sociological studies into the lives of women, and to lecture.

Returning to London, Amy is supposed to have spent some time in Birmingham, and then in London. In 1953 she returned to the Caribbean, lecturing and working with women's groups and child care organisations. She told the *Port-of-Spain Gazette* (28 May 1953) that she was 'making a survey of women in various parts of the world'. She did not find the women of Trinidad 'to be politically conscious … How will they measure up to take their place in the new nations?', she asked.

1957 saw her back in Ghana, for the Independence celebrations. From there she went back to London, where she opened a business, the Afro-Woman Service Bureau, providing laundry and mending services. With financial help from Sir Hamilton Kerr MP, she was able to purchase a house to be used as the Afro-Women's Centre – a hostel and advice centre – in London's Notting Hill area, which was soon to be the scene of anti-Black riots. Amy also planned to establish a vocational school there. The Centre became the home of the Association for the Advancement of Coloured People (AACP), set up by Amy, interestingly copying the name of the USA's National Association for the Advancement of Colored People, and not that of her ex-husband's organisation, the UNIA. While it has been impossible to ascertain exact dates, the AACP, whose secretary was CLAUDIA JONES, was certainly in existence by 1958, as it served as the headquarters for the campaigns regarding the inadequacy of police reaction to White racists. Amy was elected chairperson of the organisation set up in response to the lynching of a young Black man on the streets of Notting Hill in 1959; again her house was often used for meetings. Amy's other political involvements included serving on the editorial board of the *West Indian Gazette* and the London borough of Kensington's (which included Notting Hill) Lord Mayor's Inter-Racial Committee.

In 1960, perhaps fuelled by the need for money to finance the Centre, where the tenants were always falling behind with their rent, Amy, through the agency of her adopted daughter Eva Morris, signed an undertaking to cooperate with the Liberian government in the exploration for and the exploitation of mineral resources. Amy involved Sam Manning, who had been living in the USA for some years, not only in this enterprise, but also in plans to establish an ice factory in Kumasi and to export Duracrete, a substance superior to cement, to Ghana. The latter were soon dropped in favour of the export of diamonds from Liberia. Amy now went to Liberia, but debts and the climate drove her and Sam to Ghana, where he died of 'consumption' in 1961. Amy returned to Liberia and attempted to set herself up as a diamond broker. This, too, failed and by 1964 she was ill and in desperate financial straits in Las Palmas. She wrote to her friend Claudia Jones, asking for her possessions to be moved out of her London home, which she was about to lose due to the non-payment of the mortgage. She also asked for Claudia's help to prevent the repatriation of the remains of Marcus Garvey to Jamaica. (She had obstructed this previously, at the time of his death, claiming that Amy Jacques was not Garvey's legal wife and thus could not remove his remains.) When the Jamaican government paid her outstanding bills in Las Palmas, her fare back to London, and the Jamaican negotiator promised to fund the publication of her biography of Garvey, she signed the release papers for the remains. The biography was never published, and as with other manuscripts by Amy, has apparently been lost.

In 1965 Amy returned to Jamaica. Indefatigable, she set up the Marcus Garvey Benevolent Foundation to create and support Jamaican welfare agencies. When funds raised in Jamaica were embezzled, she went to New York in 1967 to raise more. She made a record, 'Up You Mighty Race: Recollections of Marcus Garvey', on which she read some of Marcus' speeches, in order to raise funds for the Foundation. Though unwell, she accepted an invitation from the Black Panthers to undertake a lecture tour of California. Exhausted, after a brief stop in Trinidad Amy finally returned to Jamaica in November 1968.

Amy Ashwood Garvey died of cancer in May 1969.

MS

Further reading

Martin, Tony, 'Amy Ashwood Garvey, Wife No. 1', *Jamaica Journal*, 20/3, August–October 1987.

Yard, Lionel M., *Biography of Amy Ashwood Garvey*, Associated Publishers, nd.

Marcus Garvey
(1887 – 1940)

Marcus Garvey created the only worldwide anti-imperialist movement embracing equality and self-determination for all Africans and those of African descent; he promoted self-help and Black pride in the face of persecution and ubiquitous notions of White supremacy.

Marcus Garvey was born in St Ann's Bay, Jamaica; his father was a stonemason, a deacon in the Methodist church, a lover of books and reading; his mother sold home-baked cakes and sweets in the local market. Marcus attended the local elementary school until he was fourteen, when he was apprenticed to his printer godfather.

In 1906 he moved to Kingston, obtained work as a compositor and rose to the rank of vice-president of his trade union. The young Garvey was much influenced by Dr Robert Love, the Bahamian-born US-trained physician, who had settled in Jamaica. Love's newspaper, the radical *Jamaica Advocate*, counselled race-consciousness as an anti-colonial concept, advocated land reform and Black representation in the Legislative Council; it also carried news of the Black world outside Jamaica. Garvey joined and then became the secretary of the National Club formed in 1909, which called for self-government within the Empire. After the demise of the Club in 1910, the refusal of employment after he had joined a printers' strike, and the failure of his own paper the *Watchman*, Garvey moved to London in 1912.

In London Garvey did a variety of work. For a while he was employed by DUSÉ MOHAMED ALI at the offices of his *African Times & Orient Review*, where he must have met some of the leading radical Black activists of the day.

Garvey returned to Jamaica in July 1914. Immediately he set about establishing a political organisation: with the help of AMY ASHWOOD, the woman who was to become his first wife, the Universal Negro Improvement Association (UNIA) was launched on 1 August 1914. Its aim was 'a universal confederacy among the race, to strengthen the bonds of brotherhood and unity among the races'; to 'promote racial pride and reclaim the fallen'; 'to promote conscientious Christian worship among the native tribes of Africa and assist in the civilising of backward tribes of Africa'; and to establish educational facilities and 'worldwide commercial and industrial intercourse'. Hundreds flocked to join.

An admirer of Booker T. Washington's industrial educational policies, in 1916 Garvey decided to visit the USA to spread his message and to visit Washington's Tuskegee Institute, which he intended to use as a model for an educational establishment he was planning for Jamaica. At that time, lynching and segregation were widespread in the USA; the organised struggle against increasing disenfranchisement and other limitations placed on 'Negroes' was headed by a number of Black organisations, led by middle-class men – and some women. To escape the horrors of the South, Blacks were migrating to the North in search of wartime work. West Indians also arrived: 11,000 between 1899 and 1910; their numbers doubled in the next 10 years.

However, by the time Garvey arrived, Washington was dead. So Garvey called on W.A. Domingo, an associate from the days of the National Club in Kingston. Domingo, now settled in New York, had become a socialist; he introduced Garvey to his political colleagues and soon Garvey was speaking on their platform under the aegis of the Afro-American Liberty League. Working intermittently as a printer, Garvey travelled through the States, returned to New York and set about building a branch of the UNIA. He was so successful that Kingston receded into the background. Amy Ashwood soon joined him.

African American intellectuals and their numerous organisations were constantly at odds with Garvey. His popular appeal was resented, if not feared. W.E.B. Du Bois' theory of only the 'talented tenth' being fit to take leadership roles was anathema to Garvey. The bourgeoisie feared the demagogue who could obviously arouse the masses. Many were in favour of integration, which was opposed by Garvey. Emigration, which had been debated for decades, was currently in an anti-emigration phase: by the 1920s most African Americans had decided that if not their homeland, the USA was the country their labour had helped create, and their energies should be devoted to its 'redemption' from racism. This philosophy did not prevent an Afro-American resentment of the Caribbean incomers/settlers.

Garvey opened the first branch of the UNIA in New York a year after his arrival, with a membership initially drawn mainly from his socialist and communist colleagues, many of whom were of West Indian origins. But soon he was successful in spreading his message far and wide. This included the principles enunciated in Jamaica, and the belief that the domination and exploitation of Black peoples by Whites had resulted in Blacks losing their self-esteem, their self-respect. They had to re-learn that 'Black is Beautiful' – not just White! Now thousands flocked to his banner.

The membership of the UNIA was estimated at anything from 4 million to 40,000. The only known exact numbers are for 1923, when the membership of eight branches, including Jamaica and Guatemala, totalled *c.*64,000. In the words of C.L.R. JAMES, 'there has never been a Negro movement anywhere like the Garvey movement, and few movements in any country can be compared to it in growth and intensity'. The UNIA soon started a newspaper, the *Negro World*, initially edited by W.A. Domingo, which constantly challenged entrenched notions of White superiority and advocated self-determination for Blacks. The paper's anti-colonial message was loud and clear. Correspondents from Africa and the Caribbean informed readers of the situation in their homelands.

Divisions or branches, established by adherents, functioned independently: charged with putting into action UNIA's aims, they collected membership fees (a part of which was remitted to the headquarters), paid out sickness and death benefits, and were free to embark on commercial projects. Their activities were centred around a rented or purchased Liberty Hall, where debates, lectures, educational classes, concerts and dances were held. Parades through towns featured the uniformed members of UNIA women's organisations such as the Motor Corps and Black Cross nurses, children's organisations akin to scouts and the UNIA African Legion, a paramilitary force which often served to protect UNIA and local populations from the aggression of the Ku Klux Klan and similar racist forces.

In order to enhance economic self-help, the UNIA fostered a number of commercial ventures. Many were poorly manged due to entrepreneurial inexperience. Probably the worst managed was the UNIA's own shipping line, started in 1919. It was intended to carry goods between the West Indies, the USA and West Africa, meeting the needs of West African traders who were frequently denied shipping space by the European shipping companies. The Black Star Line made the UNIA very popular among Africans. Garvey's popularity was increased by the presentation of two UNIA petitions to the League of Nations in 1922 and 1928. Both demanded the return of the African territories confiscated from Germany at the end of the First World War to their native inhabitants. The petitions, as well as the 63 letters of support from international organisations obtained by Garvey, were ignored by the League. In 1929 and again in 1931 Garvey travelled to Geneva to attempt to convince the League. He was unsuccessful.

At the first UNIA international convention in 1920, which was attended by 2,000 delegates, the Declaration of the Rights of the Negro Peoples of the World was promulgated. It reiterated the earlier principles and condemned worldwide discrimination in all its many forms and the inculcation of White superiority by the education system. It demanded 'self-determination for all peoples' and espoused 'the inherent right of the Negro to possess himself of Africa' and the 'necessity of Negro nationalism, political power and control'; the 'culmination of all the efforts of the UNIA must end in a Negro independent nation on the continent of Africa', to which all diaspora Africans could return. Garvey's surprising ignorance of the multiplicity of peoples and cultures in Africa resulted in his declaring himself Provisional President of a future independent republic of Africa.

To achieve the aims of the Declaration, in 1920 and again in 1924 Garvey sent emissaries to Liberia, the only, though only notionally, free country in West Africa. The Liberian government agreed a grant of land for a proposed immigration of between 20 and 30 thousand families. Garvey began to fund-raise for the venture. Goods and building materials began to be exported, and the construction of five settlements was begun. However, for a variety of reasons still debated by historians, hostility developed between the UNIA and President King. These reasons include a leaked memorandum from a settler highly critical of the Liberian elite; the appointment of Du Bois, who was hostile to Garvey as the USA's 'envoy extraordinary' to President King; and warnings from the neighbouring colonial powers France and Britain. The land concession was cancelled, materials were impounded and the settlers were expelled in 1924. The governor of Sierra Leone, the British colony bordering Liberia, congratulated President King for his 'vigorous action' in preventing the settlement of UNIA people whose 'avowed object [was] the fomenting of racial feelings and ill will'. The USA also had an interest: the Liberian government promptly leased the lands previously allocated to the UNIA to the US Firestone Company, for use as rubber plantations.

The UNIA emissaries of 1920 had also visited Sierra Leone, where branches, including a female division, were soon established. Sierra Leoneans in Senegal who had established a branch there were deported by the French authorities, who were also concerned about Garveyite activities in Dahomey and Cameroon. The Belgian rulers of Congo were equally fearful of Garvey's influence. There were also branches of the UNIA, and of the Black Star Line, in Lagos, Kano and Ibadan. While the initiators of the branches were in the main West Indians or Sierra Leoneans settled in Nigeria, many of the officers were Nigerians who became active in the National Congress of British West Africa and the Nigerian National Democratic Party when it was formed in 1922. The *Negro World* circulated in Kenya, Nyasaland and Uganda, much to the consternation of the British governors. Stories circulated in South Africa that the armies of the UNIA would come to free Africans; there were seven UNIA branches in Cape Town alone. However, with the debacle in Liberia and the collapse of the Black Star Line, the UNIA's immediate appeal in Africa diminished.

In 1924 Garvey also sent an emissary to Britain, where branches had been established. The British government, whose hostility to Garveyism in its colonies was profound, refused to acknowledge him. Branches had been formed in most of the West Indian colonies, which protested about local conditions. The *Negro World*, banned by the governments, was smuggled in by seamen.

The US government seized the opportunity offered by the UNIA's haphazard accounting system to deal with a man whose growing power and influence was causing concern. Allegedly with some support from his opponents among the Black intelligentsia, Garvey was charged with mail fraud. He was arrested in Janaury 1922; the Supreme Court rejected his appeal against conviction in 1925 and he was jailed for five years. In 1927 he was deported to Jamaica. Amy Jacques, his second wife, whom he married after divorcing Amy Ashwood in her absence, accompanied him. The couple had two sons, Marcus Jr and Julius.

The colony to which Garvey was forced to return was just recovering from a series of post-First World War strikes, which had resulted in the killing of three sugar workers. The dire economic situation led to an increase in emigration to the USA, which was reversed by the onset of the Depression: some 28,000 returned home between 1930 and 1934.

Almost immediately Garvey launched the Peoples Political Party, whose programme focused on labour conditions; reforms of the legal and land systems; demands for a health service, libraries and secondary schools in all the parishes; the end of electoral corruption and a 'larger modicum of self-government'. The Party published a paper, the *Black Man*, which was also the mouthpiece of the UNIA. (The *Negro World*, which continued to be published in the USA, was banned in Jamaica.) The paper carried historical articles, encouraged creative artists, supported anti-imperial movements abroad and brought news from the Black world.

The Party contested local elections of 1929. The government seized on an anti-government statement Garvey had made in an election speech to charge him with sedition and sentenced him to six months' hard labour. Thus he could not take the seat he had won in the Municipal Council. Other forms of harassment were instituted: the sellers and readers of the *Black Man* were intimidated and Garvey was denied entry to the other Caribbean colonies. Not surprisingly, he won another seat at the next elections. However, in the elections of 1930 for the Legislative Council the Party was defeated – and faded away. The UNIA continued to function, both in Jamaica and the USA.

In 1928 Garvey had visited London, prior to his appeal to the League of Nations in Geneva. The 'Petition of the Negro Race' reiterated the grievances of the Negroes which had been presented to the League in 1922 and again demanded redress. It called for a Commonwealth of Black Nations in West Africa, governed by Africans. His public meetings, at which he attacked the imperialists responsible for colonial exploitation, did not attract a large audience. However, he made contact with LADIPO SOLANKE and assigned the lease on his rented house to the West African Students' Union when he left later that year. In 1935 Garvey returned to London, this time to settle. He resuscitated the *Black Man*, which had ceased publication for some two to three years. The paper's theme remained both the emancipation of Africa from colonial rule and equality for diaspora Africans, but the virulence of his writing became muted. Garvey continued to address meetings and to speak at Hyde Park Corner, excoriating the invasion of Abyssinia by Italy, decrying the belittling film roles offered to PAUL ROBESON and other Black actors and highlighting the omission of Blacks from invitations to the 1937 coronation. However, on other issues, which included a defence of the British Empire as a system, Garvey was, C.L.R. James wrote, heckled by himself and GEORGE PADMORE.

At the UNIA conference in Canada in 1937, Garvey instituted summer schools in African Philosophy to train UNIA leaders; participants included West, East and South Africans, as well as local students. He also established a correspondence course in Black Studies in London. Back in Toronto for the 8th UNIA Convention, attended by only 110 people, the turn in Garvey's politics was obvious: the Black Repatriation Bill of White racist Mississippi senator Theodore G. Bilbo received endorsement.

By 1937 the British government found Garvey to be so harmless that he was granted permission to travel to the Caribbean. However, as in his speeches he avoided issues such as the 'labour disturbances', his West Indian audiences found him disappointing.

After two bouts of pneumonia and two strokes, Marcus Garvey died in London on 10 June 1940. He was buried in London, contrary to his wishes to be buried in Jamaica. This desire was fulfilled in 1964 when his remains were shipped home, interred in a national shrine and Garvey was named Jamaica's first National Hero.

MS

Further reading

The literature on Garvey is extensive, see for example:

Clarke, John Henrik, *Marcus Garvey and the Vision of Africa*, New York, Random House, 1974.

Hill, Robert (ed.), *The Marcus Garvey and Universal Negro Improvement Association Papers*, vols 1–5, Los Angeles, University of California Press, 1983.

Langley, J.A., 'Marcus Garvey and African Nationalism', in S.O. Mezu and R. Desai (eds), *Black Leaders of the Centuries*, Buffalo, NY, Black Academy Press, 1970.

Lewis, Rupert, *Marcus Garvey: Anti-Colonial Champion*, London, Karia Press, 1987.

Okonkwo, R.L., 'The Garvey Movement in British West Africa', *Journal of African History*, 21 January 1980.

Joseph Ephraim Casely Hayford
(1866 – 1930)

Joseph Ephraim Casely Hayford, Ghanaian, writer, lawyer, politician and Pan-Africanist, was a founder of the National Congress of British West Africa, one of the first Pan-African organisations on the African continent. He was born on 29 September 1866 at Cape Coast, at that time in the British colony of the Gold Coast in West Africa. He was the fourth son of Revd and Mrs Joseph de Graft Hayford; his father was a minister in the Methodist Church and his mother a member of the Brew family. J.E. Casely Hayford was thus a member of the coastal elite whose families often had European as well as African ancestry and European or Europeanised names.

Casely Hayford was educated locally at the famous Weslyan Boys' High School and subsequently at Fourah Bay College in Sierra Leone. After completing his studies, he was for a time employed as the headmaster of his old school in Cape Coast before in 1885 becoming a journalist on the *Western Echo* founded by his uncle James Hutton Brew. In 1888 Casely Hayford became the editor of this newspaper which was renamed the *Gold Coast Echo*, and in 1890 became the co-owner of the *Gold Coast Chronicle*. Casely Hayford's interest in the press was at least partly political; he, like many others amongst the Western educated elite, saw it as an important vehicle for voicing anti-colonial aspirations and demands. Later, in 1912, while he was in London as part of a Gold Coast Aborigines Rights Protection Society (GCARPS) delegation sent to protest to the British government about the introduction of the 1911 Forest Bill, he joined with other West Africans to temporarily take over the ownership of DUSÉ MOHAMED ALI's financially insolvent *African Times & Orient Review*. In 1912, he was the ARPS representative at Booker T. Washington's 'International Conference on the Negro' held at Tuskegee, in the US.

During the early 1890s Casely Hayford decided to study law, at first becoming an articled clerk to a lawyer in Cape Coast and then travelling to Britain to complete his studies. From 1893–4 he studied economics at Cambridge University and then was finally called to the Bar at the Inner Temple, Inns of Court in 1896. He returned to the Gold Coast to establish his legal practice, and in 1897 became legal advisor to the GCARPS during its successful campaign against the colonial government's Land Bill, which aimed at alienating land from Africans in the interests of the Crown. The GCARPS, founded in 1897, was one of the earliest anti-colonial organisations in the Gold Coast, established by local rulers and Western educated intellectuals mainly to safeguard the land rights of Africans from the colonial authorities.

During 1903 Casely Hayford was in London again and there published his first book *Gold Coast Native Institutions*, which amongst other things attacked the corruption of the colonial administration in the Gold Coast. He was a frequent visitor to London in the early part of the century, became a member of the British-based African Society in 1903 and wrote the introduction to EDWARD BLYDEN's *West Africa before Europe* which was published in London in 1905. It was in that city that his own most famous and partly autobiographical book *Ethiopia Unbound* was published in 1911. *Ethiopia Unbound*, one of the first African novels with a strong Pan-African theme was dedicated to the 'sons of Ethiopia the world wide over'. In the novel West Africa is very much at the centre of Casely Hayford's Pan-African world, a world that was based on the political traditions of JAMES HORTON and especially Blyden. Casely Hayford praised Blyden's work as 'universal, covering the whole race', designed 'to reveal everywhere the African unto himself', 'to lead him back into self respect' and to restore to him 'his true place in creation on natural and national lines'. In particular the novel is concerned with developing the 'African nationality' and encouraging 'race emancipation' and proudly claims that Africa was the 'cradle of civilisation'. It looks forward to the prospect of mobilising those of African descent throughout the world in order to modernise African society while retaining its African features, as it argues Japan had done in the recent past. He also strongly favoured the creation of a university in West Africa that might become a centre of excellence for students from the region and throughout the African diaspora. Like Blyden, he argued that such a university must provide an Africanised curriculum so as to promote African culture and overcome the Eurocentrism that accompanied the European partition of Africa and colonial rule. Casely Hayford attempted to implement some of his ideas on the promotion of African culture and self-respect, when in 1915 he established the Gold Coast National Research Association.

From 1916–25 he was appointed, by the British governor, a nominated member of the Gold Coast Legislative Council, the body that had limited decision-making powers but was largely an advisory body in the colony. In practice Africans had absolutely no political power, a fact that led to increasing demands for political reforms particularly from those like Casely Hayford who were well aware of the contradictions between notions of nationalism and self-determination being discussed in Europe at the end of the First World War and the practice of colonial rule in Africa. Casely Hayford was also appointed to several colonial government commissions and in recognition of his public service was awarded an MBE in 1919.

Even before he became a member of the Legislative Council, he had been considering the necessity of convening a meeting to bring together African political representatives from all four British colonies in West Africa. In 1914 preparations were being made for such a meeting and reflected the development of the idea of 'West African nationality' mainly amongst the urban and Western educated elite in Nigeria, Sierra Leone, Gambia and the Gold Coast. In his book, *The Truth about the West African Land Question*, published in 1913, Casely Hayford was already speaking of a 'united West Africa' and of a nationalism that demanded unity and cultural awareness amongst Africans, but constitutional political reforms that kept the colonies within the British empire, rather than self-determination or radical demands for independence. Similar ideas were also widely promoted in the press throughout the four colonies and following the formation of territorial committees in March 1920, fifty-two delegates attended the Conference of Africans of British West Africa in Accra, which after three weeks of deliberation and the passing of over eighty resolutions officially launched the National Congress of British West Africa (NCBWA).

The NCBWA was one of the first Pan-African organisations formed on the African continent and Casely Hayford became its first vice-president and subsequently its president. It claimed to speak for all the people in the four colonies and demanded specific political reforms and changes in British colonial rule, but at the same time pledged loyalty to the empire. Casely Hayford and the others associated with the NCBWA sought constitutional reforms which would allow the educated elite of merchants and professional men more say in the running of the colonies and end the discrimination they faced in relation to employment and economic opportunities. To this end in 1920 he travelled to London as the leader of an NCBWA delegation seeking such reforms. The Colonial Secretary refused to see the delegation, but it remained in London for several months, and established links with West Africans and several sympathetic organisations in Britain including the African Progress Union and the League of Nations Union. Casely Hayford's ideas of West African nationalism did have a major influence on West African students in Britain and were initially the guiding ideology of the West African Students' Union (WASU), formed in London in 1925 by LADIPO SOLANKE. Casely Hayford subsequently became one of the WASU's patrons.

The Congress met again in Sierra Leone in 1923, in the Gambia in 1925–6 and finally in Lagos, Nigeria in 1930. But it failed to enlist the support of many of the traditional rulers in the four colonies and made no attempt to gain the support of the masses, while the colonial authorities opposed its aims. Within a relatively short time, therefore, its territorial committees in the individual colonies ceased to function effectively or have widespread influence. The colonial authorities did, however, introduce political reforms in the West African colonies, at least partly as a result of the NCBWA's agitation. But as this provided a local focus for political activity its main consequence was to undermine the regional approach of the NCBWA. The notion of a 'West African nation' was also, however, an idea which continued to influence later nationalists and nationalist movements in West Africa and Britain, including KWAME NKRUMAH and the West African National Secretariat in the 1940s.

Casely Hayford remained one of the leading politicians in the Gold Coast throughout the 1920s. As secretary of the GCARPS he initially opposed the new constitution introduced into the Gold Coast in 1925 and at first refused to accept a nominated seat on the Legislative Council. Following such protests the constitution was amended and Casely Hayford stood for election in Accra in 1927. From 1927–30 he represented Sekondi-Takoradi on the Legislative Council. Until the end of his life he remained active in politics and in 1929 helped to found the Gold Coast Youth Conference, perhaps the first modern nationalist movement in the Gold Coast.

Casely Hayford died on 11 August 1930 at the age of sixty-three and was buried in the Gold Coast.

HA

Main publications

Ethiopia Unbound: Studies in Race Emancipation, London, 1911.
The Truth about the West African Land Question, London, 1913.

Further reading

Langley, J.A., *Pan-Africanism and Nationalism in West Africa, 1900–45: A Study in Ideology and Social Classes*, London, Oxford University Press, 1972.
Sampson, M.J., *Makers of Modern Ghana*, Accra, Anowuo Educational Publishers, 1969.

James Africanus Beale Horton
(1835 – 83)

James Africanus Beale Horton, physician, scientist, historian, writer and Pan-Africanist has been called 'the father of modern African political thought'.

James Horton was born in the village of Gloucester, near Freetown, in the British colony of Sierra Leone in 1835. He was the seventh of eight children born to James Horton, a carpenter, and his wife Nancy and the only child who survived infancy. Horton's parents were both 'recaptives', enslaved Igbos (from what is now eastern Nigeria), who had been liberated by the British anti-slavery squadron and released in Sierra Leone. Like many freed slaves in Sierra Leone they had taken an English name; the original Horton was an English missionary who had visited Sierra Leone from 1816–21.

James Horton was initially educated locally in Gloucester, then in 1845, Revd James Beale of the Church Missionary Society (CMS) recruited him as a pupil for the CMS Grammar School in Freetown. Horton was fortunate enough to receive a scholarship from the colony's African Chief Justice, John Carr, but he expressed the most gratitude to the missionary Beale by adopting his name. The curriculum at the school was entirely Eurocentric and a large part of Horton's education would have included the study of Latin and Greek. In 1853 he transferred to the Fourah Bay Institution in Freetown (afterwards Fourah Bay College) to train as a clergyman, and studied Hebrew and Divinity.

In 1853 the British War Office, concerned about the high mortality rates amongst European army officers, proposed to recruit and train African physicians and offer commissions in the British army serving in the West African colonies. Horton was chosen as one of three candidates and abandoned his theological training for a medical career in Britain. He was sent to Britain in 1855 and became a medical student at London University's Kings College, where he spent three years. After achieving membership of the Royal College of Surgeons, he spent a fourth year in Britain at Edinburgh University studying for his doctorate. It seems that it was while he was in Britain that Horton became more aware of his African identity. By the time he moved to Edinburgh he was signing himself Africanus. James Africanus Beale Horton became one of the first African doctors to be trained in Britain and a Member of the Royal College of Surgeons. After his graduation, he was also one of the first Africans to be commissioned as an officer in the British army, with the rank of staff assistant surgeon.

In London in1858, Horton published his Edinburgh dissertation, *The Medical Topography of the West Coast of Africa*, and thus became one of the first African scientists to research and write on Africa. He returned to Sierra Leone and was immediately posted to the British colony of the Gold Coast with the West India Regiment. In the Gold Coast he suffered from discrimination and the racism he encountered throughout his army career. He was frequently given new postings and saw service in Gambia, Lagos, and the Gold Coast as well as Sierra Leone. But Horton was determined not to be provoked, or in any way to jeopardise the careers of other Africans. He continued with his research and during the next few years published several other scientific studies on the geology and botany of West Africa.

It seems that around 1865 he became connected with the African Aid Society, formed in London in 1860, and its newspaper the *African Times*. The *African Times* served as the mouthpiece not only of various philanthropic and economic interests in Britain but also of the emerging Western educated Africans in British colonies in West Africa. In 1865 Horton wrote an address to the African Aid Society entitled *Political Economy of West Africa – The African's view of the Negro's Place in Nature*. His first political writing was prompted by the report of the British Parliament's Select Committee on the West African colonies. At the time of Britain's world economic domination, the Select Committee proposed no further colonial annexations in West Africa and spoke of ultimate withdrawal from the existing colonies. According to the report, the object of British policy should be to create the conditions that might eventually lead to self-government in West Africa. As well as writing in support of African self-government Horton also repudiated all the theories of pseudo-scientific racism then current. In particular he opposed the views of James Hunt, who in 1863 had founded the Anthropological Society in London. Hunt was the author of the openly racist publication entitled *On the Negro's Place in Nature*.

In 1867 Horton took leave from his post and travelled to England where he continued his research and writing, and with his own finances published three more books. Two of his publications were concerned with medical and scientific matters, although here too he included demands for medical and health reforms; the third was his most famous work entitled *West African Countries and Peoples, British and Native, with the Requirements Necessary for Establishing that Self-Government recommended by the Committee of the House of Commons, 1865; and a Vindication of the African Race*.

West African Countries and Peoples, published in 1868, was a revised version of Horton's 'Political Economy of West Africa'. It again contained lengthy critiques of Hunt and other Victorian racists, including Richard Burton, as well as a vindication of Africans, which borrowed freely from Armistead's *A Tribute to the Negro*. In addition, Horton provided his readers with political, economic and social information about the West African colonies and a programme for their evolution to self-government, including the proposals for compulsory education and that Fourah Bay College should become a 'University of West Africa'. He declared that his aims were to develop amongst West Africans a 'true political science' and 'to prove the capacity of the African for possessing a real political Government and national independence'.

He was thus the first modern African writer to openly campaign for self-government for the West African colonies and to champion the cause of what he referred to as 'African nationality'. He combated the racist notion that Africa and Africans were backward and incapable of improvement, and pointed to the progress made by ex-slaves in Sierra Leone. He took the view that:

> the nations of Western Africa must live in the hope that in the process of time their turn will come, when they will occupy a prominent position in the world's history, and when they will command a voice in the council of nations.

However, he was also very much a man of his time, someone who believed that 'civilisation' must come from outside Africa and could be brought by Christianity and an enlightened British government.

During his time in England, Horton met and began a correspondence with Edward Cardwell, the Secretary of State for War, that continued when he returned to West Africa in 1868. It was after his return that he became connected with the short-lived Fanti Confederation, formed to force the Dutch and ultimately the British out of the Gold Coast. The constitution drawn up by its leaders was probably influenced by Horton's ideas. He championed the Confederation, believed that it was working towards the 'self-government of the Gold Coast' and that it should be recognised by the British government. Horton also consulted with the leaders of the Accra National Confederation, formed in 1869, who told him that it represented the 'germ of that form of government' that he had advocated in his writing. Horton communicated his views on the Fanti Confederation and other matters to Cardwell and the Colonial Secretary, Lord Granville; in 1870 these letters were published in London as *Letters on the Political Condition of the Gold Coast*.

In 1872 Horton was temporarily appointed Civil Commandant of Sekondi in the Gold Coast and in the same year he unsuccessfully applied for the post of Administrator of the Gold Coast. He had for some time been local magistrate and held other responsible positions but he was also passed over for promotion on many occasions. In 1875 however, he was promoted to Surgeon-Major and in 1879 he was appointed Head of the Army Medical Department of the Gold Coast, but at the end of the following year he retired from the army and embarked on a business career. In 1880 he bought several gold mining concessions throughout the Gold Coast and became connected with the London-based Gold Coast Mining Company. In the next few years he attempted to supply credit facilities to West African traders and after fourteen months of negotiations launched the Commercial Bank of West Africa in 1882. Horton became one of the richest men in West Africa, but suddenly contracted a fatal skin infection and died on 15 October 1883 at the age of forty-eight. After his coffin had lain in state in St George's Cathedral, he was buried in Freetown.

HA

Main publications

West African Countries and Peoples, British and Native, with the Requirements Necessary for Establishing that Self-Government recommended by the Committee of the House of Commons, 1865; and a Vindication of the African Race (1868), republished edition edited and introduction by George Shepperson, Edinburgh, Edinburgh University Press, 1969.

Letters on the Political Condition of the Gold Coast since the Exchange of territory Between the English and Dutch Governments on January 1 1868, together with a short account of the Ashantee War, 1862–4 and the Awoonah War, 1866 (1870), second edition with an introduction by E.A. Ayandele, London, Frank Cass, 1970.

Africanus Horton: The Dawn of Nationalism in Modern Africa, with introduction and commentaries by Davidson Nicol, London, Longmans, 1969.

Further reading

Fyfe, C., *Africanus Horton 1835–1883 – West African Scientist and Patriot*, New York and Oxford, Oxford University Press, 1972.

W. Alphaeus Hunton
(1903 – 70)

Hunton, according to KWAME NKRUMAH, had spent his life 'sacrificing and working so hard for the cause ... He was grand and selfless. I always had great respect for him …'. The 'cause' was the freedom of Africa from imperial domination, Pan-Africanism and socialism.

Alphaeus' father, the son of an escaped slave, was born in Chatham, Ontario. Trained as a teacher, he migrated to the USA after working for the Canadian Indian Bureau for a while. He worked for the rest of his life for the YMCA, finally as the Secretary of its International Committee. Addie Hunton, his wife, also worked for the Y, and with the National Association of Coloured Women, as well as the International Red Cross in Europe during the First World War. She managed to maintain her political involvements and struggles for women's rights, even when she became the sole breadwinner on the death of Alphaeus' father in 1916. This internationally (especially Africa)-oriented upbringing set Alphaeus on his life's journey.

The young Alphaeus worked his way through high school and Howard University. In 1926, with an MA degree from Harvard, he returned to teach at his *alma mater*. He taught English language and literature at this premier university for Black students, which, however, only appointed its first Black president that year. Hunton also became involved politically, for example in the anti-lynching crusade, and in organising a branch of the Teachers' Union on campus as 'a viable instrument for academic and social progress'. He was also the chair of the Labour Committee of the Washington branch of the American Federation of Teachers and served on the national executive board of the National Negro Congress (NNC), an organisation agitating for Black rights. Hunton organised picket lines, mass demonstrations, parades, public meetings, and produced bulletins and leaflets regarding issues such as the various and multitudinous forms of 'Jim Crow oppression' (which continued after the outbreak of the Second World War, for example by excluding Blacks from well-paid defence industry jobs), and police brutality. In 1940 he was the main organiser of the NNC annual conference, attended by 1,300 delegates.

While continuing to teach, from 1934 to 1938 Hunton worked for his PhD at New York University, where he came under the influence of a leading Marxist, Dr Edwin Burgum. This influence is reflected in his dissertation, which examined the influence of Britain's imperial role on the poet Tennyson and on the contemporary British public. During this period he married and divorced twice; his final marriage to Dorothy took place in 1943.

By 1943 Hunton was frustrated at Howard: he needed a larger forum to express his political and racial dissatisfactions; he had become convinced, according to his Howard and NNC colleague Doxey Wilkerson, that 'the basic ills of our country and the world called imperatively for a socialist reconstruction of society'. The offer of the Educational Directorship of the Council on African Affairs (CAA) provided him with an opportunity to attempt this 'reconstruction'. Initially called the International Committee on Africa, the Council had been formed in New York in 1937 by Max Yergan, who had recently returned to the USA from many years' work in South Africa as a 'missionary' for the YMCA. Reorganised in 1941, PAUL ROBESON became the chairperson; Yergan remained executive secretary. Despite the heavy workload he undertook at the CAA, Hunton retained his seat on the NNC Executive and on the editoral board of its monthly journal, *Congress View*, until the demise of the NNC in the post-war years.

It was Robeson and Hunton who did most of the publicity work for the Council, speaking in the major US and Canadian cities. For example, 4,000 people attended a meeting on Toronto in January 1944 at which Hunton spoke on 'Africa – a continent in bondage'. However, while they succeeded in arousing interest in Africa, and certainly in educating their audience about the realities of the continent, they did not succeed in broadening the Council's membership. This always bothered Hunton, who would have preferred to turn the CAA into a 'mass based' organisation.

Hunton edited the CAA's *New Africa* (later *Spotlight on Africa*), a monthly source of information and analysis. Again, to quote Wilkerson, Hunton used the journal to work for the ending of 'the despoliation and devastation in [Africa] that last bastion of colonial imperialism'. The monthly magazine carried news and long reports from around the world of important events touching Africa. Hunton had informants not only in the USA, Africa and the Caribbean, but also in London, and must have subscribed to newspapers from around the world as well as to official British, US and UN publications, and clearly read every book published anywhere on Africa. All these were deposited in the Council's library, which was open to researchers. One can, perhaps, judge *New Africa*'s effectiveness by its banning in Kenya, South Africa and the 'Belgian' Congo. Hunton also sent news releases to 62 foreign papers and 67 US newspapers, sometimes two or three times a week. He also helped with the day-to-day administration of the CAA.

As Education Director and later as Secretary, Hunton was part of the team which planned the CAA's many activities, some of which were responses to emergencies such as the shooting of miners in Enugu, Nigeria; famine in South Africa; and the trial of Jomo Kenyatta by the colonial government in Kenya. Hunton helped organise the many conferences held by the CAA, for example that on 'Africa – New Perspectives' in 1944, at which one of the speakers was the then student, Francis (later Kwame) Nkrumah. In June, October and November 1946 there were meetings (one in the huge Madison Square Gardens) on South Africa, and pickets outside the South African consulate. In April 1947 there was a People's Rally Against Imperialism which included a play on colonial struggles, films, and songs by Robeson. Hunton was also the CAA's 'observer' at the United Nations, attending sessions relevant to the CAA's concerns, preparing documents for its General Assembly and Trusteeship Council, and acting, when possible, as a go-between for colonial delegates.

Hunton also wrote a number of pamphlets. In *Stop South Africa's Crimes* published in 1946, he outlined the USA's involvement in the South African economy. Then he enumerated the resolutions passed at a meeting the CAA had called the previous October, for the US government and the United Nations to:

- reject South Africa's annexation of S-W Africa
- press for racial equality (including Indians) in South Africa
- limit the periods of new 'trusteeship' agreements
- place the colonies of Spain and Portugal under UN supervision
- guarantee political autonomy and self-determination within a definite time limit
- provide for the representation of African colonial peoples in the UN.

Readers were urged to write to the UN and the US government in approval of these resolutions and to press for their implementation.

Resistance Against Fascist Enslavement in South Africa (1953), reprinted the African National Congress' Memorandum to the United Nations, and added a long section by Hunton, which again detailed the USA's involvement in South Africa and urged readers to write to their Congressmen in support of a CAA resolution which had been sent to the US President 'to halt US assistance in any form to the Government of the Union of South Africa and to denounce publicly that government's racist program as an international menace'.

No copies are available to this writer of the following pamphlets by Hunton: *Africa Fights for Freedom* (1950), *Seeing is Believing – The Truth about South Africa* (1947), which was sent to the UN General Assembly; *Africa Fights for Freedom* (1950); *Bandung: Asian-African Conference* (1955); *Review of the Asian-African Conference* (1955).

Clearly a man of vast commitment, Hunton was also a founder of the radical Black journal *Freedomways*, to which he also contributed articles. He also wrote for the radical newspaper *People's Voice*, and for the journals *Masses and Mainstream* and *Political Affairs*, in which, for example, he suggested that the Central African Federation had been at least partly formed to attract US capital to its 'white settler' member states. (*Political Affairs*, April 1959) He also bemoaned the absence of economic issues at the All-African People's Conference and the spending of large sums by some of the newly independent states on 'non-essentials'. (*Political Affairs*, December 1959)

The arrival of the Cold War in 1946/7 also witnessed major upheavals at the CAA, which was accused by the red-baiting press of communism. Yergan turned FBI informer and disrupted the Council's work. He was eventually ousted after a bitter struggle. Hunton became Secretary, Robeson remained Chair, and W.E.B. DU BOIS became vice-chair. Kwame Nkrumah wrote to Hunton from Accra in November 1948 saying that he was 'glad the CAA had been renewed under your leadership'; he was willing to 'co-operate with you in order to accelerate the dawn of freedom in Africa'. But such enthusiasm from Africa was not matched by support at home: membership waned, despite attempts to establish local chapters.

In 1949 Hunton testified against the formation of NATO to the Senate Foreign Relations Committee; the following year he campaigned for the return of Paul

Robeson's passport which the US government, having already instructed concert halls and recording companies not to give him a platform, had withdrawn. In 1951 he, the Robesons and CLAUDIA JONES were amongst the signatories of a petition to the United Nations charging the USA with the genocide of African Americans.

When Hunton himself was questioned in 1951 by the House Committee on Un-American Activities, he refused to give the names of the donors to the Civil Rights Congress' Bail Fund. He was imprisoned for six months for his adamant refusal. The jailing drew protests from many Black leaders. On his release Hunton once again took up the cudgels on behalf of Africa: he organised support, for example, for the liberation movements in North Africa and in Kenya. The government now launched a thorough investigation of the CAA, demanding to see all documents, etc. With no funds to support what would be a protracted struggle, the CAA decided to dissolve itself in June 1955.

Financially supported (as always) by his wife Dorothy, Hunton now concentrated on writing a book, *Decision in Africa* (1957). In this he outlined the existing situation in Africa and delineated answers to questions he posed: who was benefiting from the much-vaunted increased production of minerals and crops? Under what conditions was production being increased? And what will be the consequences? As ever he was concerned to get his readers involved in the issues he raised. Americans had a 'responsibility', he argued, to voice their 'opposition to the continued imperialist domination in Africa … Americans and their government … [must] take their stand unequivocally … on the side of *African freedom*' (p.238).

As now all university appointments were denied him, Hunton did what work he could, for example in the fur trade and as a seasonal IBM employee. With financial assistance from friends he was able to attend the historic All-African People's Conference organised by GEORGE PADMORE in Accra in December 1958. Prime Minister Kwame Nkrumah arranged for him to tour Ghana and then to visit Nigeria, Guinea and the Ivory Coast, where he was made welcome by the many who had read CAA publications or had received Council support. From West Africa he travelled to London, and saw his erstwhile colleague Paul Robeson perform in *Othello* at Stratford-upon-Avon. Joined by Dorothy, he then travelled to Moscow, and through Europe back to London, and then to the USA.

In New York the Huntons faced a situation as bleak as the one they had left behind. Hunton was offered a few speaking engagements, but no employment. Dorothy returned to the sewing machine. They were saved by an invitation from President SÉKOU TOURÉ to Hunton to teach at the only *lycée* and then at the university just being established. The Huntons left for Conakry, Guinea in April 1960. At the beginning of the school year, Dorothy was also drafted in to teach English. During the school vacation they visited Sierra Leone, where they called on CONSTANCE CUMMINGS-JOHN, whom Hunton had known and supported during her sojourn in the USA.

In August 1961 the Huntons were invited to return to the USSR, partly for a medical check-up, as both had suffered from the African coastal climate. After two months they returned to Conakry, but soon an invitation arrived from Du Bois, then settled in Accra, where he had begun work on an *Encyclopaedia Africana*. At the age of ninety-three, Du Bois, who had been a none-too-appreciative colleague of Hunton's at the CAA, now felt he needed a trustworthy assistant. Nkrumah welcomed the Huntons warmly.

Hunton drew up discussion documents on the proposed *Encyclopaedia*, which, after approval by the Advisory Committee, were further discussed at a conference attended by 150 delegates. Five regional committees were established to gather information; Hunton served as coordinator. When Du Bois died in August 1963, the project was incorporated into the Ghana Academy of Sciences. Hunton left on a visit to the Regional Committees of North and East Africa and then travelled to Hungary where he was a guest at the inaugural dinner of the Hungarian Academy of Sciences. On his return, Hunton resumed work on the *Encyclopaedia*. An international Editorial Board was set up and met in September 1964; ten volumes were outlined and it was planned to publish the first three by 1970. Hunton himself began working on volume 3, biographies.

But the workload was too heavy and in October Alphaeus was hospitalised with a heart attack. On his recovery, the Huntons accepted an invitation to visit China, where Alphaeus received further medical treatment. On their return to Ghana Hunton was appointed to the directorship of the *Encyclopaedia* project by its Standing Committee, but the Academy of Sciences refused to accept the appointment, replacing him with a Ghanaian and also stripping him of his responsibilities as administrator. But worse was to come: Nkrumah was overthrown in February 1966 and later that year the Huntons were ordered to leave Ghana. They returned to New York.

In February 1967 President Kenneth Kaunda invited the Huntons to Zambia as his guests. The President instructed the Zambian representative on the *Encyclopaedia* Committee to investigate the possibility of continuing the work. As this proved impossible, he asked Hunton to commence working on a history of the nationalist movement in Zambia. As Zambia hosted many South African (and other) freedom fighters, Hunton began writing a column under the name of 'Optimist' in *Mayibye*, the bulletin of the African National Congress.

Hunton's health continued to deteriorate. He was flown to London, where his condition was found to be inoperable. Alphaeus Hunton died in Lusaka on 13 January 1970. President Kaunda attended the funeral, after which Dorothy Hunton returned to New York.

MS

Further reading

Hunton, Dorothy, *Alphaeus Hunton: the Unsung Valiant*, Chesapeake, Eca Associates, 1986.

Von Eschen, Penny M., *Race Against Empire: Black Americans and Anti-colonialism*, Ithaca, Cornell University Press, 1997.

Wilkerson, Doxey, 'William Alphaeus Hunton: a life that made a difference', *Freedomways*, 3rd Quarter, 1970.

C.L.R. James
(1901 – 89)

Cyril Lionel Robert James, author, eclectic intellectual and political activist, is probably the best known figure of Caribbean birth on the world stage. He has been the inspiration – and the source of ongoing debate and controversy – to many Black intellectuals (and others) for half a century. His life and writings encompassed Africans and the Diaspora.

C.L.R., as he was ubiquitously known, was the grandson of the first 'coloured' engine driver on the Trinidad Government Railway. His father was a school teacher; his mother a lover of literature who introduced him to the classics of European writing. One of his boyhood friends was Malcolm Ivan Nurse, better known as GEORGE PADMORE. At the age of ten he won one of eight annual scholarships to Queen's Royal College, Trinidad's premier secondary school. There he became a prize pupil, an outstanding athlete and the holder of the national high-jump record. He also played and loved cricket, but realised early that he was not of world-standard. On graduation he was invited to teach at the school; among his pupils was the future Prime Minister, ERIC WILLIAMS. In his unpublished autobiography James claims that it was MARCUS GARVEY who made him 'aware that to be black was something of political importance'.

By the 1920s C.L.R. was involved in the publication of the *Beacon*, a literary/ political journal, and was working on a novel, *Minty Alley* (not published until 1936). In 1932, at the invitation of his erstwhile cricketing colleague Learie Constantine, then resident in Nelson, Lancashire, James moved to Britain. With Constantine's recommendation he become a cricket writer for leftish daily, *The Manchester Guardian*. Constantine also offered financial support for the publication of *The Life of Captain Cipriani* (a labour/political leader in Trinidad) (1932), which James used to promote Trinidad's independence from colonial bondage. C.L.R. repaid Constantine by helping him with his *Cricket and I*.

Soon involved in the international Marxist movement, C.L.R. joined the Independent Labour Party, becoming a branch secretary and a proselytiser on colonial issues. In 1935, when the proposed invasion of Ethiopia by imperialist Italy became imminent, he founded the International Friends of Abyssinia (IAFA) (later 'of Ethiopia'); among its officers were Jomo Kenyatta, AMY ASHWOOD GARVEY and ex-Comintern official George Padmore, recently extradited from Hamburg. The IAFA campaigned against the Italian invasion of that free African country, emphasising the duplicity and savagery of European imperialism. This organisation, whose members included African activists temporarily in Britain, evolved into the International African Service Bureau, much involved in African independence movements. The Bureau published a monthly journal, *International African Opinion* edited by James. C.L.R. was also involved in the welfare-oriented League of Coloured Peoples, organised by professional Blacks in 1931 under the leadership of HAROLD MOODY, which he tried to revolutionise. He also attended and spoke at meetings of the West African Students' Union.

On leaving the ILP in 1936 James joined the minuscule anti-Stalinist Trotskyist movement and united its disparate strands, publishing a joint paper, *Fight*. With the publication of his *World Revolution: the Rise and Fall of the Communist International* (1937; Dorothy Pizer, Padmore's partner, was his secretary at the time), James established himself as a leading theoretician and critic of Stalinism. As one colleague recalled, 'he could think mightily for himself ... [he was] the outstanding British Trotskyist in the 1930s'.

During these years in Britain James published *A History of Negro Revolt* (1938), a pan-Africanist survey, and *The Black Jacobins: Toussaint L'Ouverture and the Haitian Revolution* (1938), a seminal historical study. It ends with an analysis of imperialism, which 'vaunts its exploitation of the wealth of Africa for the benefit of civilisation. In reality ... it strangles the real wealth of the continent – the creative capacity of the African peoples'. Transmogrified into a play in 1936, with Paul Robeson leading the cast, *Toussaint* remains James' only published play.

Invited to lecture in the USA by the Socialist Workers Party, James left the UK in 1938. Joining the US Trotskyists, he went to Mexico to meet with the exiled erstwhile Soviet leader Leon Trotsky, to try to convince him of the importance and validity of the *autonomous* Black movement in the USA and worldwide. This encounter and the intellectual turmoil caused by the Hitler–Stalin pact led him and a group of close associates to re-examine the fundamental Marxist texts and the formulation of theories in support of autonomous workers' councils and Black youth and women's movements. James gained first-hand experience by working with sharecroppers, coalminers and auto-workers attempting to set up their own organisations. During this period he wrote innumerable articles under the name of J.R. Johnson. He left the Trotskyists in 1951.

In 1950, having divorced his Trinidadian wife Juanita, James married Constance Webb; the couple had a son, but the marriage did not last long.

Threatened with deportation during the McCarthyite anti-communist witch-hunts of the 1950s, James was imprisoned on Ellis Island, where he wrote *Mariners, Renegades and Castaways: the story of Herman Melville and the World We Live In* (1953), a classic political study of Herman Melville's *Moby Dick*. He was deported to Britain in 1952.

In 1957 James was a special guest at Ghana's independence celebrations. KWAME NKRUMAH had met James while he was a student in the USA and it was an introductory letter from James that led to the long association between Nkrumah and George Padmore. He was also a special guest of the President when Ghana became a republic in 1960. However, some years later James publicly broke with Nkrumah over his intervention with the judiciary. *Nkrumah and the Ghana Revolution* (1977) is his chronicle and his critique of events in Ghana and elsewhere in newly independent

Africa, as well as suggestions for the future. He believed that 'democracy must involve the population. Africa will find that road or continue to crash from precipice to precipice'.

Eric Williams, then Chief Minister of the colony of Trindad, in 1958 invited his old friend and mentor to Port-of-Spain to edit his party's newpaper, *The Nation*, and to become secretary of the West Indian Federal Labour Party, the ruling party of the Federation of the West Indies. James, with his third wife, Selma, whom he had married in 1956, moved to Trinidad. Selma helped edit the paper. However, ideological and other differences led to James' resignation from *The Nation*, and departure in 1962, before the independence celebrations. (Perhaps the main difference between the two men revolved around James' belief in the fundamental importance of involving the masses in the political process, and in the necessity of racial unity in Trinidad.)

Back in Britain, James now pondered the long-lasting effects of colonialism coupled with his experiences in Trinidad. The result was *Beyond the Boundary*, published in 1963. Part autobiography, part meditation on the art and aesthetics of cricket, it is probably also the first socio-political analysis of sport, delineating how not only social relations but personal attitudes are formed by the game, on and off the cricket pitch. True to his love and study of literature, he also gave a series of six lectures on Shakespeare on the BBC's Caribbean Service.

In March 1965 James returned to Trinidad as a cricket correspondent for British newspapers. Williams had just declared a State of Emergency in response to a major strike by sugar workers, probably supported by the left-wing Oilfields Workers' Trade Union (OWTU). Though there was not a shred of evidence that James had been involved in the strike in any way, Williams promptly placed him under house arrest.

On his release James decided to stay in Trinidad. He joined the Indian-based Democratic Labor Party (DLP), which opposed Williams. When the leader of the DLP decided to support Williams' anti-strike Industrial Stabilisation Act, James and the DLP deputy leader Stephen Maharaj formed the Workers' and Farmers' Party (WFP). However, the WFP was unable to attract support either from the workers or from the major left-wing activists (with the exception of the OWTU president) who remained loyal to Williams. In the 1966 elections the WFP only got 3 per cent of the popular vote. James returned to Britain.

In 1968 James accepted an invitation to give some lectures at Makarere College in Uganda, where he spoke on the rejection of European philosophy and politics by Caribbean writers such Wilson Harris, Alejo Carpentier and AIMÉ CÉSAIRE. His hosts at Makarere arranged for James to meet President NYERERE, whose Ujamaa philosophy had deeply impressed James.

Returning to Britain he acted as advisor to the West Indian United Association of Manchester, and continued speaking on platforms around the country and writing for mainstream/liberal journals such as the British *New Society*, *Journal of Commonwealth Literature* and *The Cricketer*, as well as for US journals such as *Radical America* and the *Black World*.

James' outspoken advocacy of left-wing and Black Power movements led to his banning by a number of Caribbean governments – bans which were not lifted until the mid-1970s. However, the US government permitted James' return when he was asked to join the faculty of Federal City College in Washington. He stayed there for almost ten years, also teaching courses and giving lectures at other universities. His Washington home became a meeting place for the city's young Black activists and intellectuals. The College honoured him with a doctoral degree.

In 1969 his 1938 *History of Negro Revolt* was republished with an essay bringing it up to date. In this James wrote of the economic subordination of the newly independent African states and sought to analyse the 'abrupt disintegration and resort to crude military dictatorship in African state after African state'. He saw this as due to the search for support by nationalist leaders among the civil servants (the middle class) of the colonial state – thus all that happened was that the old imperialist power was replaced by a new Western-educated and -oriented elite in thrall to Western economic powers. James espoused FANON's prescription that only 'uncompromising revolt against black nationalist regimes [would] rid Africa of the economic and psychological domination by Western civilisation'.

The ongoing situation in Africa so distressed James (and others) that in 1971 he met with a small group of West Indian political activists and intellectuals in Bermuda to discuss the holding of a Pan-African congress in Africa. He then travelled to Nigeria, Ghana and Tanzania, and to Guyana and Trinidad, and twice to Jamaica, to publicise the urgent need for the conference. However, it was only when Tanzania's ruling Tanganyika African National Union (TANU) party promised to underwrite the conference that a *Call* was promulgated in 1974 for a meeting to discuss the difference between mere political independence (under which international finance capital dominated the ex-colonies) and true socio-economic independence. In contrast to the 5th Congress, James and Nyerere planned for the Congress to discuss how to achieve complete control over economic and financial life, freedom for Southern Africa and self-reliance. (*Race Today*, April 1974) The 6th Pan-African Congress met in Dar-es-Salaam, as Tanzania was then 'viewed throughout the African world as one of the most important working models of self-reliance'. But James did not attend in protest at the decision by Caribbean governments and/or the International Steering Committee to only permit official representatives to attend. (President Nyerere attacked the governments' decision in his opening speech at the Congress.) According to a clearly grossly disappointed James, the Congress 'left *no* particular doctrine behind it … It stood for nothing in particular' (*At the Rendezvous of Victory*, pp.245–6).

In 1976 James addressed the First Congress of All African Writers, in Dakar, Senegal. His lecture was entitled 'Towards the Seventh: The Pan-African Congress – Past, Present and Future' *At the Rendezvous of Victory* (1984), which outlined the Congress' history, beginning with the first, organised by HENRY SYLVESTER WILLIAMS in London in 1900. Maintaining that the 'national state is no longer a viable political entity', he called for a West African and a Southern African federation; for policies to prevent the development of an African elite; for a new focus on the peasantry; for inculcating a sense of responsibility among the educated for the uneducated; and for women's equality.

On his retirement from teaching in the USA in 1980 James experimented with returning to live in Trinidad in a house offered by the OWTU, but this proved uneasy, and he once again relocated to London. C.L.R. and Selma were divorced in 1982. He continued to lecture, to write articles and essays, and appeared in a series of televised lectures. In the spring of 1983 he addressed a Pan-African meeting in Accra. In 1988 the Trinidad Prime Minister announced the award of the Trinity Cross, the country's highest honour, to James, and asked him to return home to live. The offer was refused, but James promised to visit. This was not to be: C.L.R. James died on 30 May 1989, in London. He was buried in Trinidad on 13 June.

MS

Main publications not cited in the text (London editions)

Notes on Dialectics (1948), London, Allison & Busby, 1980.
The Future in the Present, Selected Writings vol. 1, London, Allison & Busby, 1977.
Spheres of Existence, Selected Writings vol. 2, London, Allison & Busby, 1980.
The C.L.R. James Reader, London, Blackwell, 1992.

Further reading

Buhle, Paul, *C.L.R. James: The Artist as Revolutionary*, London, Verso, 1988.
La Guerre, John G., *The Social and Political Thought of the Colonial Intelligentsia*, Mona, ISER, 1982.
Young, James D., *The World of C.L.R. James*, Glasgow, Clydeside Press, 1999.

Claudia Jones
(1915 – 64)

Claudia Jones worked to achieve racial equality in both her adopted countries, the USA and Britain. She also wrote and campaigned against imperialism and for women's rights worldwide.

Claudia Cumberbatch was born in the Belmont section of Port-of-Spain, the capital city of the British colony of Trinidad on 21 February 1915. According to her own account, her mother's family were landowners and her father Charles' in the hotel business, but the family's financial circumstances declined when the price of cocoa dropped on the world market. In 1922, hoping to improve their prospects, Mr and Mrs Cumberbatch emigrated to the USA; their four daughters followed two years later. Claudia was attending Harriet Beecher Stowe Junior High School when her mother, a garment worker, died three years after their arrival. Poverty and overcrowding led to a year's hospitalisation with tuberculosis.

After completing high school, Claudia worked at a variety of menial jobs; she also played tennis and joined the New York Urban League's drama group. In 1936, prompted by the Communist Party's defence of the Scottsboro Boys, nine 'Negro' youths charged, without any evidence, of raping a white girl, Claudia joined the Young Communist League (YCL). The Party was then also very active on the streets of Harlem, where Clauda lived, helping the evicted and the jobless suffering the ravages of the Depression coupled with racism. The Party also took a public stance for racial equality and against imperialism. Claudia was offered a job on the Party's newpaper, the *Daily Worker*, and by 1938 she was editor of the YCL's *Weekly Review*. She was also appointed state education director for the YCL, and served as its state chairperson.

In 1945 Claudia became a member of the Party itself, and by 1948 was elected to the National Committee of the Communist Party of the USA (CPUSA). She continued working as a journalist on the Party's papers, wrote pamphlets and theoretical articles and went on US-wide recruitment drives. She was such a magnetic public speaker that she could hold Madison Square Gardens spellbound.

Though Claudia occasionally wrote articles about the Caribbean, the focus of her attention during this phase of her life was the Party and its theoretical disputes, to which she contributed. There is no evidence that she was interested in the Council on African Affairs, a specifically anti-imperialist organisation established in 1937 under the chairmanship of PAUL ROBESON. Claudia was friendly with Robeson and his wife, and probably also knew fellow-communist ALPHAEUS HUNTON, who became the CAA's Education Director in 1943.

After the Second World War, the US government embarked on an anti-communist witch-hunt: one of its victims was Claudia, who was imprisoned for a year on fraudulent charges. As she had never been granted citizenship because of her communist affiliation, she was deported to Britain in December 1955. She arrived in London seriously ill, having already been hospitalised in New York with heart disease.

On her arrival, Claudia knew no-one except one or two fellow White communist exiles from the USA. Naturally she expected to be embraced by the British Communist Party (CPGB), to whom she had been recommended by the CPUSA. Though the Party helped by obtaining medical treatment and accommodation, it appeared not to know what to do with this outspoken and highly experienced woman from the leadership of the US Party. She was given work as a typist for the inexperienced (and apparently) incompetent man heading the Party's China News Agency.

Claudia attended the Party's 25th Congress in 1957, and despite obstacles put in her way, questioned it about its lack of policy regarding the 'special problems facing colonial peoples in Britain in the present economic situation'. She advocated a 'joint struggle against the common evil of imperialism' in Britain and her colonies. The CPGB at this time had no great interest in imperialism at home or abroad, or in Britain's Black population, and certainly had no program to combat racial discrimination.

In the 1950s the racial situation in Britain was deteriorating almost daily as the numbers of immigrants arriving from the colonies and India increased. (There has been a more or less scattered population population of African – and later Indian – descent in Britain since at least the sixteenth century.) Though the government itself as well as private employers were recruiting these workers, nothing had been done to win the support of the trade union movement or the British people. Caribbeans and Indians were met with anti-immigrant campaigns and fascists organising on the streets. The Ku Klux Klan had branches in Britain. The move to curtail immigration, despite the labour shortage, began in Parliament as early as 1952. By1958 sporadic attacks had escalated into anti-Black riots which swept many British cities. In 1959 a Black man was killed on a London street by a gang of White youths for no reason other than that he was Black. This was Britain's first post-Second World War lynching.

The Party, in effect, did nothing. So Claudia moved outside the Party to organise resistance. This was a tremendous step for a woman who had been nurtured by communism, and who was a stranger in Britain. Having left the Caribbean as a child, she could not even claim immediate solidarity from Trinidadians. Using all the skills she had acquired in the USA, Claudia formed groups. She formed groups into coalitions. She persuaded Caribbeans, Africans and Indians to cooperate. She organised meetings, marches, demonstrations, petitions, lobbies, hunger-strikes. She worked with other anti-imperialist organisations. And all the while she was in and out of hospital being treated for heart disease and the consequences of her childhood TB.

One of these groups, the Inter-Racial Friendship Co-Ordinating Council, organised a huge public funeral and then a memorial meeting for the murdered Kelso Cochrane. It obtained an audience with the Home Office, in charge of the police, whom Claudia charged with racial discrimination. The deputation, *inter alia*, asked that racial discrimination should be made illegal. The Home Secretary announced in Parliament that he would take no such action as it 'might not be effective'.

Though there were no more lynchings, racial discrimination in many forms (e.g. housing, employment, education) continued and the move to restrict immigration gained momentum. To counter this Claudia next formed the Committee of Afro-Asian Caribbean Organisations (CAACO), which campaigned on all these issues. The CAACO also organised on international issues: it held a solidarity march with the 1963 March on Washington demanding civil rights; it campaigned for the release of Rhodesian leader Joshua Nkomo and for military action against Ian Smith's unilateral declaration of independence; it demanded economic and political sanctions and the release of political prisoners in South Africa; and it demanded the restoration of the deposed government in British Guiana and the release of political prisoners there. Claudia spoke on many platforms against the war in Vietnam and on the civil rights demands in the USA. She worked closely with the Committee of African Organisations and was a member of its Boycott Sub-Committee, the forerunner of the Anti-Apartheid Movement; she helped organise the first five-day fast outside South Africa House to protest against apartheid.

Realising the urgent need for a pan-Africanist oriented newspaper, with very little financial support (and none from the CPGB), Claudia published and edited the *West Indian Gazette and Afro-Asian-Caribbean News* from 1958. A monthly paper that covered British and world political, economic and cultural news, the *Gazette* was also a campaigning tool. It contained articles written by and about Black leaders around the world. It analysed situations in Britain and elsewhere affecting Black peoples; it brought news of other current affairs, of campaigns and protests. Claudia's approach can perhaps be best summarised by excerpts from her editoral on the visit of Dr MARTIN LUTHER KING to Britain in 1964:

> We can agree that there is enough that is similar [between the situation of Black people in the USA and the UK] to draw certain lessons. One such lesson is the necessity to uphold a principled stand on every issue of discrimination ... Dr King could not have known that there are some ... who seek to obscure the main issue of racial discrimination by counter-posing the so-called question of the growing 'ghettoes' ... If the root causes of racial discrimination are obscured, the 'scapegoat' theory remains untouched ... Discrimination is man-made and is based on the exploitation for profit at the expense of colonial and newly-independent peoples as an integral part of the imperialist system, which oppresses other nations using racialism to disrupt working class unity ... Commonwealth citizens [must] organize and unite – the better to effectively challenge the disabilities confronting us.

> (*Gazette*, January 1965)

The *Gazette* also carried book reviews and reviews of cultural events, and for a while hints on beauty-culture. It was distributed to agents in the major British cities, from whom it was not easy to collect the moneys gathered by them; thus the *Gazette* was constantly in dire financial straits and all its staff worked as volunteers.

Additionally, the *Gazette* office served as an advice bureau for Black peoples as well as a discussion forum for visiting Black political figures such as Jamaica's Norman Manley, Martin Luther King and W.E.B. DU BOIS. The phone was ringing constantly and there was never enough staff to deal with all the matters of urgency.

And all the while Claudia was in and out of hospital.

But Claudia was undeterred. Always culture-conscious, probably since her days with the New York Urban League drama group, and through her friendship with Paul Robeson, Claudia recognised that art and culture can be used for political purposes. So she organised talent quests and beauty contests in the days when the teachings of MARCUS GARVEY had been forgotten and that a Black woman could be beautiful was an unknown (and unacceptable to many Whites) concept. She not only raised morale with these shows, but got jobs for people in the entertainment and fashion industries. She introduced African American artists and writers to a Black British audience. In all this she had the support of Paul Robeson, who in 1958 had returned to live in Britain.

To further this notion and to demonstrate to the British that the Caribbean was not at all cultureless, from 1959 Claudia organised a replica of Trinidad Carnival. Held indoors in February, these proved hugely successful, attracting many well-known Caribbean musicians, and thus proved another showcase for Caribbean (and African) talent. The carnivals were held annually until her death.

It was not until 1962 that Claudia was granted a passport by the British government. She then travelled to Moscow, at the invitation of *Soviet Woman* magazine – not under the auspices of the CPGB, to which she still belonged and which now occasionally tried to use her expertise. She toured factories, schools, hospitals, etc. in Moscow, Leningrad and Sevastopol, and had a holiday in the Crimea, where she met up with Henry Winston, another senior CPUSA official, just released from long imprisonment. Exhaustion resulted in another bout of illness: she was hospitalised for a month. The following year she was back in the USSR, to attend the World Congress of Women. How this trip was financed is not known. Claudia reported both her trips in the pages of the *Gazette,* speaking favourably of the USSR.

This was the period of the great Sino-Soviet split. But Claudia was no longer under the diktat of a communist party; she was learning freedom of thought. Thus she accepted the invitation to attend the Tenth World Conference Against the Hydrogen and Atomic Bombs, meeting in Japan in 1964. How she was financed is again unknown. But that she was her own woman is clear: she was registered as attending as a representative of Trinidad, not of any communist party! She worked there as the vice-chair of the drafting party, which produced the Conference declaration. This called for 'common action' against the manufacture and use of nuclear weapons, the dismantling of all foreign military bases and US withdrawal from Indo-China. Claudia is remembered by the Haitian delegate to the Conference as 'standing up against the tendency to set up water-tight barriers between our peoples of Asia, Africa and Latin America ... In a large measure the success of the conference was her work'.

Claudia was among the group of Conference delegates invited to visit China. She spent seven weeks there and toured five cities in order to be shown and to learn about

China's road to socialism. She interviewed Madame Soong Ching Ling, the widow of Dr Sun Yat-Sen and sent very favourable reports back to the *Gazette*.

But it all proved too much. Within two months of her return, on Christmas Eve 1964, Claudia died in her sleep. Among the many paying tributes to her was Raymond Kunene of South Africa, who stated that her death 'has deprived the liberation movements all over the world of one of the most dynamic and most militant fighters'. Alphaeus Hunton wrote from Ghana that he thought of her as 'always in the vanguard of the march of oppressed peoples towards freedom'.

MS

Main publications

Pamphlets:

Jim Crow in Uniform, New York, New Age Publishers, 1940.

Lift Every Voice and Sing, New York, New Age Publishers, 1942.

An End to the Neglect of the Problems of the Negro Woman, New York, New Century Publishers, 1949.

Ben Davis: Fighter for Freedom (with an introduction by Eslanda Goode Robeson), New York, National Committee to Defend Negro Leadership, 1954.

Articles, excluding those appearing in the USA pre-1958:

'The Caribbean community in Britain', *Freedomways*, Summer 1964.

Further reading

Johnson, Buzz, *'I Think of my Mother': Notes on the Life and Times of Claudia Jones*, London, Karia Press, 1985.

Sherwood, Marika, *Claudia Jones: A Life in Exile*, London, Lawrence & Wishart, 2000.

Martin Luther King Jr
(1929 – 68)

Martin Luther King Jr, leader of the civil rights movement in the USA, political activist, clergyman, writer and orator, has become one of the most famous Americans of the twentieth century. Since 1986, 20 January is annually celebrated as Martin Luther King day, a public holiday in the USA.

Martin Luther King junior was born Michael King junior on 15 January 1929 in Atlanta, Georgia in the USA. He was the first son and second child of the Reverend Michael King Sr and Alberta Williams King. Five years after his birth both he and his father were officially registered as Martin Luther King Sr and Jr. Martin Luther was born into a prosperous middle-class family. His father was an active member of the National Association for the Advancement of Coloured People (NAACP) and a well-respected figure in Atlanta's Black community.

M.L. King Jr was educated locally and then in 1944 at the age of fifteen he was admitted to the famous Morehouse College in Atlanta, where his father was one of the trustees. At first he decided to study medicine and then sociology before deciding to become a clergyman. In 1948 he was ordained as a Baptist minister in his father's Ebenezer Baptist Church. He then attended Crozer Theological College in Pennsylvania, graduating in 1951, before studying for a doctorate in philosophy at Boston University, which he successfully completed in 1955.

As a student King had already begun to believe that social justice could be defined in Christian terms and that Christianity could provide a critique of capitalism and social ills. He was particularly inspired by the 'Social Gospel' ideas of the late-nineteenth-century theologian Walter Rauschenbusch. He also began to believe that the moral power of non-violence, as practised by Gandhi, might also bring about social change as well as being a means to control and harness individual anger. King embraced the Gandhian philosophy of Satyagraha and thought that it could be applied to the problem of racism in the USA. Hatred, he came to think, might be defeated by social love and personal suffering.

In 1953 King married Coretta Scott and began to think about future employment. He considered teaching theology but decided to become a preacher first. In 1954 he moved to Montgomery, Alabama to become the minister at Dexter Avenue Baptist Church. King took over his ministry at a time of great change in the USA. In May 1954, the Supreme Court outlawed segregated schools and ushered in the beginning of the civil rights era. King joined the Montgomery NAACP and became known as a local activist. Then in December 1955 he became involved in the famous Montgomery bus boycott, occasioned by the arrest of Rosa Parks for violating the city's segregation laws. King was elected president of the Montgomery Improvement Association (MIA), the body that organised the successful 381-day boycott. It was during the boycott that King further developed and preached his ideas on non-violent direct action, and discovered and honed his oratorical powers. King continued to lead the MIA despite arrests and intimidation and even a bombing of his house.

The boycott made him a nationally and internationally known figure, particularly when the US Supreme Court ruled in favour of the MIA at the end of 1956. In 1957 he was listed in *Who's Who in America* and was selected as one of the 'outstanding personalities of the year' by *Time* magazine. In the same year he was awarded the NAACP Springarn Medal and several other awards and honorary doctorates. By 1960 he had more than fifty such awards and honorary degrees.

In March 1957 King went to Ghana, invited by KWAME NKRUMAH to attend the independence celebrations. King was inspired by the struggle for independence in Ghana and other African countries but shocked at the poverty he witnessed in Nigeria during his return journey to the USA. He began to take a great interest in African affairs and following his journey he corresponded with several political activists in southern Africa, especially Albert Luthuli. In 1957 he joined the New York-based American Committee on Africa (ACOA), which included amongst its leading members Bayard Rustin and A. Philip Randolph. The ACOA focused its efforts mainly in supporting the anti-apartheid struggle in South Africa but also took a more general interest in anti-colonialism throughout the African continent. King became a member of the ACOA's National Committee, and subsequently during the early 1960s he was connected with the founding of the South Africa Emergency Committee in 1960 and the American Negro Leadership Conference on Africa in 1962.

King believed that 'at bottom both segregation in America and colonialism in Africa were based on the same thing – white supremacy and contempt for life', and he argued that, 'We realise that injustice anywhere is a threat to justice everywhere. Therefore we are as concerned about the problems of Africa as we are with the problems of the USA'.

In August 1957 King convened a conference that established the Southern Christian Leadership Council in Atlanta, an organisation based on the church and the experience of the Montgomery bus boycott, which could organise a mass struggle for civil rights throughout the southern states. King was unanimously elected president and the SCLC began to organise voter registration in its 'Crusade for Citizenship'.

In 1958 King's first book, *Stride Toward Freedom: The Montgomery Story*, was published. In it he recounted not only the story of the bus boycott but also some autobiographical details and his philosophy of a non-violent approach to social change. But it was while autographing copies of the book in New York that he was stabbed, and for a time was close to death. His assailant, an African American woman, was subsequently committed to an institution for the criminally insane.

After a trip to India in 1959, King returned even more committed to the Gandhian philosophy of non-violence and determined that the SCLC should mount a full-scale assault on all forms of racial segregation. In order to develop this work King moved back to Atlanta, became co-pastor in his father's church and the leader of a growing civil rights movement, often led by young students, that was adding sit-ins and freedom rides to its arsenal of non-violent weapons. King was being asked to speak throughout the country and often commented on the fact that students were as much inspired by the struggles for freedom in Africa as they were by events in the USA. In 1960, he and the SCLC called a student conference in North Carolina. Out of the conference grew the Student Non-violent Co-ordinating Committee (SNCC), which mobilised students and youth throughout America to combat segregation and discrimination.

In the same year King gave his support to John Kennedy in the presidential elections, after Kennedy had not only made promising speeches on civil rights, but also helped King get released on bail from prison. But following Kennedy's election in 1961, King was critical of the US-backed invasion of Cuba and government inactivity on desegregation. In that year King supported the campaign initiated by Congress of Racial Equality (CORE) of Freedom Riders, who were travelling throughout the South to force desegregation on interstate buses. Press and media coverage of the bloody encounters that often took place persuaded the Federal government to take some action in their support, and persuaded King himself of the importance of the media and the need to stage dramatic events that would get nationwide or even international coverage.

But King's tactic of provoking violence against civil rights protestors and engineering the arrest of himself and others ended in failure in Albany, Georgia in 1962 and led to criticism of King's leadership from some SNCC activists. The SCLC campaign against segregation in Birmingham, Alabama, in 1962–3, went according to plan and led to mass arrests and police violence that outraged public opinion throughout much of the USA. King's own arrest led to his famous 'Letter from Birmingham Jail' directed at that city's White clergymen, in which he defended his belief in non-violence and resistance to unjust laws, and presented himself as the moderate alternative to 'black nationalist' organisations such as the Nation of Islam.

The Birmingham campaign considerably increased King's stature. It was increased again in August 1963 by his involvement with the March on Washington, when a quarter of a million people marched to pressure the US Congress to pass the Civil Rights Bill proposed by President Kennedy. It was on this occasion that King delivered his 'I have a dream' speech, one of the most famous speeches of the twentieth century.

Martin Luther King was thereafter seen as the principal spokesman of the civil rights movement. In 1964 he appeared on the cover of *Time* magazine and in the same year he witnessed the signing of the Civil Rights Act by President Johnson and was awarded the Nobel Peace Prize, the first African American to receive that honour.

While he was on his way to Stockholm to receive the Nobel Prize, King travelled to London in December 1964 to encourage Caribbean, African and other organisations to unite to fight racism and discriminatory legislation in Britain. King explained, 'I think it is necessary for the coloured population in Great Britain to organise and work through meaningful non-violent direct action approaches to bring these issues to the forefront of the conscience of the nation wherever they exist.' Subsequently immigrant and other organisations in Britain founded the Campaign Against Racial Discrimination.

However, King also had his critics. Many activists in the SNCC and other organisations opposed his devotion to non-violence in all circumstances, his publicity-seeking tactics and what were viewed as the limited and integrationist goals of the SCLC. His most influential critic was Malcolm X, who before his assassination had formulated his own political programme which stressed the need for self-defence and political struggle waged 'by any means necessary'. For many, the apogee of King's career was reached during the historic protest march for voting rights from Selma to Montgomery, Alabama in 1965. The murderous attacks launched against the supporters of the march caused further public outrage and led President Johnson to announce a Voting Rights Act, which would guarantee such rights for African Americans in the southern states.

The passing of the Civil Rights Act that same year was seen as a triumph for the tactics of non-violent direct action but also as the effective end of an inter-racial movement for legal changes. But after 1965 King also began to widen his critique of American society, denouncing US involvement in Vietnam and expressing his concern over the poverty and oppression faced by African Americans and other Americans in the country's major cities. In 1966 King attempted to stage non-violent demonstrations against segregation and discrimination in Chicago. But he met with little success and renewed criticism from members of the SNCC and other organisations who had begun to demand 'Black Power', which King criticised as simply a 'gratifying slogan' with violent connotations. King's increasingly outspoken criticisms of the US war in Vietnam drew criticism from more conservative supporters of civil rights in the NAACP as well as other organisations and from sections of the press.

King was convinced that the USA required fundamental changes in economic and political power and began to formulate the need for a Poor People's Campaign to pressurise Congress to enact a Bill of Rights for the Disadvantaged. He supported workers striking for union recognition and hoped for united action between the anti-war movements and those seeking improved conditions for poor and working people.

However, in April 1968 King was assassinated on the balcony of a motel in Memphis, Tennessee. His death led to rioting and violence in more than 130 cities in the USA and resulted in a new Civil Rights Act passed a week after his death.

HA

Main publications

Why We Can't Wait, New York, Harper and Row, 1964.
Where Do We Go From Here: Chaos or Community?, New York, Harper and Row, 1967.
Trumpet of Conscience, New York, Harper and Row, 1968.
The Martin Luther King Papers, Carson, Claybourne, (ed.), 1992.
The Autobiography of Martin Luther King, Carson, Claybourne (ed.), London, Little Brown & Co., 1999.

Further reading

Fairclough, Adam, *Martin Luther King*, London, Sphere Books, 1990.
Garrow, David J., *Bearing the Cross: Martin Luther King, Jr. and the Southern Christian Leadership Conference*, New York, Morrow, 1986.
Lewis, David L., *King: A Biography*, 2nd rev. edn, Urbana, University of Illinois Press, 1978.
Oates, Stephen B., *Let the Trumpet Sound – The Life of Martin Luther King Jr.*, London, Search Press, 1982.

Toussaint L'Ouverture

(c.1743 – 1803)

The leader of the revolt of the almost half million enslaved Africans on the island of St Domingue, Toussaint L'Ouverture attained his people's freedom and created the first independent country to rise out of the oppressions of slavery. His revolution struck fear in the hearts of imperialists and gave courage to the enslaved everywhere.

In 1492 Cristoforo Columbo had stumbled across an island he named Santo Domingo during his search for the riches of the East. It was soon settled by the Spanish; the French gained a toehold on the eastern end of the island and were the acknowledged rulers there in 1697. By the the time Toussaint was born, it was the colony producing the most wealth for its 'mother country'. In the 1790s there were some 30,000 Whites, 24,000 free Blacks (mainly of mixed descent) and 450,000 slaves on the island. The free Blacks, many of whom owned plantations and slaves, did not have full rights of citizenship and were lower in the strict social hierarchy than all Whites. The colony was ruled directly by France.

Toussaint was one of eight children born to an enslaved African couple on the plantation known as Breda. His father being a very privileged slave, the young creole-speaking Toussaint was allowed to learn French, Latin, and reading and writing from Pierre Baptiste, his godfather, a slave working at the nearby hospital run by the Fathers of Charity. Toussaint also became a Roman Catholic. At first assigned to work with the estate animals, L'Ouverture became coachman to the estate manager and then steward of all the livestock. He married and had a number of children.

The French Revolution in 1789 deposed the French monarch, and promulgated the Declaration of the Rights of Man (*liberté, egalité, fraternité*); it also granted the right for local Assemblies in the French Colonies. In St Domingue this encouraged the free Blacks to begin a struggle for full equality, which was opposed by the royalists. The ensuing civil war resulted in the massacre of thousands of Whites in August 1791. Further fighting broke out when the Assembly declared that only those free Blacks born of free parents were to be granted the new Rights.

The slaves, led by Oge, also rebelled in 1790, but were suppressed and Oge was executed. However, probably because the acculturated slave population had been augmented by the arrival of 100,000 newly enslaved Africans in the period 1788–91, the Blacks, led by a 'voodoo' priest named Boukman, fought on. The Assembly in France, needing the revenue from St Domingue products (sugar, coffee, tobacco), sent an army to restore control. Caught in the innumerable cross-fires, the French had to proclaim emancipation in August 1793. Infuriated, the royalists sought British support to restore slavery.

The events in France – including the horrors of civil war and the Reign of Terror instituted by the National Convention's Committee of Public Safety – were mirrored in St Domingue: the Whites were split between royalists and republicans; the free Blacks supported whichever faction promised them equality and power; and the slaves followed whoever appeared to guarantee freedom. Added complications were the Spanish in the other half of the island, who would have liked to gain control.

At first Toussaint did not join the revolt; he had donned the mask of obsequiousness worn by so many slaves as a means of survival. In fact, he helped his master (the estate overseer) to escape to America. Until they began intriguing for British support, Toussaint supported the royalist faction on the island. However, he then swopped sides, joined in the ubiquitous fighting and on Boukman's death, shared the command of the ex-slaves with Dessalines. By 1793 he was in control of central St Domingue.

However, in 1794 Port-au-Prince, the capital, surrendered to the British. It took yellow fever and four years of struggle by L'Ouverture, now in undisputed control, to defeat them. The peace treaty permitted the remaining British troops to leave and promised St Domingue neutrality while Britain was at war with France. A secret clause permitted the exchange of St Domingue products for British and American goods.

The French Assembly confirmed emancipation in 1794, but attempted to retain control over the colony. While circumventing French control, L'Ouverture also had to deal with the invading Spaniards. He put down a revolt of the 'mulattoes' in 1796 and was rewarded for this efforts by being made Lt. Governor of the colony by the French overlords.

But the tortured history was to continue. The French encouraged Anore Rigaud, a 'mulatto' who had fought with L'Ouverture against the British, to lead a rebellion. Rigaud refused the offer of a share of power by L'Ouverture. The Americans, interested in getting trading rights, sent aid to L'Ouverture. Rigaud was beaten by July 1800. A reign of terror on 'people of colour' was instituted by Dessalines, governor of the South, but was stopped by L'Ouverture.

September 1801 saw another revolt, this time of Blacks. In the North, it was led by Moise, a one-time supporter, who had come to believe that his uncle L'Ouverture had been favouring the Whites; he also shared the resentment of many ex-slaves who were being forced to work in almost slave-like conditions on the plantations, most of which were still owned by Whites and 'mulattoes'. The revolt was crushed, Moise was captured and executed.

The revolt was a symbol of the growing internal opposition to L'Ouverture, who faced immense problems in setting up an administration. Years of war had devastated the country. Probably up to one-third of the Black population had perished. The violence of slavery had been superseded by new forms of social control, almost as savage. Neither L'Ouverture nor any of his colleagues had any experience of national administration, especially in the face of mounting lawlessness. Moreover, he was surrounded by constantly changing and warring factions in St Domingue while France inflicted its own chaos on the colony. Spain, Britain and North America intrigued with and against him. Naturally, Whites and 'mulattoes' resented a powerful Black man. Equally naturally, the ex-slaves did not want to continue working the land. But St Domingue needed to produce so that it could trade.

The only solution was what amounted almost to a military dictatorship. Labourers were forced to return to their plantations and to work for their keep plus a quarter of the produce. Hours of work were limited and flogging forbidden. The military ensured both sides of the bargain. In 1801 L'Ouverture set up an Assembly, but its six district representatives were all Whites and mulattoes and thus inspired little confidence in the population. The Assembly passed a constitution which, *inter alia*, abolished slavery, removed the colour bar in employment, preserved the planters' rights to their land and established municipal government. L'Ouverture was made governor-for-life, with the power to name his successor.

Despite the ongoing mayhem, L'Ouverture managed to establish a military and civil administration which previously had been sent out by France. Courts of law and of appeal were instituted and taxation systematised. He attempted to convey and impose standards of personal industry, social and public morality, education and religious toleration, racial equality and free trade.

L'Ouverture understood that the manipulations around him were following the principle of 'divide and rule'. He believed – and told his French overlords – that people of all colours must live under and obey the same laws. He fought against racial stereotyping, writing to the Directory (the French government at the time) in 1797 that 'if because some blacks have committed some cruelties it can be deduced that all blacks are cruel, then it would be right to accuse of barbarity the European French'. Victor Schoelcher, whose biography of L'Ouverture was published in 1899, wrote that L'Ouverture had proposed 'to descend upon the African continent with a thousand of his soldiers ... to try to abolish slavery'. Such views were anathema – and represented a great threat – to the rulers of the world.

Thus Napoleon Bonaparte, who came into power in France in 1799, dreamed of reinstating slavery and capturing L'Ouverture. As soon as he had signed a peace treaty with Britain in 1801 he turned his attention to St Domingue. The next year he sent his brother-in-law General Charles Leclerc with a fleet of 56 ships and 43,000 men to retake the colony. Toussaint, though he knew of the fleet, was unaware of its size, or its intentions. The major ports were only lightly defended and were quickly taken by the French invaders. As by now there was considerable resistance to aspects of L'Ouverture's rule in much of the country, it was soon overrun by Leclerc's troops.

At the time of the invasion Toussaint himself was inland at Ennery, his plantation. Leclerc, who had brought with him two of L'Ouverture's sons, who had been sent for education to France, sent the sons as hostages to bribe their father to surrender. He refused. The boys were returned to Leclerc; their fate is unknown. Leclerc now tried outright bribery. L'Ouverture again refused. Over-confident of total victory, Leclerc issued an order reinstating slavery. This rallied many to the side of L'Ouverture; with Dessalines' leadership the French were now beaten and Leclerc was forced to sue for peace. However, there was no clear victory for either side, and the war and the French policy of extermination had further devastated much of the country.

L'Ouverture now announced his retirement to Ennery. However, the French lured him to Gonaives, arrested him there and shipped him to France. His wife and at least some of his remaining children were taken on the same vessel, but separated from him. On arrival L'Ouverture was allowed to see his family before being taken to the exceedingly damp castle of Joux, high up in the Jura mountains; Napoleon's obvious intentions were to humiliate him and procure his death by malnutrition, lack of heat and of medical attention. L'Ouverture died on 7 April 1803. The fate of his family is unknown.

The fighting continued in St Domingue under Dessalines, who had replaced the French flag with one of red and blue bearing the words 'Liberty or Death'. France and Britain were again at war, thus weakening the French position in St Domingue. The few French who had not been killed in the fighting or by disease were expelled, only to be captured by the British. On 1 January 1804 Dessalines announced the independence of St Domingue and renamed it Haiti.

This, and the 15-year struggle to attain it, had caused consternation in the White imperialist world and had given hope to the many Blacks under White domination. For example, the British in Jamaica were not only fearful of the spread of such revolutionary ideas, but of actual invasion by L'Ouverture. The Americans voiced similar fears and many states banned Haitian immigrants. However, they ultimately gained from the success of the revolution, as Napoleon gave up his dream of an American empire and sold them 'his' colony of Louisiana. The millions of enslaved Africans in the Americas looked to L'Ouverture as an example; among these were leaders such as Gabriel Prosser and the White abolitionist John Brown; in 1826 the demand of slaves rebelling on the US vessel *Decatur* was to be taken to Haiti. In mid-century African Americans considered emigration policies to Haiti, the nearest free African-led country.

MS

Further reading

James, C.L.R., *The Black Jacobins*, London, Secker & Warburg, 1938.
Parkinson, Wenda, *'This gilded African': Toussaint L'Ouverture*, London, Quartet Books, 1978.

Patrice Émery Lumumba
(1925 – 61)

Patrice Émery Lumumba led the struggle for the independence of the Congo (now the Democratic Republic of the Congo) and became that country's first Prime Minister. He was brutally murdered just six months after independence, but his anti-imperialist stands and political principles made him a symbol of the African and Pan-African struggles throughout the world.

Lumumba was born in Wembonya village in the Katoko-Kombe district of Sankuru, Central Kasai province of what was then the Belgian colony of the Congo. He was educated in local missionary schools, both Protestant and Catholic.

After completing his studies, Lumumba worked as a clerk in the colonial tax office and then in the post office where he became an assistant post-master, and as the manager of a brewery. As a member of the educated elite or évolués, Lumumba began writing and agitating for the Congolese anti-colonial movement and wrote articles for such anti-colonial publications as *La Croix du Congo* and *La Voix du Congolais*, as well as being the editor of the official post office paper *L'Echo* and a contributor to the Belgian newspaper *L'Afrique et la Monde*. He was also an activist in the Cercle Libéral, the founder and president of the Amicale de Postiers (Post Office Workers Friendly Society), secretary and then president of the Association of Congolese Government Employees, and involved in other organisations including the African Staff Association, the Committee of the Belgo-Congolese Union based in Stanleyville (now Kisangani) and several African cultural groups.

In 1956 Lumumba wrote the book *Congo, My Country* (originally entitled *Is the Congo, the Land of the Future Threatened?*). This book aimed to address the problems facing the Congo, and convey the 'ideas and aspirations of the Congolese people'. Lumumba spoke for many Congolese when he demanded, after interviewing different sections of the population, that land appropriated by the colonial authorities should be returned to the people of the Congo as it was their 'common patrimony'. Much of Lumumba's book seems to be only demanding reforms to the colonial system, not the end of colonial rule itself, but, it also contained progressive views on the status of women in Congolese society, was a powerful indictment of colonialism and envisioned the development of the anti-colonial movement and future independence. Lumumba's anti-colonial activities brought him to the attention of the Belgian authorities, which attempted to steer his political development into harmless channels by sending him to Belgium in 1956 on a goodwill visit.

In 1958, following proposals for decolonisation made by General De Gaulle in the neighbouring French Congo, Lumumba and others sent a memorandum to the governor-general of the Belgian Congo demanding independence and African involvement in the discussions being held in Belgium on Congo's future. This demand was followed by the founding the Mouvement National Congolais (MNC), the first anti-colonial organisation to be formed in the Congo that included all of the country's nationalities and drew its support from workers' organisations not just the elite. The main aim of the MNC was to liberate Congo from colonialism but it also had a vision of a new society based on the needs of the people and it condemned the exploitation of man by man. Lumumba became the MNC's first president and under his leadership it transformed itself into a mass political party and attempted to unite all the anti-colonial forces in the country.

In 1958, Lumumba travelled to Accra, Ghana, to attend and speak at the All African Peoples Conference that had been convened by KWAME NKRUMAH and the government of newly independent Ghana. Here Lumumba met Nkrumah and many other African leaders and became a member of the Conference steering committee. He returned to tell a mass rally of 7,000 that the MNC entirely agreed with the view of the Conference that no African country should remain under foreign domination after 1960. He then declared that 'the independence that we claim in the name of peace cannot be considered any longer by Belgium as a gift, but on the contrary is a fundamental right that the Congolese people have lost'. He explained that the main objective was to organise the masses of the Congolese people for 'the liquidation of the colonial regime and the exploitation of man by man'.

On this basis Lumumba and the MNC worked to unite all Congolese in one anti-colonial movement. In 1959 seven other anti-colonial organisations joined the MNC during its April congress and passed a resolution demanding the installation of a Congolese government by 1960 as a step towards independence. When rioting broke out in the Congo in November 1959, Lumumba was held responsible, arrested and sentenced to six months' imprisonment, but he was released following the demand of all the Congolese organisations attending the Belgian–Congolese Round Table Conference held in Brussels, Belgium in January 1960.

At the conference the Belgian government was faced with a united front of all the Congolese anti-colonial organisations led by Lumumba. It therefore agreed to grant the Congo independence at the end of June 1960, following elections to be held in that year. The Belgian and other monopolies operating in the Congo felt threatened by the political orientation of Lumumba and the MNC, and did everything they could to promote and finance other Congolese political organisations, especially those which might create instability or be in a position to demand regional autonomy or secession. Belgium even declared a state of emergency and sent troop reinforcements to the Congo. But even in these circumstances, the MNC, which campaigned for a united Congo, won the June elections and became the largest parliamentary party, winning 37 out of 137 seats. The Belgian government was at first reluctant to accept the result and tried to encourage other parties to form a government but on 23 June 1960 Lumumba became Prime Minister and in one of his first speeches proclaimed that the independence of the Congo marked 'a decisive step towards the liberation of the whole African continent'.

Only a few days after independence, Belgian army officers provoked a mutiny amongst the 24,000 African soldiers in the Force Publique and the Belgian government sent troop reinforcements to the Congo. Lumumba demanded that this invasion must be stopped and appealed to the United Nations for support; at the same time he appointed new African commanders of the gendarmerie and promoted all the Congolese non-commissioned officers. However, the mutiny continued and while Belgian troops were occupying the country, Moise Tshombe, the leader of the Confederation of Tribal Associations of Katanga, declared the independence of the copper-rich Katanga region, the most valuable and economically developed part of the Congo. Tshombe was backed by the Belgian government and its troops and the big multinational monopolies such as Union Minière, which was controlled by French, Belgian, British and US capital. The foreign monopolies completely dominated Congo's economy and felt that their profits were now being threatened by Lumumba and his government. At this time Congo produced over half of Africa's tin and silver, over 85 per cent of its diamonds and was an important producer of uranium.

Lumumba cut off diplomatic relations with Belgium and issued an ultimatum demanding that their troops be withdrawn within twelve hours, at the same time appealing to the UN for assistance. A UN Security Council resolution unanimously agreed that Belgian troops should be withdrawn and sent in UN forces to evict them. But the UN troops failed to fulfil this role, never entered Katanga and instead began to disarm the Congolese army not the Belgians. As a consequence Lumumba felt justified in appealing for African and even Soviet support. Lumumba received promises of military support from Ghana and some other states, and even signed a secret agreement to establish a political union with Ghana, but these plans came to nothing. Then in September 1960 Kasavubu, who had been named President of Congo, tried to remove Lumumba from office, to dissolve parliament and to establish a new government. Lumumba recalled parliament and with its support and full emergency powers attempted to continue to govern the Congo and free it from foreign intervention.

In the midst of the crisis Colonel Mobutu, formerly one of the commanders of the Force Publique appointed by Lumumba, announced that this force, renamed the Armée Nationale Congolaise, had staged a coup. Behind Mobutu was the hand of the CIA and US imperialism which had the aim of ousting Belgium from its dominant position in the Congo. Lumumba found that the UN then closed all Congolese airfields and even closed down the capital's radio station in order to prevent aid from the Soviet Union from reaching him and to prevent him from broadcasting. He was put under house arrest and guarded by UN troops. Still Lumumba decided to fight on for the independence of the Congo. With the aid of his supporters he managed to escape from house arrest and travelled to Stanleyville to establish a new government and a new army. Lumumba's government began to gain increasing influence throughout Congo, including some areas of Katanga, but Lumumba was again apprehended by Mobutu's troops and taken to Katanga by a Belgian plane to meet his fate.

Since 1961 there has been great speculation about exactly who was responsible for Lumumba's execution and the deaths of his two comrades Maurice Mpolo, a government minister, and Joseph Okito, vice-president of the Congolese Senate. Mobutu and Tshombe were clearly directly involved. But it appears likely that representatives of the US and Belgium governments were indirectly and possibly directly involved too. Recent research shows that Lumumba's execution was supervised by Belgian military and police officers. Lumumba was finally assassinated in January 1961, although news of his death was not announced until some three weeks later by a representative of the government of Katanga. Lumumba's death was condemned and mourned all over Africa and indeed all of the world. He came to symbolise the struggle for genuine African unity and independence. Songs were composed about him and a university in Russia named after him. His death at the young age of thirty-six also exposed the nature of the UN which did nothing to support the duly elected Prime Minister and government of an independent state, but connived with those foreign governments and financial interests that wished to intervene in the Congo for their own sordid reasons. As the President of Ghana, Kwame Nkrumah, expressed it, Lumumba and his comrades died because they 'put their faith in the UN and because they refused to allow themselves to be used as puppets or stooges for external interests'.

HA

Main publications

Congo, My Country, London, Pall Mall Press, 1962.
Lumumba Speaks: The Speeches and Writings of Patrice Lumumba, 1958–1961, edited by Jean van Liede and translated from the French by Helen R. Lone, Little, Brown & Co., Toronto, 1972.

Further reading

De Witte, Ludo, *The Assassination of Lumumba*, London, Verso, 2001.
Lumumba, London, Panaf Books, 1970.

Ras T. Makonnen
(*c.* 1900 – 83)

Ras T. Makonnen spent his whole life devoted to securing rights for Black peoples around the world, whose 'wrongs arise from the world's neglect of certain fundamental truths and whose hope of redress depends on the building of a world community in which those truths will be accepted in practice'. (*Pan-Africa*, 1/2, 1947)

George Thomas Nathaniel Griffith was born in the village of Buxton in British Guiana; his father, who Makonnen claimed was of Ethiopian descent, was a miner of gold and diamonds. After (probably) graduating from Queen's College in Georgetown, he seems to have gone to Texas to study mineralogy. A part-time involvement with the YMCA in Beaumont, Texas soon became a full-time post, which included establishing services for the Black population of the town, including services to businessmen – and even a brass band for the 60,000 Black workers of the Magnolia Petroleum Company. This resulted in speaking engagements around the USA and attendance at YMCA international conferences. At one of these Griffith met Max Yergan, who had been a YMCA 'missionary' in South Africa; this was probably Griffith's introduction to Africa.

From Texas in 1932 Griffith went north, to Cornell University, where he briefly studied agriculture and worked in the library. Cornell's student body included a number of Ethiopians, with whom he discussed the looming Ethiopian crisis. It was at this time that Griffith changed his name to Makonnen. His holidays were spent in Harlem, New York City, where he claims to have participated in the agitation against high rents. He and his West Indian and African friends (including Nnamdi Azikiwe) formed the Libyan Institute, where the members 'read learned papers on aspects of Africa'. (*Pan-Africanism from Within*, p.93) He also listened on the street corners and at other meetings to Black socialists and communists, including GEORGE PADMORE, 'but never became a party man; [though] I borrowed a lot from them' (p.103). He also lent his energies to the Brookwood Labour College, working on 'a primer on American history and a dictionary of terms essential to the workers' movement' (p.105). Makonnen's reading, to judge by his memoirs, was broad; it is known, for example, that he and Kenyatta visited Jamaican-born Theophilus Scholes to thank him for the great stimulus they had derived from reading his books, which were critical studies of British imperialism and racism.

Wanting to assess the developing situation in Europe for himself, Makonnen transferred to the Royal Agricultural College in Copenhagen, where he could also further his interests in the cooperative movement. Passing through London he re-met

George Padmore at an International African Friends of Abyssinia (IAFA) meeting in Trafalgar Square, where he contributed to the discussion. After about 18 months he was deported from Denmark for suggesting that the mustard sold by Denmark to Italy was being used in the manufacture of the mustard gas being used in Abyssinia. A fellow passenger on the boat to England was PAUL ROBESON .

Makonnen visited Russia, perhaps in the company of Jomo Kenyatta – but never espoused communism. Not that he wanted to prevent 'Africans from reading literature on Marxism. On the contrary.' But he did not want them to join the British Communist Party, whose leader, he claimed, 'was not in politics to break up the British Empire any more than Churchill' (p.159). He advised that if you were interested in communism, fine; but work out for yourself how to apply its principles, don't let someone else dictate to you.

In London Makonnen probably became a founder member of the first attempt to form a Pan-African Federation in mid-1936, which brought together representatives from North, South, East and West Africa, and the Caribbean. The Federation's secretary was 'Tomasa Rwaki Griffith', who signed himself 'Tomasa R. Makonnen' in a letter (September 1936) to Tufuhin G.E. Moore of the Gold Coast, who was in London protesting against low cocoa prices.

Makonnen naturally also became involved with IAFA, which was chaired by C.L.R. JAMES; one of its leading members was Jomo Kenyatta. After the Italian conquest of Abyssinia, IAFA transformed itself into the International African Service Bureau (IASB), under the chairmanship of Padmore, with Makonnen as 'executive and publicity secretary'. Makonnen drafted the constitution. The IASB stood for 'the progress and social advancement of Africans at home and abroad; full economic, political and racial equality; and for self-determination'. The Bureau aimed to 'co-ordinate and centralize' Black organisations around the world and link them 'in closer fraternal relations' with one another, and with 'sympathetic' White organisations. Membership of the IASB was restricted to Blacks, but Whites could become associate members.

The office of the IASB, which was administered and funded through the efforts of Makonnen, was a 'regular mecca for all revolutionaries from all the colonies and a rendezvous for the Left'; it also provided a place to stay for colonials. '[Makonnen] did a colossal job', C.L.R. James wrote, 'he cooked, and cleaned the place himself … [And] he was no mean agitator himself'.

The IASB was in touch with colonial organisations such as the Gold Coast Aborigines Rights Protection Society, which solicited its support for its 1935 petition regarding monopolistic control of cocoa exports. It organised various protest meetings in Trafalgar Square and sent speakers, including Makonnen, as far afield as Belfast and Scotland. On the Sunday platforms at Speakers' Corner in Hyde Park Makonnen and other IASB speakers drew a crowd by using Prince Monolulu as the first speaker. Monolulu, who earned an occasionally lucrative living as a race-course tipster, had a 'kind of Rasputin tone [and] traded in subtle vulgarity of a high order'. (Né Peter McKay, Monolulu was probably born in the Caribbean; he was one of the funders of the IASB.) Makonnen himself is described by NKRUMAH as a 'gifted speaker'. There, and at left-wing and other meetings, Makonnen assiduously sold the IASB's newspaper.

In July 1937 the Bureau had begun to publish a duplicated paper, *Africa and the World*, whose 14 August 1937 (and apparently final) issue noted that Makonnen had been among the speakers at a Trafalgar Square meeting regarding the situation in the West Indies, where there was widespread agitation for civil and trade union rights. He also spoke to peace groups, on socialist/labour platforms, and to the Left Book Club. By 1938 seemingly enough money had been raised not only to publish a printed monthly paper, *International African Opinion* (*IAO*) but also a number of pamphlets which were sold in Britain and sent surreptitiously overseas to colleagues in the West Indies and East and West Africa. In its February–March 1939 issue the *IAO* published an article by Makonnen entilted 'A plea for Negro self-government', which analysed the economic motives for the subjection and exploitation of Black peoples everywhere and advised 'African peoples of the West to aim in political philosophy and corresponding action at the establishment of the complete economic, social and political control of their own destinies'. The *IAO* was soon banned in East Africa and probably elsewhere in the British colonies.

Clearly Makonnen's contribution as treasurer must have been immense – according to C.L.R. James, he did all the organising for the IASB, acted as a publicity agent – and provided the finance.

The life of *IAO* was as brief as that of its predecessor: the final issue was published in February–March 1939. However, the IASB did not cease publishing: the treasurer raised enough money to continue publishing pamphlets, whose authors included Kenyatta and ERIC WILLIAMS. Makonnen served as an advisory editor.

Probably in 1938 Makonnen moved to Manchester, where he opened a number of restaurants and an exclusive nightclub, all of which did exceptionally well, especially after the arrival of US, especially African American, troops in the area during the Second World War. Among his 62 employees was Jomo Kenyatta. He also opened a bookshop, which catered to the students at the nearby Manchester University, and eventually owned a number of houses which he let to Black people.

Makonnen also furthered his interests in the cooperative movement by studying at the Co-operative College in 1939–40 and lecturing on the movement to local organisations. For a while he was also a student at Manchester University taking a course in British history; a fellow student believed he was an 'Ethiopian noble exile ... he was an older man, kept very much to himself ... He did not continue with the course'. Makonnen also became an active member of the local Labour Party and was even invited to speak at the prestigious County Forum, where his talk on 'The Myth of Empire' must have evoked some criticism. At about this time he formed the African Co-operative League with Sierra Leonean Laminah Sankoh, which he wanted to link 'with our traditional African form of co-operation', in the hope of replacing purely exploitative, capitalist enterprise among Africans.

The Pan-African Federation (PAF) was re-formed in Manchester in 1944 under the presidency of Dr Peter Milliard, a politically active physician of British Guianese origins; Makonnen was the secretary. The PAF organised a Pan-African Congress, convened in Manchester in July 1945, with delegates and representatives from the Black world. The principal political organiser of the Congress was George Padmore, assisted by the recently arrived Francis (Kwame) Nkrumah. In order to maintain continuity with previous Congresses, W.E.B. Du Bois, who had called four of them, was invited to chair the Manchester Congress. 'One important thing that came out of the Congress', Makonnen believed, was 'that the struggle was not to be found in Europe for the majority of us. The old idea that you could do more work for liberation outside Africa was being laid aside'. (*Pan-Africanism from Within*, p.168) Both Nkrumah and Kenyatta were soon to return to Africa. At the Congress Makonnen had spoken about Ethiopia, attacking British policies which he claimed were aimed at dismembering Ethiopia in order to both enlarge the British empire and restore some sovereignty there to Italy to enable Italy to repay a British loan.

In mid-1946 Makonnen began to advertise the 'Panaf Service' as 'importers and exporters, publishers, booksellers, printers, and manufacturers' representatives', based at his premises at 58 Oxford Road, Manchester, which was also the PAF's home. Profits from these new activities went to finance the PAF, which maintained old contacts and made new ones with political groups and activists in Africa and the Caribbean whose concerns were publicised and whose delegations to Britain were helped when possible. The PAF attempted to break down 'clannish' and tribal divisions both in Britain and Africa, which Makonnen felt were 'obstacles to pan-Africanism' (ibid., p.190). It also organised many political meetings, for example criticising the British government's non-cooperation with the UN's attempts to introduce democracy to the colonies, supporting the 1945 strike in Nigeria and celebrating the centenary of Liberian independence. The PAF set up an Asiatic-African United Front Committee to foster cooperation between all 'subject peoples' and attempted to set up a Pan-African Committee in Paris.

The PAF Secretary, after holding a meeting on the issue and consulting widely (for example with Kobina Sekyi of the Aborigines' Rights Protection Society in the Gold Coast, with whom Makonnen and the PAF had a long relationship), sent a memorandum to the United Nations about the appointment of Barbadian Grantley Adams to the Trusteeship Council. Adams had recently publicly defended British imperialism. Makonnen questioned the UN about the appointment, as 'colonial people' had not been consulted about it; and Adams had not consulted them about the stance he should take on issues affecting them.

The PAF also got involved in the ever-increasing racial incidents in the UK. For example, it – or Makonnen – stood bail for Black seamen accused of mutiny in Plymouth. As the PAF had little faith in White British barristers, in 1946 it raised the funds to bring the eminent Jamaican Norman Manley to Britain to defend a Jamaican airman accused of murder. (The man was acquitted.) In 1948 it demanded a government investigation of the racial riots which had taken place in Liverpool. Makonnen himself corresponded with the city's mayor and obtained an interview with the chief constable. Always using his profits to help his fellow Blacks, Makonnen gave £5,000 to the founding of a home for the abandoned children fathered by Black servicemen with White women who did not want to keep their 'coloured' babies.

Makonnen maintained his involvement with Ethiopia which had begun with the campaigns against the 1935 invasion. He had helped to organise the exiled Emperor Menelik's retinue. Post-war, he raised funds for the Princess Tsehai Memorial Hospital. In 1946 the PAF questioned the British government over the unkept promises which had been made to Ethiopia, and Makonnen supported the pro-Ethiopia campaigns organised by Sylvia Pankhurst, for example for the restoration of Eritrea and Somalia to Ethiopia. At this 19 June meeting he argued that the problems of Africa were 'attributable to Europe's master-race principle'.

In 1947 Makonnen began to publish a journal, *Pan-Africa*, a 'monthly journal of African life, history and thought'. He was its publisher and managing editor; the editor was Dinah Stock; Padmore, Kenyatta and Nkrumah were among the associate and contributing editors. The journal sought and attracted articles from and readership in the colonised world as well as the USA. By October 1947 the Belgian Government banned the journal from the 'Belgian' Congo; within another few months it was banned by the East African colonial governments as seditious. This loss of readership resulted in the journal's demise in early 1948. Though no copies have remained, it appears that the journal also published news-releases (which reached, for example, the Gold Coast) and a copy of the petition to the United Nations, 'Statement on the Denial of Human Rights to Minorities in the Case of Citizens of Negro Descent in the USA'. The journal, also funded by Makonnen, was – naturally – based at 58 Oxford Road.

Having 'no ties with Guyana', and as 'all my travelling … was to get knowledge to prepare me for working in the West Indies or Africa', in 1957 Makonnen emigrated to Ghana. As he had been very critical of Nkrumah in 1948, because of Nkrumah's pro-communist associates in London, this move either indicated a change of perception, or hopes induced by Padmore's presence there. Serving Nkrumah as co-founder director of the African Affairs Centre in Accra (whose buildings he probably paid for), he arranged and gave some specialised lectures for the 'hardened freedom fighters' three times a week there. He 'explained to them the nature of British, French and other imperialists', using Padmore's and Nkrumah's books. However, after Padmore's death:

> Barden was made secretary of the Bureau of African Affairs … He was just a police boy who had managed to worm his way into Kwame's favour … [So] the opportunity was lost of using the Bureau as a truly pan-African instrument of policy-making.
>
> (*Pan-Africanism from Within*, p.209)

Makonnen was also head of the national press set up by Nkrumah, the Guinea Press. There his distress at the level of corruption suffusing the various institutions with which he was familiar increased. He also experienced considerable hostility as an 'outsider'. Nevertheless, he was one of the emissaries from Ghana who toured a number of African states in preparation for the 1963 Organisation of African Unity (OAU) conference in Addis Ababa, which he then attended and addressed. After some disagreement with Nkrumah, perhaps over corruption, or the lack of socialist planning to match the socialist rhetoric, Makonnen was demoted to the post of director of hotels and tourism, and then director of state bakeries. Even this did not wholly dampen his creativity, as he set about attempting to introduce more nutritious bread than was generally available.

After the fall of Nkrumah, Makonnen was imprisoned for nine months. He was released, after some international protest, the most influential from President Kenyatta. He moved to Kenya, from where he wrote to Nkrumah in Conakry that he 'would like to join' him. 'If we are clear and dedicated on the path we intend to travel, I am sure we would arrest disaster [i.e. counter-revolution] and bring happiness to mankind', he wrote. Nkrumah's reponse is unavailable, but must have been negative as Makonnen lived in Kenya from 1967 until his death.

Given some land by his old comrade Kenyatta, Makonnen hoped to start:

> the sort of institution Africa has too fequently failed to provide for visiting Africans and blacks of the New World: a reception and instruction centre for the many blacks who cannot get to grips with Africa from the confines of its tourist hotels. It is intended at the same time to be a repository for pioneer work by blacks and whites on the African past, to offer an ongoing forum of criticism and discussion of the African present.
>
> (*Pan-Africanism from Within*, pp.xxi–xxii)

How much of this he accomplished is not known. His life-long activism was not wholly forgotten: he was asked to give occasional lectures at the university, and attended the Pan-African Congress in Dar-es-Salaam in 1974, where a photograph shows him discoursing with young people.

MS

Main publication

Pan-Africanism from Within, Kenneth King (ed.), Nairobi, Oxford University Press, 1973.

Malcolm X
(1925 – 65)

Malcolm X was probably one of the brightest and most courageous men of his generation. He moved from being a hoodlum to being the chief spokesperson for the Nation of Islam in the USA – a position which made him a world-renowned 'hate figure' to the Western world. Then, rethinking his philosophy and politics, he left the Nation and began to advocate a wholly new, Pan-Africanist, socialist-leaning philosophy. Stalked by assassins throughout his highly public life, his premature death at their hands robbed the Black world of a man who well might have helped lead it along the path of true freedom.

Malcolm was the child of Earl and Louise Little. She was an immigrant from Grenada settled in Montreal, who met her husband at a UNIA meeting in Canada. Earl Little, a Baptist minister, was a builder who could get no regular work in Lansing, Michigan because of his Garveyite beliefs. Mrs Little earned money by dressmaking and crochet-work. On the night of 28 September 1931 Mr Little was murdered in the town, probably for no other reason than that he was seen as an 'uppity nigger'. A judge in Lansing who coveted the family's smallholding outside of town exerted considerable pressure on Mrs Little to sell it. But Mrs Little refused, and continued to attempt to raise her family of eight children in the strict West Indian fashion, and to support them with the little she could earn. GARVEY, who had apparently visited the family many times, was not by this time in a position to help; the authorities succeeded in declaring Louise Little insane and confined her to an institution. The judge got the smallholding; the children were placed in separate foster homes.

Though the Little children kept in contact with each other, and many visited their mother regularly, not surprisingly Malcolm began to steal and misbehave in school. This led to his being placed in a 'detention home' at the age of 13, followed by more foster homes until his step-sister Ella obtained legal custody of him and young Malcolm moved to Boston. There he was soon caught up in Black night life while earning a living as a shoe-shine boy, soda-fountain clerk, busboy, dishwasher/waiter on the Boston–New York railway and then in Small's Paradise, Harlem's premier bar/restaurant. Little now took to gambling and acted as a 'fence' for stolen goods; after losing his job at Small's for pimping, he sold marijuana and bootleg liquor. He also acquired a nickname, 'Detroit Red'. By acting crazy, which in some ways he was, as he was addicted to marijuana and cocaine, he avoided being drafted for the Second World War. Back in Boston, constantly high on drugs for which he paid with the proceeds of robberies, Little was arrested and sentenced to 10 years' imprisonment in February 1946.

Influenced by his brothers Philbert and Reginald, and then his other siblings, Little began to take an interest in Islam as preached by Georgian-born Elijah Muhammad, the leader of the Black Muslims, also known as the Nation of Islam. As Little was to discover later in his life, this version of Islam bore very little relationship to any of its forms practised by Muslims elsewhere in the world. Little began to study the writings of Muhammad, who represented himself as the 'messenger of Allah' in the USA. According to the Messenger, the Black man's troubles in the States stemmed from the 'devil white race'. These devils had brainwashed the 'so-called Negro' until he was 'mentally, morally and spiritually dead'. History had been 'whitened', by simply leaving the Black man out of the books. Elijah Muhammad demanded strict discipline to ensure that 'true knowledge' was acquired; this would return the Black man to his true place in society, 'at the top of civilisation'.

Responding to his mother's injunction, 'Now that this has happened, Malcolm boy, don't serve time, let the time serve you!', conveyed to him by his eldest brother Wilfred, Little began to educate himself by reading through the prison library's unusually large stock – history, philosophy, science, anthropology, international relations. He attended classes and participated in debates.

When he was released from prison in 1952, Little headed for Detroit where his brother Wilfred had arranged a job for him as a salesman in the furniture store he managed. Wilfred also took him to the Black Muslim Detroit Temple Number One, from where the congregation went to Chicago to hear Elijah Muhammad speak. Little was mesmerised. He applied for and received his 'X', which the Black Muslims used as a symbol of their lost African names, and began work to recruit members for the Detroit Temple. He was named Assistant Minister in the summer of 1953. Malcolm X became Elijah Muhammad's favourite, most erudite disciple and was soon appointed to head Temple Seven in New York.

In 1956 Betty X, a graduate of the Tuskegee Institute now studying nursing in New York, began to attend Temple Seven. She and Malcolm were married in January 1958. The couple had three daughters and one son; twin daughters were born some months after Malcolm's death.

Malcolm X, whose oratory was magnetic, soon became the *bête noire* of the US White world. It was said that he 'could stop a race riot – or start one'. He was front page news, on talk shows and panel discussions, and addressed huge rallies from one coast of the USA to the other, defending and explaining Elijah Muhammad's version of Islam and criticising the 'white devils' and their pride in the miniscule steps they were then taking on civil rights issues. What Blacks wanted, demanded, was human rights, he argued. Malcolm preached separation from the 'white devils' who were intent on keeping Blacks on the lowest levels of society. Black people needed their own land. Blacks had also to own their own businesses to demonstrate what Black people could do for themselves. Malcolm praised the wisdom of Elijah Muhammad and castigated other Black organisations which, he claimed, accepted support from Whites and were thus controlled by them. Membership of the Black Muslims increased during Malcolm's stewardship from c.400 to c.40,000. The American right-wing offered rewards for his death.

Then Malcolm began to think for himself, to think through and beyond the Nation of Islam. He became critical of the Black Muslim policy of talking and not doing. He was confounded by the escalating rumours of Elijah Muhammad's betrayal of the strictures of Muslim morality, which many Muslims felt to be a betrayal of their faith. Recognising that he was seen as a leader by the non-Muslims as well as the Muslims of Harlem, he began to create an organisation of his own, an activist organisation. First would come a new mosque – but before that, he had to learn about true Islam.

In April 1964 Malcolm went on *Hajj*, pilgrimage to Mecca. According to his own account, 'the colour-blindness of the Muslim world's religious society and the colour-blindness of [its] human society' began to 'persuade' him 'against my previous way of thinking'. A common, sincere belief, he learned, could make all men 'brothers'. Malcolm became the guest of Prince Faisal of Saudi Arabia while he was in Mecca. He held discussions with high ranking Saudi and Sudanese officials and other pilgrims and met local people. He concluded from all these that 'the single worst mistake of the American black organizations ... is that they have failed to establish direct brotherhood lines of communication between the independent nations of Africa and the American black people'. (*Autobiography*, p.399)

Malcolm went from Mecca to Beirut, then to Lagos, Ibadan and Accra. He spoke at Ibadan University, on Nigerian radio and television, at the Ghana Press Club, the Ghana Club and the University of Ghana, emphasising 'the need for mutual communication and support between Africans and Afro-Americans, whose struggles were interlocked'. In Ghana he talked with Ghanaian ministers and was granted a brief audience by President NKRUMAH, as well as the ambassadors of Algeria, China, Cuba and Mali. Then Malcolm had breakfast with 'Dr MAKONNEN' with whom he 'discussed the need for the type of Pan-African unity that would also include the Afro-Americans'. (*Autobiography*, pp.407–8) Sadly, we may never know what the subject of these discussions were; but they clearly bore heavily on the evolution of Malcolm's thinking.

Back in the USA in May 1964, Malcolm began to hold public meetings open to all, telling his audience that he 'firmly believe[d] that Negroes have the right to fight against [white] racists by any means that are necessary'. (*Autobiography*, p.422) He confirmed that he would work 'with anybody who is sincerely interested in eliminating [the] injustices that Negroes suffer'. He accepted invitations to speak at the Militant Labor Forum of the Socialist Workers Party, where at the 29 May meeting he told his audience that 'the system of this country cannot produce freedom for an Afro-American ... [A]ll the countries that are emerging today from under the shackles of colonialism are turning toward socialism ...'. (*Malcolm X Speaks*, pp.68–9) Media attention continued and visitors from the many countries he had visited called on him in his Harlem office.

In June 1964 Malcolm announced the formation of the Organization of Afro-American Unity (OAAU), based on 'ideas' he had accumulated from his 'travels and observations of the success that our brothers on the African continent were having in their struggle for freedom'. (*Two Speeches by Malcolm X*) Membership would be open to 'all people of African descent in the Western Hemisphere, as well as our brothers and sisters on the African Continent'. The Statement of Basic Aims included the 'determin[ation] to unify the Americans of African descent in their fight for human rights and dignity', and to 'build a political, economic and social system of justice and peace'. The OAAU was 'dedicated to the unification of all people of African descent in this hemisphere' and it planned to set up schools and voter-registration drives; to support rent-strikes; to set up housing self-improvement programmes; and work for a cultural revolution that will be 'the means of bringing us closer to our African brothers and sisters', a 'journey to our re-discovery of ourselves'. (*Last Year of Malcolm X*, p.110) The motto of the new organisation was 'By Any Means Necessary'.

Malcolm returned to Africa a month later, on 9 July. His tour began with attendance at the Organization of African Unity (OAU) meeting in Cairo, where he was housed with the liberation fighters from the unliberated world. Having been granted 'observer' status, Malcolm was permitted to submit a memorandum to the assembled heads of state. This began by stating that the OAAU had been patterned after the OAU. He pleaded with the leaders of the independent African nations to be the:

> shepherd of *all* African peoples everywhere ... [as] our problems are your problems ... It is a problem of human rights ... We beseech [you] to help us bring our problem before the United Nations ... The United States government is ... incapable of protecting [our] lives ... [O]ur deteriorating plight is becoming a threat to world peace.

> (*Malcolm X Speaks*, pp.72–7)

By seeking to approach the United Nations, Malcolm was following in the footsteps of PADMORE's *Manifesto on Africa in the Post-War World* presented to the founding meeting of the UN in 1945, and the petition against US genocide signed by HUNTON, CLAUDIA JONES and the ROBESONS in 1951.

The OAU passed a resolution, which, *inter alia*, stated that the OAU was:

> deeply disturbed by the continuing manifestations of racial bigotry and racial oppression against Negro citizens of the United States of America ... .Urges the Government authorities in the United States ... to intensify their efforts to ensure the total elimination of all forms of discrimination based on race, colour, or ethnic origin.

Though the resolution was not presented to the UN in 1964, probably because, as Malcolm feared, 'our African brothers' were indeed 'held in check by American *dollarism*'. However, Malcolm's arguments were used by African spokesmen in the Congo debates at the UN in December that year: for example, Kojo Botsio of Ghana argued that the USA had no more business in the Congo than Ghana would have intervening 'to protect the lives of Afro-Americans ... tortured and murdered for asserting their legitimate rights'. (Goldman, p.241)

After a stay of many weeks in Cairo, Malcolm travelled through fourteen nations. He met with many heads of state, Jomo Kenyatta, JULIUS NYERERE, Milton Obote and SÉKOU TOURÉ, and even more old and new revolutionaries. Addressing meetings everywhere, he spoke on international issues such as Cuba, Vietnam, 'Red' China and the Congo, as well as the domestic US situation. An African American group following in his footsteps a few weeks later found that 'Malcolm's impact on Africa was just fantastic. In every country he was known and served as a main criteria [sic] for categorizing Afro-Americans and their political views'. (*Malcolm X Speaks*, p.85)

Malcolm returned to Europe in November to speak in Paris at the invitation of the journal *Présence Africaine*. He told the overflowing audience that the OAAU had evolved from his study of 'the tactics and the strategy that our brothers and sisters were using in Africa'. Explaining the tactics that had been used to make sure the Negro hated himself and divorced himself from Africa, Malcolm went on to attack the hypocrisy of the USA which 'preaches integration and practices segregation'. (*The Militant*, 7 December 1964) A few weeks later he was in Oxford, participating in a debate at the highly prestigous Oxford Union. From there he went to address Manchester University students on 4 December. Interviewed by the *Manchester Evening News* (4 December 1964) he lambasted the US involvement in the Congo and stated that 'it was the threat of spreading Mau Mau activity that made most of Africa free'. Then it was back to New York to publicise and rally support for the OAAU and to promulgate his ever-developing interpretations of the Black world.

In February 1965 Malcolm was back in London to attend the first conference of the Committee of African Organisations, one of whose earliest (or even founder) members had been Claudia Jones. Giving the closing speech at the conference, he argued that:

> British imperialism and other European partners could not exist for a single day without the support of the United States of America. Hence the significance of the role of the Afro-Americans against this enemy of all mankind ... US imperialism is forcing all its satellites, Britain, France, Germany, Italy and Belgium into line ... [T]he stronger and more united Africa becomes, the more respect will be accorded to the people of African origin. [Malcolm emphasised that] a person should not be judged by his colour but by what he does.
>
> (*West Indian Gazette*, February 1965, p.4)

Malcolm had been invited to address a meeting in Paris convened by the Congress of African Students on the US involvement in Vietnam and in the Congo, but was refused permission to land at Orly Airport. Interviewed by one of the organisers over the telephone, Malcolm stated that:

> the Afro-American community in France and in other parts of Europe must unite with the African community ... [W]e must restore our cultural roots ... Unity will give our struggle strength ... to make some real concrete progress ... a positive program of mutual benefit ...
>
> (*Final Speeches*, pp.39–40)

Presumably, he had also intended to meet with the OAAU chapter in Paris, which had twenty or so members. Returning to London, he spoke to students at the London School of Economics. He reiterated that he was 'not for violence, but the people who have violence committed against them should be able to defend themselves'. The

Black community in the USA was attacked by 'an element among whites' who were racist and had a 'strong influence in the power structure', which found many ways of attacking and controlling Blacks. He analysed and condemned the US involvement in the Congo and in Vietnam; he dissected US involvements in southern Africa and the growing US influence in the whole of Africa. (*Final Speeches*, pp.46–64) The next day he was filmed by the BBC walking around Smethwick, where a Conservative, whose election slogan had been'If you want a nigger for a neighbour, vote Labour', had recently been elected to Parliament. He likened the treatment of Black people in the town to that of Jews under Nazi Germany.

Back in the USA, Malcolm explained his evolving new philosophy on many platforms. He attacked the US government for its lack of wholehearted support for civil/human rights for African Americans, and for its neo-colonialist attitudes abroad, as well as for its plausible involvement in the murder of PATRICE LUMUMBA. The Basic Unity Program of the OAAU, announced in February 1965, just a week before Malcolm's death, reiterated the need for the unity of Africans and Afro-Americans; the OAAU intended publishing newspapers and using all other media to foster this unity. African Americans had to educate themselves about Africa and the world in order to be able to 'clarify [their] roles, rights and responsibilities'. The study of 'philosophies, psychologies, cultures and languages that did not come from our racist oppressors' was essential to the liberation of their minds. As the protection offered by the UN Charter of Human Rights was denied to African Americans, they had to affirm their right to defend themselves. Eight committees would be set up to put these aims into practice. (*Last Year of Malcolm X*, pp.113–24)

On 13 February Malcolm X's home was bombed; he and his family narrowly escaped death. The assassins, held to be Black Muslims, succeeded on 21 February 1965: Malcolm X was gunned down at an OAAU meeting at the Audubon Ballroom, Harlem, New York City. Some 22,000 people filed passed his coffin. In losing Malcolm, Ossie Davis said in his funeral oration, we African Americans have lost 'our manhood, our living black manhood … our shining prince'.

MS

Further reading

Breitman, George, (ed.), *Malcolm X Speaks*, New York, Grove Press, 1965.
Carew, Jan, *Ghosts in Our Blood*, Chicago, Lawrence Hill Books, 1994.
Goldman, Peter, *The Death and Life of Malcolm X*, Urbana, University of Illinois Press, 1979.

Nelson Rolihlahla Mandela

(1918 –)

Nelson Rolihlahla Mandela, first African President of South Africa, was born in the Transkei, South Africa on 18 July 1918. One of thirteen children, he was the son of Gadla Henry Mandela, a chief of the Thembu, and the third of his four wives Nosekeni. Nelson Mandela was educated at the universities of Fort Hare and Witwatersrand and, while in prison, by correspondence course at the University of London.

In the 1940s Nelson Mandela came into contact with the African National Congress (ANC), the organisation which had been formed in 1912 to lead the struggle against racism and White minority rule in South Africa. He joined the ANC in 1942, and in September 1944 was one of a group of radical younger men, including Oliver Tambo and Walter Sisulu, who formed the ANC Youth League (ANCYL). Mandela and the ANCYL espoused a militant brand of African Nationalism. They had become dissatisfied with the slow pace of change and the moderate constitutionalism of the ANC and were determined to turn it into a mass movement that could take direct action to force political change.

Mandela became one of the leaders of the Youth League. He was elected Secretary in 1947 and was one of those responsible for drafting the Programme of Action adopted by the ANC at its annual conference in 1949. The Programme of Action was an immediate response to the racist policy of Apartheid being introduced by the National Party government, brought to power in all-White elections in 1948. The Programme of Action advocated employing boycotts, strikes, civil disobedience and non-cooperation as weapons to force political change and bring about full citizenship, a universal franchise and, amongst other things, a redistribution of land in South Africa. Members of the ANCYL began to take over the leadership of the ANC and in 1950 Mandela was elected to the ANC's National Executive Committee.

In 1952 the ANC launched its Campaign for the Defiance of Unjust Laws and Mandela was elected National Volunteer-in-Chief. He travelled throughout the country organising mass resistance to discriminatory laws including the Suppression of Communism Act, a law that aimed to suppress not only the Communist Party in South Africa, but all opposition to the government. Mandela had at first been wary of communism and the Communist Party, just as he was initially wary of Indian and White influence in the ANC. He described his own early political beliefs as 'militant African nationalism', but through discussions with communist members of the ANC he gradually changed and broadened his views. In subsequent years he became close to the newly formed South African Communist Party, its leaders and many of its views, but was never a member. For his part in the Defiance Campaign Mandela was arrested and given a suspended prison sentence.

The Defiance Campaign turned the ANC into a mass organisation and Mandela was recognised as one of its leaders and elected First Deputy President in 1952. He had already been elected President of the Youth League and of the Transvaal region of the ANC. His prominence also meant continual repression from the government and the first of several banning orders, that aimed to hamper his political activities and which continued until his eventual imprisonment.

In 1954 Mandela was one of the organisers of the Congress of the People, which united the ANC with the South African Indian Congress, the Coloured Peoples' Organisation and the Congress of Democrats, collectively known as the Congress Alliance. He helped to draft the Freedom Charter which was acclaimed by the Congress of the People in 1955, before it was broken up by the police and 155 leaders of the Congress Alliance were arrested on charges of high treason.

The Treason Trial continued until 1961 when Mandela and other leaders were declared not guilty. It was during this period that Mandela's first marriage broke up and in 1958 he met and married his second wife Nomzamo Winifred Madikizela. Winnie Mandela as she became known, was to become one of the most prominent leaders of the ANC during Mandela's subsequent long imprisonment.

In 1960, Mandela was one of the main organisers of the ANC's protests following the Sharpeville massacre, and was one of over 2000 arrested when the South African government declared a state of emergency and then banned the ANC and other anti-apartheid organisations. Even though the ANC was an illegal organisation it continued to organise throughout South Africa. In 1961, Mandela was the secretary of the organising conference for the Maritzburg Conference, which gathered together 1,440 delegates from 145 different groups throughout South Africa and was seen at the time as the biggest political meeting of Africans in the country's history. Mandela made his first public speech since 1952 and called for a national convention and threatened a three day stay-at-home protest. He would not speak again on a public platform for 29 years. Shortly afterwards Mandela began his life underground and was sometimes referred to in the press as the 'Black Pimpernel'. By this time he was becoming an internationally known figure who, in the wake of Sharpeville, was reassessing the ANC's continued adherence to non-violence. Not for the last time in his political career Mandela publicly voiced his reservations about ANC official policy and in private put forward his plan for a military wing of the ANC. The new military organisation was named Unkhonto we Sizwe (MK) and Mandela became its first commander-in-chief.

In 1962 Mandela secretly left South Africa and embarked on a tour of Africa to seek support and military training for MK, and in order to speak at the meeting of the Pan-African Freedom Movement of East and Central Africa (PAFMECA), the embryonic Organisation of African Unity (OAU), in Ethiopia. During his trip Mandela met with several African leaders including SÉKOU TOURÉ and President Tubman of Liberia who both offered financial support. During his time abroad Mandela visited the ANC's external leader, Oliver Tambo, in London and then returned to Ethiopia for a short course of military training.

Shortly after his return to South Africa, Mandela was arrested and charged with leaving the country illegally and incitement to strike. He conducted his own defence and using the court to make political statements, began to appear as a symbol of the freedom struggle in South Africa. Mandela was found guilty and given the heaviest ever sentence for a political offence, five years' imprisonment.

Mandela served only eight months of this sentence before he was back in court in the famous Rivonia trial, named after the ANC's secret headquarters, charged with sabotage, an offence that could carry the death penalty. Mandela and some of the others accused were fully prepared to admit their involvement with sabotage and MK, and decided to refuse to appeal whatever the sentence. Mandela again wanted to use the court to make a powerful statement that would carry weight not only in the country but also throughout the world. He spoke from the dock for four hours and ended with the famous words:

> During my lifetime I have dedicated myself to the struggle of the African people. I have fought against white domination and I have fought against black domination. I have cherished the ideal of a democratic and free society in which all persons live together in harmony with equal opportunities. It is an ideal I hope to live for and achieve. But if needs be it is an ideal for which I am prepared to die.

In the event Mandela, aged forty-six, and seven others were sentenced to life imprisonment and were taken to the notorious Robben Island maximum security prison. In prison Mandela remained a powerful symbol of protest, who resisted the inhumanity of both the prison system and individual prison guards. He fought for the rights of political prisoners, assisted other prisoners with legal advice, established political education classes at the 'university' of Robben Island and refused to compromise his political principles.

Nelson Mandela became the world's most famous political prisoner, the man who personified the struggle against apartheid and for a democratic South Africa. This was especially so when a major international campaign to 'Free Mandela' was launched by the ANC in 1980, and even gained the support of the UN Security Council. In 1979 Mandela was awarded the Nehru Prize for International Understanding and in 1980 he was awarded the freedom of the Scottish city of Glasgow. The following year his name was proposed as the next Chancellor of London University and in subsequent years there were further honours and numerous solidarity events organised throughout the world.

The South African government also took note of his growing international reputation. In 1974 Mandela was offered an early release from prison if he would recognise the Bantustan government in the Transkei. Not surprisingly Mandela refused this offer and those subsequently made, including that made publicly in 1985 when President P.W. Botha demanded that he renounce violence as a 'political instrument'. Mandela made it clear that he would not give any undertaking at a time when 'the people are not free'. Nevertheless the South African government took measures to create the conditions for a dialogue with Mandela. He was moved from Robben

Island to Pollsmoor prison in April 1982 and was permitted to meet various Western statesmen in 1984 and members of the Commonwealth Eminent Persons Group in 1986. In 1988 he was given his own private bungalow in the grounds of Victor Verster prison, a move which was effectively preparation for his eventual release.

In 1985 Mandela made the decision to begin direct personal talks with the South African government, initially even without the approval of the ANC leadership. He had come to believe that the struggle for democracy could not be won by military means and that South Africa was facing a destructive and bloody civil war. Regular secret talks began in 1987 and in 1989 Mandela met both the outgoing president P.W. Botha and his successor F.W. de Klerk. These talks culminated with the release of many of the leading political prisoners and in 1990 with the un-banning of the ANC and other organisations. Mandela was himself released after '10,000 days' imprisonment in February 1990.

Shortly after his release, Mandela and the other leaders of the ANC suspended the armed struggle and began the difficult negotiations with the South African government that culminated in a universal franchise and South Africa's first democratic election in May 1994. In 1991 Mandela was elected president of the ANC and in 1993 became the third Black South African to be awarded the Nobel Peace Prize. In 1994 Mandela and the ANC won a landslide victory in the election and he became the first Black President of South Africa. Mandela's main aim was to avoid further bloodshed in the country, to restore international confidence and to encourage reconciliation. He included former adversaries in his cabinet both from the National Party and the Zulu-based Inkatha Freedom Party. He established the Truth and Reconciliation Commission, headed by Archbishop Desmond Tutu, in an attempt to investigate but not bring to justice those responsible for political crimes during the period of apartheid. Mandela remained President of South Africa until his retirement from public life in 1999. Immensely popular abroad during his many visits, he also managed to retain great personal popularity in South Africa despite growing criticism of his government, high levels of corruption and crime, and the slow pace of economic and social change. Nelson Mandela became something of an icon in the last quarter of the century, almost universally respected and admired for his personal sacrifices, qualities and principles rather than the policies of his government.

HA

Main publications

No Easy Walk to Freedom, Ruth First (ed.), London, Heinemann, 1965.
The Struggle is My Life, London, International Aid Fund for Southern Africa, 1978.
Nelson Mandela Speaks: Forging a Democratic, Non-racial South Africa, New York, Pathfinder, 1993.
Long Walk to Freedom, London, Abacus, 1994.
In the Words of Nelson Mandela, Jennifer Crwys-Williams (ed.), London, Penguin, 1997.

Further reading

Benson, Mary, *Nelson Mandela – The Man and the Movement*, London, Penguin, 1994.

Gregory, James, *Goodbye, Bafana: Nelson Mandela My Prisoner, My Friend*, London, Headline, 1995.

Hagemann, Albrecht, *Nelson Mandela*, Johannesburg, Fontein Books, 1996.

Meredith, Martin, *Nelson Mandela – A Biography*, London, Penguin, 1997.

Schneider, Martin (ed.), *Madiba: Nelson Rolihlahla Mandela: A Celebration*, Johannesburg, Martin Schneider & Co., 1997.

Sampson, Anthony, *Mandela – The Authorised Biography*, London, HarperCollins, 1999.

Harold Moody
(1882 – 1947)

Harold Moody devoted his life to the struggle in Britain for the rights of Black peoples everywhere. A frequent correspondent and visitor to the Colonial Office, he confused the bureaucracy, who could not decide whether he was 'woolly but well-meaning or astute and mischievous'.

As his father was a prosperous druggist in Kingston, Jamaica, though Harold was one of six siblings, he was sent to obtain a good secondary education at Woolmer's School. On graduation he worked in his father's business; his free time was devoted to the Congregational Church. In three years he saved enough money to sail to England to enter London University as a medical student in 1904. He gained his degree in 1912, having won a number of prizes over the long years of study. By then he had married, despite her family's objections, a White woman, Olive Mabel Tranter.

Having failed to obtain a hospital post because of racial discrimination, Moody decided to set up his own private practice. Despite a growing family (there were to be six children altogether) and a busy medical practice, Moody devoted a considerable amount of time to Congregational activities and to those of the Colonial Missionary Society, to whose Board he was appointed in 1912. He was made chairman in 1921, which necessitated travel throughout the UK. Already aware of the many levels of discrimination faced by Black people of all classes in London, he now found that the same situation existed everywhere he went. A growing concern for his fellow Blacks' plight led Moody, who had given at least one lecture previously at Friends' House, to the Friends Service Council conference on the colour bar in November 1929. The conference set up a Council to Promote Understanding Between White and Coloured People; its vice-chair was Dr Harold Moody.

However, in 1931 Moody decided to set up his own organisation, the League of Coloured People (LCP), whose aims were to:

> promote and protect the social, educational, economic and political interests of its members; to interest members in the welfare of coloured peoples in all parts of the world; to improve relations between the races; to co-operate and affiliate with organisations sympathetic to coloured people.

The LCP's membership comprised mainly students from the British Empire and Whites associated with religious organisations; however, the officers were all Black. Moody was named president. Moody defined 'coloured' as meaning 'of African descent' which barred Indians from membership, though their conditions in Britain and at home were also 'colonial'. Throughout the life of the LCP its membership, undoubtedly partly because of its moderate tone, and also because of the existence of the West African Students' Union, was predominantly West Indian.

By 1933 the LCP was strong enough to issue a quarterly journal, *The Keys*, and to hold its first conference. The lectures at the conference looked not only at the situation of Black peoples in the Empire, but also in the USA.

Moody's model for the LCP was the USA's National Association for the Advancement of Coloured People. This slow and legalistic approach to the situation in the colonies and for colonials in Britain was soon challenged not only by more revolutionary, Marxist-oriented students, but also by C.L.R. JAMES, then a Trotskyist, who tried to re-orient *The Keys* by writing for it, and by Barbados-born Arnold Ward, chairman of the communist-led Negro Welfare Association (NWA); and later by Peter Blackman, NWA and Communist Party member.

The LCP, by the mid-1930s, also began to take up a fairly wide range of political issues, by sending protests and deputations to the government. These issues included the Scottsboro case; the suspension of a Bechuana chief by the governor; the proposal to incorporate Bechuanaland, Basutoland and Swaziland in South Africa; the invasion of Abyssinia by Italy; and the classification of colonial seamen as 'aliens' in Cardiff, thereby depriving them of employment.

By 1936 Moody was also president of the Christian Endeavour Union of Great Britain and Ireland. This entailed even more travel, which he used partially to interest his Christian contacts in the work of the LCP, and to address the race question from the pulpit. 'The great and the good' whom he met on his travels were often invited, along with members of the Colonial Office and of course the LCP itself, to garden parties, usually held at the suburban home of an LCP supporter, Barbados-born Dr Cecil Belfield Clarke. These informal gatherings were used to persuade guests of the rightness of the LCP's advocacy on colonial and racial matters.

Despite the differences in political outlook and tactics, the LCP cooperated on some issues with other Black organisations in Britain. The 'disturbances' which swept the English-speaking Caribbean in the late-1930s evoked joint memoranda by all these organisations critical of the government's response, and of the social, economic, political, educational, health and employment conditions in the Caribbean. The LCP convened a comprehensive meeting in June 1938 to agree a resolution to be sent to the government. This called for the distribution of land, free education, universal adult suffrage and the same civil liberties as those in Britain. It concluded by demanding a federation of the West Indies with complete self-government. The Colonial Office also received LCP delegations both before and after the Royal Commission's report on the West Indies was published.

The war saw further instances of discrimination in the workplace, whether aboard a British ship, in a British factory or a British colony. The LCP always investigated and demanded that wrongs be set right, and policies changed by the government. In 1941 the announcement of the terms of what came to be called the Atlantic Charter, agreed by President Roosevelt and Prime Minister Churchill, resulted in a further round of collaborative meetings. The Charter promised to 'restore sovereignty and self-government to those who had been forcibly deprived of them'. Naturally, colonials interpreted this as applying to them. Churchill vehemently disagreed, limiting it to Europe. Moody swung into action: letters were despatched, public meetings organised. It was all to no avail.

By 1944 Moody had given up on the Atlantic Charter and produced a much milder one of his own, the Charter for Coloured Peoples. It had been thoroughly discussed before it was sent to the British and allied governments and religious and sympathetic organisations at home and abroad. The Charter called for political, educational, social and economic development, the latter in the interests of the people; 'full self-government at the earliest possible opportunity'; and for 'Imperial Powers to account for their administration to an International body'.

With the arrival of colonial delegates to the World Federation of Trade Unions meeting in February 1945, another round of discussions were held to formulate proposals to be put to the forthcoming United Nations Conference of International Organisations. These were discussed by the LCP and then by the members of the Pan-African Federation, re-formed for the Pan-African Congress held in Manchester in July 1945. (The LCP was not a member and did not attended the Congress.) Based on the Atlantic Charter and the People's Charter, the Manifesto on Africa in the Post-war World was sent to the UN and disseminated widely. It repeated the demands of the LCP Charter, but added the 'achievement of full self-government within a definite time limit', the eradication of illiteracy, and that 'the former Italian colonies [should] have the same treatment as the rest of the African territories'. The manipulations of imperialists prevented a consideration of the Manifesto; Lord Cranborne, the British Colonial Secretary, for example, believed that:

> at the bottom rung ... there are the most primitive peoples capable at present of taking only a limited part in the administration of their own affairs ... We are all of us in favour of freedom but freedom for many of these territories means assistance and guidance and protection ... Colonial empires were welded into one vast machine for the defence of liberty. Could we really contemplate the destruction of this machine?
>
> (*West African Review*, July 1945, p.23)

Concern with refashioning the post-war world did not prevent Moody from also directing his attention to local issues. He used his year as chairman of the London Missionary Society, his membership of the Council of the Save the Children Fund and service on the Executive Committee of the Native Races and the Liquor Traffic Committee to proselytise against racial discrimination and the exploitation of colonial peoples, for example by the sale of cheap liquor. Moody was also co-opted to the Conference of British Missionary Society's West India Committee, formed in 1940. He presented a memorandum to the CBMS in 1942, which instructed the Society on the realities of life in the Caribbean and argued that many churches supported repressive government policies. In order to develop economically, the islands should be formed into a self-governing federation in order to form a trading block; industrial development should be financially supported and trade union laws should be further reformed. Political development had to be based on universal franchise to elect a federal legislature.

An LCP branch was set up in Liverpool because of the multitude of problems there, caused by the racist reactions to the presence of war-workers from the West Indies, colonial seamen and African American servicemen. Among the most urgent problems that had arisen was the placement of children fathered by Black men; some married their children's mothers, but others did not; African American servicemen were prohibited from marrying White women. What was to be done with children the mothers did not wish to keep? The LCP's survey found about 100 children needing placement, and others whose mothers were in dire need of financial assistance. The LCP and other Black organisations forced the government to acknowledge the plight of the children, unwanted in a racist society. The government's reaction was masterly inaction. The League attempted to run its own home for at least a few children, but pervasive illness in the home led to its closure.

The LCP commissioned another survey, whose results were published as 'Race Relations and the Schools'. This made groundbreaking recommendations on the training of teachers, classroom practice and the content of text-books. Moody was also appointed a member of the government's Welfare of Coloured People in the UK Advisory Committee, where he fought to have the remit of the Committee broadened from purely welfare issues (e.g. hostels for workers and servicemen) to include racial equality.

In March 1944, perhaps in response to the growing number of Black peoples in Britain due to the war, Moody announced that he wanted to establish a Colonial Cultural Centre, which would also include a hostel, and aimed to promote good relations between 'coloured' and White people. In 1946 he and his wife left for a fund-raising tour to the Caribbean and the USA. Though he was well-received in the Caribbean, his fund-raising efforts among an impoverished population were not successful. His sojourn in the USA did not meet with greater success, and he returned to London an ill and disappointed man. He died on 24 April 1947. The fund started in 1950 for a memorial resulted in a bust by Harold's sculptor brother, Ronald, being placed in the London Missionary Society's Livingstone Hall in June 1953.

The LCP, bereft of its dynamo, became relatively ineffectual and died a few years after its founder.

MS

Further reading

The Keys, 1933–39 (reprint), Millwood, Kraus-Thomson Organization, 1976.

Macdonald, Roderick J., 'Dr Harold Arundel Moody and the League of Coloured Peoples, 1931–1947', *Race*, 14/3, 1973.

Sherwood, Marika, 'Quakers, Colonies and Colonials, 1938–48', *Immigrants & Minorities*, 10/3, 1991.

Sherwood, Marika, ' "Diplomatic Platitudes": the Atlantic Charter, the United Nations and Colonial Independence', *Immigrants & Minorities*, 15/2, 1996.

Vaughan, David A., *Negro Victory*, London, Independent Press, 1950.

Jamal Abd al-Nasir [Nasser]
(1918 – 70)

Jamal Abd al-Nasir [Nasser], President of Egypt, was a leading figure in the Arab world and in the Non-Aligned Movement, and also played a key role in the anti-colonial struggle in Africa and in the development of the Organisation of African Unity.

Nasser was born on 15 January 1918 in Alexandria where his father worked as a post office clerk. Nasser was born at a time when Egypt was still a British colony, a situation which led to the growth of the movement for Egyptian independence led by the Wafd, a broadly-based anti-colonial front, the revolutionary upsurge of 1919–21 and in 1922 a limited independence which left Egypt still dominated by Britain. Nasser was educated in Cairo and Alexandria and as a schoolboy began to take part in student politics and demonstrations against the monarchy, especially when he attended the Al Nahda al Misria secondary school in Cairo. He became the chairman of the executive committee of Cairo school students and immersed himself in the study of politics and the works of Arab nationalists and other anti-imperialist writers. While he was still at school Nasser came into contact with many of the main nationalist parties in Egypt including the Wafd, the National Party and the Misr el Fatat, or Young Egypt Party. In 1935 in Cairo, Nasser organised school student demonstrations against continued British interference in Egyptian affairs. When police opened fire on the demonstrations two students were killed and Nasser himself was shot and wounded. Political agitation in Egypt led to a new treaty with Britain, which still limited Egyptian sovereignty and gave Britain the right to maintain an occupying force of 10,000 troops in the country.

After leaving school Nasser briefly studied law and then in 1937 was admitted to the Military Academy in Cairo, which he graduated from with distinction a year later. He became a second lieutenant in the infantry and began the military career that would lead him to political power. It was as a young army officer that Nasser and others formed the Free Officers' organisation to overthrow 'imperialism, monarchy and feudalism', between the late 1930s and early 1940s. Nasser and other officers began planning and recruiting for the time when they could restore the national dignity of Egypt, end British occupation and rid themselves of a corrupt monarchy and political system. In 1942 Nasser wrote, 'once the Imperialist realises that Egyptians are ready to shed their own blood and meet force with force, he will beat a hasty retreat like any harlot rebuffed'.

At the end of the Second World War Egypt was still in the grip of British imperialism and Nasser, who had become a captain in the army, and the Free Officers continued with their preparations, alongside many other anti-imperialist organisations determined to gain Egyptian independence. Anti-imperialism in Egypt was fuelled by the changes in the international situation following the Second World War and the weakening of the old colonial powers such as Britain and France. It also developed as a consequence of specific events in the Middle East, such as the partitioning of Palestine and the creation of Israel. Nasser and many others from the ranks of the Free Officers were part of the Egyptian army which fought in Palestine in 1947 and during this conflict he developed many of his thoughts on the necessity of Arab unity in the struggle against imperialism.

In 1949 Nasser, at that time a major, and the Society of Free Officers stepped up their plans for a rebellion led by the military against the monarchy and foreign rule, and began to disseminate their views more widely. The struggle of the existing Egyptian government against British occupation also intensified, especially in regard to control of the Suez Canal, and produced a major political crisis in the country. It was in these conditions that Nasser and the other officers launched their coup on 23 July 1952 and forced the abdication of King Faruq. According to Nasser's later writing, he saw the army merely as a vanguard in a political revolution that would subsequently have a truly popular character and usher in a second social revolution, a new economic and political system, as well as ridding the country of British rule.

Whatever their original intentions, Colonel Nasser and the other officers in what became known as the Revolutionary Command Council assumed supreme political power in Egypt, with Nasser taking the post of Deputy Prime Minister and Minister of the Interior. Political parties were banned. Following an attempt on his life in 1954, Nasser moved against possible rivals, including General Najib who had been the country's first President following the coup. In 1954 Nasser became Egypt's Prime Minister and after a new constitution in 1956 he received overwhelming support for his nomination as President.

Nasser's Egypt provided the President with immense executive power. The most radical economic policies after 1952 involved the limiting of landholdings and rents and some redistribution and nationalisation of land, especially foreign-owned land after 1956. In 1960 one of the biggest private monopolies, Bank Misr, was nationalised; nationalisation of the press occurred in the same year. The following year many of the other leading monopolies were also nationalised so that the state controlled most economic activity. 'Arab Socialism', as this type of economy came to be known, was codified in Nasser's Charter for National Action in 1962, which called for the establishment of a new political organisation, the Arab Socialist Union, which de facto became the only political party. In 1964 a new constitution declared the UAR to be 'a democratic socialist state based on the alliance of the working forces'. Nasser's government also instituted some reforms of a progressive character. The right to vote and run for public office was extended to women in 1956 and women were entitled to equal pay and paid maternity leave. Healthcare, education and other social services were substantially expanded but political rights were limited, many political organisations including the Egyptian Communist Party were suppressed, and the opposition to Nasser grew throughout the 1960s.

If Nasser's domestic policies ushered in a new era in Egypt his foreign policy was even bolder. His government managed to negotiate the withdrawal of British troops from the Suez Canal in 1954; it took a strong stand against the British-backed Baghdad Pact and began to emerge as a country with a strong anti-imperialist orientation. In the midst of the Cold War, and after unsuccessful negotiations for financial support with the USA and Britain, Egypt began to seek economic and military support from countries such as Czechoslovakia and the Soviet Union. Then in 1956, to the consternation of Britain and France, Nasser announced that the Suez Canal would be nationalised in order to assist the financing of the Aswan Dam. Nasser's defence of Egypt's interests, which had also led to growing conflict with neighbouring Israel, led to the British, French and Israeli plan to topple his government, the invasion and bombing of Egypt and the so-called Suez Crisis of 1956. The events of 1956 were a major debacle for Britain and France, but following international condemnation and the withdrawal of their troops, Nasser's prestige soared and he became seen as a key figure in the Arab world. After attending the Bandung Conference in Indonesia in 1955 he was also viewed as a leading international figure, especially in the emergent 'non-aligned movement', and the 'Afro-Asian bloc'. By the time of the Belgrade conference of the Non-Aligned Movement in 1961, Nasser had been able to establish himself as one of the leaders of this movement, alongside Nehru, NKRUMAH, Tito and Sukarno.

Nasser's Egypt also played a key role in the anti-colonial movement in Africa. In his book *Egypt's Liberation: The Philosophy of the Revolution*, written in 1955, Nasser had written:

> Can we possibly ignore the fact that there is an African continent that fate decreed us to be a part of, and that it has also decreed that a terrible struggle exists for its future – a struggle whose results will either be for us or against us with or without our will?

Despite this fatalistic view of the world, Nasser's government turned Egypt, one of only a few independent African states at the time, into a place of refuge for many of Africa's leading anti-colonial fighters and their organisations, including those from Cameroon, Uganda, Somalia, Angola, South Africa and many other countries. Nasser sometimes spoke of the rest of the African continent in paternalistic terms, and saw Egypt bringing enlightenment to the rest of Africa, but there can be no denying the support given by the Egyptian government and its media to the anti-colonial struggles, especially in North Africa, but also throughout the continent. Nasser's Egypt was a particularly strong supporter of the anti-colonial movements in Morocco, Tunisia and Algeria and it was the main external base for the Algerian FLN. Radio broadcasts from the 'Voice of Free Africa' in Cairo were influential throughout the continent and broadcast in Hausa, Swahili and Amharic. Egypt also became a major education centre for thousands of students from other African countries and the venue for many important anti-colonial conferences including the first 'Quit Africa' Congress.

In 1958 Nasser's Egypt, renamed the United Arab Republic (UAR) after union with Syria, joined with seven other African states at the first Conference of Independent African States held in Accra, Ghana, and soon afterwards established its credentials as one of the radical African states, along with Ghana, Guinea, Mali and Algeria. Subsequently Nasser supported the government of PATRICE LUMUMBA in the Congo and sent and then subsequently withdrew UAR troops as part of the UN contingent to the Congo. Following the coup in the Congo, Nasser retaliated by nationalising Belgian property in the UAR. At the famous Casablanca Conference, and at the third All African Peoples Conference in 1961, Nasser made a strong call for African unity, and he was a strong critic both of the UN and the imperialist powers and the disunity that had emerged amongst African states over the crisis in the Congo. Although Egypt's radical leadership role was increasingly filled by Algeria after 1962, Nasser continued to play a major role in the negotiations that culminated in the founding of the Organisation of African Unity in Addis Ababa in 1963, and he can be seen as someone who played a key role in maintaining the unity of North and Sub-Saharan African states in this period.

On the international stage Nasser attempted to weld together both the Arab states and the Afro-Asian states, so as to end their marginalisation in world affairs and to combat the domination of the two superpowers and their respective blocs. But in the difficult period of the Cold War and instability in the Middle East, he was always especially concerned both to try to preserve Egypt's position of non-alignment and to secure allies, including African ones, in case of renewed hostility with Israel. But Nasser's foreign policy led to increasing difficulties for Egypt throughout the 1960s. In 1961 a coup in Syria effectively dissolved the UAR. The following year Egypt became embroiled in a civil war in Yemen, which dragged on for several years and which increasingly created economic and political, as well as military, difficulties. Then in 1967 following a new Syrian–Egyptian defence pact and mounting tension between Israel and Syria, Egypt was invaded by Israel during the Six-Day War. Much of the country's air force and significant sections of its armed forces were destroyed and Israel occupied Egyptian territory. Nasser tendered his resignation but massive street demonstrations persuaded him to remain in office. However, despite continued Egyptian offensives, Israel remained in control of the occupied territories and the whole region was plunged into warfare and even greater instability. It was this regional instability, and in particular the struggle of the Palestinians, that led to the civil war in Jordan in 1970. It was immediately after he had played a leading role in negotiating a settlement between the Jordanian government and the Palestinians, that Nasser suffered a major heart attack and died in September 1970.

His death provoked mass demonstrations of grief in Egypt and his funeral was attended by millions of Egyptians.

HA

Main publication

Egypt's Liberation: The Philosophy of the Revolution, Washington DC, Public Affairs Press, 1955.

Further reading

Farid, Abdel Majid, *Nasser: the Final Years*, Reading, Ithaca Press, 1994.
Stephens, Robert, *Nasser: A Political Biography*, London, Penguin, 1971.
Woodward, Peter, *Nasser*, London, Longman, 1992.

Francis Nwia Kofi Kwame Nkrumah
(*c.*1909 – 72)

Francis Nwia Kofi Kwame Nkrumah, Pan-Africanist, one of the founders of the Organisation of African Unity and the first leader of independent Ghana, was born in Nkroful in the Nzima region of what was at that time the British colony of the Gold Coast. Although his father, a goldsmith, had many wives, Nkrumah was the only child born to his mother. He was educated in local missionary schools and then in 1926 attended the Government Training College in Accra (known as Achimota College from 1927) where he trained as a teacher. After graduating in 1930 Nkrumah worked as a teacher but also considered training for the priesthood. In 1935 Nkrumah journeyed to Britain and then to the USA to study at Lincoln University. He then completed post-graduate studies at the University of Pennsylvania. After completing his studies, Nkrumah was employed as a teacher of political science at Lincoln University.

It was during the time he spent in the USA that Nkrumah became politically active, no doubt influenced by those he came into contact with at university and the meetings of various political organisations including GARVEY's UNIA, the Council on African Affairs and the Communist Party. It was also in the USA that Nkrumah became active in the African Students' Association, which was formed in 1941 by West African students, the majority of whom were from Nigeria and the Gold Coast. Nkrumah was elected president of this organisation, wrote for its publication *African Interpreter* and spoke at numerous meetings. In 1942 he demanded that the ASA should be open to all Africans, not just students. It seems that it was also during this period that he began to advocate many of his Pan-African views, often in opposition to other ASA members.

In 1945 Nkrumah went to London ostensibly to study at London University. He became an active member of the West African Students' Union and was soon elected its vice-president. He met and worked with the Trinidadian Pan-Africanist, GEORGE PADMORE of the Pan-African Federation, and threw himself into organising the historic Manchester Pan-African Congress. It seems that it was in Britain that he began using the name Kwame and to associate with all those in the anti-colonial and anti-imperialist movement. Nkrumah played a prominent role in the planning of the Pan-African Congress and claimed to have drafted the famous 'Declaration to the Colonial Peoples of the World', which called for the unity of all colonial peoples against imperialism.

Following the Congress, Nkrumah was one of the founders and general-secretary of the West African National Secretariat, formed 'with a view to realising a West

African Front for a United West African Independence', and was the 'chief editor' of the WANS' *New Africa*. He also became the leader of the 'Circle', a secret revolutionary organisation dedicated to establishing a Union of African Socialist Republics. During this period Nkrumah travelled to Paris to meet SENGHOR and other African members of the French National Assembly, and to discuss plans for West African Unity. During his time in Britain, Nkrumah also became closely involved with the British Communist Party. It was also during his time in Britain that Nkrumah published *Towards Colonial Freedom*, an analysis of colonialism and imperialism, and the call for 'the organisation of the colonial masses' to achieve independence. Nkrumah speaks of the need for 'the complete national unity of the West African colonies' to achieve independence; at this stage he seems to have been more preoccupied with West African rather than continental African unity, viewing the former as 'the lever' to achieve the latter.

In 1947 Nkrumah left Britain when he was asked to become the general-secretary of the anti-colonial United Gold Coast Convention (UGCC), which had been formed by constitutional nationalists in the Gold Coast in August of that year. On his way back to the Gold Coast, Nkrumah held several meetings with political and trade union leaders in Sierra Leone, and Liberia, and continued to campaign for West African unity.

In 1948, rioting and demonstrations by workers and ex-servicemen led to the declaration of a state of emergency in the Gold Coast. The UGCC had not organised the riots, although it did seek to make political capital out of them, and Nkrumah and six other UGCC leaders were arrested and detained. The arrests raised Nkrumah's profile but also highlighted political differences between him and the other more conservative UGCC leaders. These differences led to Nkrumah's demotion to treasurer and prompted him to first establish the Committee of Youth Organisation and found the *Accra Evening News*, and then in June 1949 to found the Convention Peoples' Party (CPP).

The CPP demanded 'Self-Government Now' and began to mobilise trade unionists, farmers, youth and ex-servicemen's associations for this goal. In 1950 Nkrumah announced a campaign of 'positive action', along the lines discussed at the Manchester Pan-African Congress, which led to a series of strikes and demonstrations throughout the colony. The colonial authorities again declared a state of emergency and he was arrested and sentenced to three years' imprisonment. Even in prison Nkrumah's leadership role and popularity were undiminished and he successfully stood in the 1951 general election, winning over 90 per cent of the votes cast. In 1951 he was released from prison to become Leader of Government Business and from 1952 Prime Minister. Nkrumah and the CPP continued to win elections held in 1954 and 1956 and led the country to 'internal self-government' and then formal independence in March 1957. Ghana, as the Gold Coast was renamed, became the first sub-Saharan African colony to gain independence. In 1960, following a referendum, the adoption of a new constitution and a general election, Nkrumah became Ghana's first President and was re-elected to this post unopposed in 1965.

Nkrumah had declared that 'the independence of Ghana is meaningless unless it is linked up with the total liberation of the African continent'. With this view in mind he convened the Accra conference of independent African states in 1958 and at the end of the same year the first All African Peoples' Conference, a precursor of the Organisation of African Unity. The following year Nkrumah helped to establish an economic union with the former French colony of Guinea and in 1960 this union was joined by independent Mali, another former French colony. Nkrumah began to draft plans for a wider union of African states but his ideas were opposed by more conservative African countries at the second conference of African states held in Ethiopia in 1960. Nkrumah was an enthusiastic supporter of LUMUMBA during the crisis in the Congo, and as a consequence of his dissatisfaction with the conduct of the UN in the Congo he approached nine other African states with the intention of forming an African 'Joint High Command' that might intervene in future African crises. In 1961 Nkrumah took part in the famous Casablanca Conference of progressive African states which condemned 'neo-colonialism', and, despite the differences that emerged between the 'Casablanca group' and more conservative African states, he was able to play a significant role in the creation of the Organisation of African Unity in Ethiopia in 1963. Nkrumah's Ghana not only gave support to those fighting against colonial rule in Africa but also to those opposed to pro-Western or reactionary governments. He adopted a policy of non-alignment in foreign affairs and forged close ties with some socialist countries, including China and the Soviet Union.

Nkrumah had declared in his autobiography the need for a socialist society for a newly independent nation, but despite attempts to industrialise and diversify the economy, his government found it increasingly difficult to solve those economic, political and social problems that were a legacy of colonial rule. Some of the economic measures he introduced were openly opposed through strikes and Nkrumah's popularity waned as a consequence of economic problems, continued interference by Britain and the USA and an increasingly corrupt and dictatorial government. In 1961 there were bomb attacks and in the following years a number of attempts to assassinate Nkrumah, who in 1964 banned opposition parties and declared a one-party state. In 1966 when Nkrumah was on his way to a peace mission in Vietnam his government was overthrown by a military coup. Nkrumah went into exile in Guinea where SÉKOU TOURÉ made him co-president. For a time Nkrumah called on his compatriots to overthrow the military regime, but when such appeals went unheeded he spent much of the remainder of his life writing. After some years of ill health he died of cancer in Bucharest, Romania in 1972. Even after his death Nkrumah continued to be a controversial figure. He was at first buried in Guinea and then in his home village in Ghana. In 1994 he received an official re-burial in a special mausoleum in Accra.

HA

Main publications

Autobiography, London, Panaf Books, 1957.
I Speak of Freedom, London, Panaf Books, 1961.
Towards Colonial Freedom, London, Panaf Books, 1962.
Africa Must Unite, London, Panaf Books, 1963.
Consciencism, London, Panaf Books, 1964.
Neo-Colonialism: The Last Stage of Imperialism, London, Panaf Books, 1965.

Challenge of the Congo, London, Panaf Books, 1967.
Dark Days in Ghana, London, Panaf Books, 1968.
Voice from Conakry, London, Panaf Books, 1968.

Further reading

Milne, June, *Kwame Nkrumah – A Biography*, London, Panaf Books, 1999.
Sherwood, Marika, *Kwame Nkrumah: The Years Abroad 1933–47*, Legon, Ghana, Freedom
    Publications, 1996.

Julius Kambarage Nyerere
(1922 – 99)

Nyerere, the first President of independent Tanganyika, the creator of Tanzania and a founder of the Organisation of African Unity (OAU), is one of the few world leaders of the late twentieth century whose name has remained unsullied by accusations of corruption, and who retained a life-long allegiance to socialism.

Born in Butiama on the shores of Lake Victoria in the then British trusteeship territory of Tanganyika, Nyerere only began attending school at the age of 12. He was so bright that the priests ensured his rapid progress. After gaining a teacher's certificate at Makerere College in Kampala he taught at a Catholic school at Tabora, Tanganyika from 1946 until 1949. Then, on a government scholarship, he took an MA (then an undergraduate degree) at Edinburgh University, graduating in 1952. He was the first Tanganyikan to gain a university degree. As a student he was involved with the Scottish Council for African Questions, which was then lobbying against the increasing White domination of the Central African Federation. Influenced by Fabian socialism and wide reading, he 'evolved the whole of [his] political philosophy while at Edinburgh'. On his return in 1953 Nyerere resumed teaching and married Maria Magige; they had five sons and two daughters.

Based on a philosophy of socialism and traditional African communalism, Nyerere formed the nationalist Tanganyika African National Union (TANU) in 1954. The Union faced huge obstacles. Tanganyika was a poor country: its soils are poor; its rainfall sparse and unreliable; much of the land is suitable only for sparse grazing; it had few mineral resources. The little Western-style education available was in the hands of Christian churches (approx. 30 per cent of the population was Muslim) which espoused the ongoing tutelage of Africans. There were 120 cultural and linguistic groups. In 1957, only 5 per cent of the eligible population was attending 'upper' primary school and the adult literacy rate was much less than 10 per cent. The most productive lands were in the hands of the few White settlers. On taking over from the Germans after the First World War, the British had instituted indirect rule, creating chieftaincies where none existed. Hardly any Africans were employed by the government administration.

TANU's aims at this stage were not independence but an amelioration of living and working conditions. Tanganyikans flocked to join: by 1957, membership totalled 200,000. The colonial government was hostile, and tried every possible means to suppress TANU, even encouraging the formation of a rival political party, supported by local European and Asian businessmen. Nevertheless, pressured by Britain, in 1958 the colonial government was forced to hold the first ever elections to the

Legislative Council. TANU-supported candidates, including Nyerere and European and Asian candidates, won all 15 seats. Though Nyerere immediately raised the issue of self-government, generally TANU policy was cooperative: this resulted in a broadening of the franchise, a reformed Legislative Council with an elected majority, and responsible self-government after new elections in 1960. TANU won these also and Nyerere was appointed Chief Minister.

Nyerere now petitioned the UN and initiated discussion with Britain on independence. With most unusual alacrity Britain granted independence in 1961. Nyerere was now Prime Minister. He set about instituting a 'democratic and socialist form of government ... democracy by discussion among equals'. He realised he had to 'safeguard the unity of the country from irresponsible and vicious attempts to divide and weaken it'; these could include external forces as well as 'irresponsible individuals [whose only] policy is self-aggrandisement'. A one-party state, which permitted 'freedom for opposition [but not] an organised opposition' was necessary in order to preserve the new, fragile unity.

Nyerere clearly foresaw independent Africa's future problems. He warned in 1961 that a new 'Scramble for Africa' would be instituted by the Western powers, which would 'divide nation against nation ... If an African state is armed, then, realistically, it can only be armed against another African state'. He believed that both socialist and capitalist countries were using their wealth for purposes of power and prestige, not to alleviate poverty. Thus African peoples had to develop their own form of socialism and had to beware, in a world divided between the rich and the poor, that they were not used as 'tools' by either. 'The danger to African Unity', he warned, 'is going to come from these external forces'.

There was opposition to some of his policies, for example to the granting of citizenship to all born in Tanganyika irrespective of race, and the necessarily slow Africanisation of the civil service; there were strikes over low pay. In 1962 Nyerere resigned, stating that he wanted to 'leave government to be an effective teacher'. He toured the country extensively, building up TANU membership. He also published three pamphlets, laying out his philosophy, which included a rejection of all forms of exploitation and the prevention of income differences.

Prime Minister Kawawa followed Nyerere's nationalist, socialist and egalitarian policies. New elections were held in December 1962; Tanganyika was declared a republic with Nyerere as its first President. Development projects were immediately begun, financed by aid from Britain and the USA. These included import-substitution manufacturing and huge growth in primary and secondary education. A university college and a Civil Service Training Centre were established; and the government ministries also set up training courses. In June 1963 Nyerere was appointed the chancellor of the University of East Africa and two years later he sponsored an International Congress of African Historians at Dar-es-Salaam. As there were not nearly enough places in tertiary education to train the personnel urgently required, Nyerere joined with Mboya, Kenneth Kaunda and Joshua Nkomo in arranging placements for students in the USA: by 1963 there were 1,011, including 132 women, in the USA, and 100 in Canada.

Nyerere during all this time was also involved in pan-African politics. In March 1958, while attending the first anniversary celebrations of Ghana's independence, he discussed with GEORGE PADMORE and KWAME NKRUMAH the convening of what became the All African Peoples' Conference (AAPC) later that year. Also present were Tom Mboya and Joseph Murumbi of Kenya; the three men discussed the possibility of a regional grouping. In September Nyerere and Tom Mboya of Kenya took the lead in establishing the Pan-African Movement for East and Central Africa (PAFMECA), which was a loose grouping of political parties which espoused freedom, democracy and regional federation. That regional unity could be a precursor to all-African unity was then accepted by the AAPC at its December meeting in Accra. The AAPC resolutions stated the 'ultimate objective of African nations is a Commonwealth of Free African States … linguistic and other divisions should be subordinated to the over-riding demands of African Unity'. These principles were not endorsed by the subsequent four meetings of the Conference of Independent African States.

In 1962, with the addition of Ethiopia and Somalia to the group, PAFMECA became PAFMECSA and lent active support to liberation movements in the region. Though heavily dependent on TANU for financial support, and much weakened first by the resignation of its general-secretary Mbiyu Koinange in 1963 (he returned to Kenya on its independence) and then by the formation of the OAU, PAFMECSA survived until 1977. (Its collapse was at least partially due to differences between Nyerere and Jomo Kenyatta regarding strategies towards the situation in Uganda, and different approaches to development.)

In 1963 Nyerere, before the convening of what became the OAU, reiterated that 'African Unity must come, and it must be a real unity. Our goal must be a United States of Africa'. However, the radicals (who included NASSER, Nkrumah and Nyerere) lost the argument at Addis Ababa and no plan for unification (as opposed to statements of hope) were discussed. Despite Nyerere's attempts to find common ground and his rejection of 'conquest to facilitate union', many of the leaders were not even prepared to consider the possibility of political union. The OAU was generally impotent and purposeless until the 1970s.

In Zanzibar, which had been granted independence by Britain in 1963, a bloody coup led by the Umma Party, overthrew the government. The Umma was a communist-oriented offshoot of the Afro-Shiraz Party, a combination of native and mainland Africans united against the minority but dominant Arab population. Both African parties had links with TANU, and a pact of union, which left considerable power in the hands of the Umma Party's leader Sheikh Abeid Karume, was signed in 1964. Tanzania was born – and Nyerere was now caught up in the West's Cold War: British and American aid dried up.

Nyerere's political position had to move from a pro-Western stance to a more non-aligned position. An avowed anti-imperialist, he hosted nationalist movements then struggling for independence, such as the ANC and the PAC of South Africa, Frelimo of Mozambique and Zanla of the then Southern Rhodesia. Refugees were accepted from Mozambique, Rwanda, Burundi and Zaire. Tanzania boycotted South African goods and would not permit flights going to South Africa to land on Tanzanian territory. In 1965 Tanzania was one of only seven countries to follow the OAU resolution to sever diplomatic relations with Britain if she would not use force against Ian Smith's unilaterally declared independence for Rhodesia. (This meant the loss of a $42.5 million interest-free loan from Britain.) Nyerere opposed the American participation in the war in Vietnam and American and Belgian interventions in the Congo.

Nyerere now sought aid from middle-ranking European powers, from China, and, somewhat futilely, from the Soviet bloc. This alienated the Western block even further. However, aid was crucial. Nyerere's political stance cost the country millions: 83 per cent of the development budget for 1964–5 was to come from overseas. The economy had not improved and development was not progressing as fast as he would have liked. Class divisions were emerging in Tanzania, as was the corruption of officials and signs of authoritarianism. Strikes were again taking place, including one by the military which Nyerere could only contain with the temporary help of British forces.

In 1967 Nyerere announced the Arusha Declaration which espoused socialist doctrines for self-reliance and for leadership; and for the nationalisation of key aspects of the economy. Strategies were put in place for attempt to ensure that these paths were followed, but unfortunately some had to be enforced. Among these were the 'villagisation' programmes intended to curb individual peasant acquisitiveness; and the leadership rules, which TANU asked the National Assembly to enforce in 1972. (The leadership rules forbad participation in any form of capitalist actitvity by TANU leaders of any rank.) That year also saw the decentralisation of administration, and the beginning of efforts to increase mass participation in local councils. Development programmes were also pursued, still financed by foreign aid despite Nyerere's fear of pressures from donors. These included piped water for rural dwellers; dispensaries and a 'barefoot doctor' scheme for rural areas; and a further increase in educational provision, so that by 1975 79 per cent of boys and 60 per cent of girls aged 7–13 were in school.

In 1972 Sheikh Karume, considered by many to have been a blood-thirsty dictator, was assassinated. This resulted in the merging of TANU and the Afro-Shiraz Party into the Chama Cha Mapinduzi (CCM), under the chairmanship of Nyerere. (Why Nyerere apparently took no actions to curb Karume is not understood by many; did he perhaps fear a reduction in aid by those who had initially supported Karume?)

The economy continued to decline. Industrialisation, which Nyerere believed would naturally follow from free education did not happen. The management of the tea and coffee plantations, confiscated from their (mainly White) owners, and the marketing of produce through inefficient state marketing boards was so inexpert that these primary industries all but collapsed. The drought of 1979 was followed by floods in 1980, the international increase in petrol prices, the reduction in the prices of Tanzania's main exports, and an explosion in the numbers of civil servants. Nevertheless, Nyerere remained vastly popular with his people, whom he had welded into one, largely overcoming ethnic divisions. He was universally known as *Mwalimu*, 'teacher' in Swahili, the national language. In the 1980 presidential elections, he won 93 per cent of the votes.

While the situation in Tanzania deteriorated, Nyerere was part of the African leadership which forced apartheid-dominated South Africa to leave the Commonwealth. In 1974 he hosted the sixth Pan-African Congress, which had been initiated (but not attended by) C.L.R. JAMES, then teaching in the USA. James was very impressed by Nyerere's attempts to curb the power of the elite and to build a socialist state. In 1979 Nyerere was the key founder of the Southern African Development Community (SADC), formed to lessen dependence on South Africa by building economic self-reliance.

Continuing his ever-principled stand, Tanzania helped oust Uganda's military dictator Idi Amin in 1979. This was a breach of OAU principles, but as Amin had been universally condemned and as his action was supported by most Ugandans, Nyerere was not disciplined. This was not the first time that Nyerere had transgressed OAU principles: in 1968 he had extended diplomatic recognition to Biafra, on the basis that international powers were 'determining the situation ... Nigeria, Britain and the oil companies are on one side'. Nyerere had also long recognised that the boundaries 'which divide African states are nonsensical', as they had been arbitrarily drawn by Europeans in 1885. In 1984 he was elected chairman of the OAU.

Tanzania's economic situation, exacerbated by the success of health measures which resulted in an almost doubling of the population between 1957 and 1978, continued to deteriorate. Financial problems increased with the expenses of the war against Amin, which totalled almost $1 billion. Dependency on foreign aid, which contradicted Nyerere's philosophy of socialist self-reliance, increased. In 1979 Tanzania was forced to apply for an IMF loan; by 1981 it had to accept the usual IMF Structural Adjustment Programme stipulations. In 1986, Tanzania's external debt was $3.7 billion to be repaid by a population of 18 million!

In 1984 the presidency of Tanzania and the chairmanship of the CCM were separated and the Prime Minister was given increased power over domestic issues. Nyerere retired, settling on the farm given to him by the government near his birthplace. He concentrated on writing, translating Shakespeare plays into Swahili, and bookbinding – as well as on the ruling party which he continued to chair until 1990. His international activism also continued, primarily in the fields of conflict resolution, for example in Burundi; in 1987 he had become one of the founders of the South Commission, which attempts to bridge the gap between the rich and the poor countries by working closely with the Group of 77 (the developing countries) at the UN. At his death he was mourned worldwide as one of the greatest leaders of modern Africa.

Julius Nyerere died of leukemia in a London hospital on 14 October 1999.

MS

Main publications not mentioned in the text

Freedom and Unity, Oxford, Oxford University Press, 1966.
Ujamaa – Essays on Socialism, Dar-es-Salaam, Oxford University Press, 1966.
Freedom and Socialism, Dar-es-Salaam, Oxford University Press, 1968.
Freedom and Development, Dar-es-Salaam, Oxford University Press, 1973.
Crusade for Liberation, Dar-es-Salaam, Oxford University Press, 1978.

Further reading

Legum, Colin and Geoffrey Mmari, *Mwalimu: the Influence of Nyerere*, Trenton, Africa World Press, 1995.

George Padmore
(1902 – 59)

George Padmore probably has a much more rightful claim to the title of the Father of Pan-Africanism than W.E.B. Du Bois, on whom the title was bestowed. His life was devoted to the true emancipation and unification of Africans and those of African descent.

The son of a government agricultural advisor and teacher, Malcolm Ivan Nurse was born on 28 July 1902 in Tacarigua in the British colony of Trinidad. He attended Trinidad's model elementary school, Tranquillity, and then St Mary's Roman Catholic College (1915–16) and the private Pamphylion High School. (At that time there were no state, only private and denominational secondary schools in Trinidad.) He was a boyhood friend of C.L.R. James; the fathers of the boys were also friends. Young Malcolm probably got his early introduction to politics and Pan-Africanism from his father, a voracious reader, who had attended the meetings organised by Henry Sylvester Williams during his brief return to Trinidad in 1901, and who roomed with Mrs Williams after Williams' premature death in 1911. Hubert Alfonso Nurse held what for a Black man was a remarkable post in the colonial government: that of government instructor in agriculture. At first his son worked as an apprentice pharmacist, and then as a journalist on the Trinidad *Guardian*.

Nurse married Julia Semper, who was pregnant when Nurse left Trinidad in 1924 for Fisk University, Tennessee, USA. (All West Indians wanting post-secondary education had to leave their homes as there were no tertiary institutions anywhere in the British colonies.) He enrolled as a medical student in 1925. After two years he moved to Howard University in Washington to study law, in order, he wrote on his registration form, 'to practice law in Liberia'. He continued to write, both for the Trinidad press and for the journals of the universities he attended. He also joined the Communist Party (USA), whose leadership then was advocating racial equality. He adopted the *nom-de-guerre* of George Padmore, in order to protect his family from repercussions for his political activism. As 'Padmore' he spoke on communist platforms and wrote for the communist press.

In 1929 he was sent by the CPUSA to the Communist International-sponsored Second Congress of the League Against Imperialism (LAI); he was elected to the committee (the International Trade Union Committee of Negro Workers – ITUCNW) being set up to organise a conference of Negro workers. Some months after his return to the USA, in December 1929, Padmore accompanied the CPUSA leader to Moscow, where he remained as a member of the Profintern (the Red International of Labour

Unions) and was soon named head of the newly formed Negro Bureau. In 1930 he was detailed to aid in the organisation of the conference which had been suggested at the LAI meeting, and was eventually held in Hamburg in July 1930, under the chairmanship of the African American, James Ford. As no full list of delegates was published, it is unclear exactly how many Africans were present. Padmore definitely made a trip to West Africa to recruit delegates, as four West Africans are listed among the speakers; whether he also travelled to South and East Africa is uncertain. The conference's resolutions included the development of an 'efficient working class leadership' and the formulation of demands to include 'equal pay regardless of race, nationality and sex' and 'against racial barriers in trade unions'.

Padmore wrote six long pamphlets for the ITUCNW, including what was really a book, the *Life and Struggles of Negro Workers*, published in 1931. This analysed the situation of Black workers and soldiers in Africa and the Americas, and their political current 'awakening'. The solution he advocated for their dire situation was naturally the communist 'line' of the time: the building of 'revolutionary trade unions of blacks and whites' which would lead the 'united front struggles of the working class against the offensive of the capitalists' (p.123).

It was probably towards the end of 1931 that Padmore replaced Ford as head of the ITUCNW and also as editor of its monthly publication, the *Negro Worker*. In the *Worker*, which was despatched to interested and/or activist Black peoples around the world, Padmore attempted a mass education programme on the importance, functions and organisation of trade unions and collective action against exploitation. The *Worker* also carried news of struggles and the situations faced by Black peoples (as workers) around the world, and inveighed against imperialism and racism. Banned by most colonial governments, Padmore arranged for seamen visiting Hamburg to smuggle the *Worker* into the colonies.

In 1934 Padmore resigned from the Comintern because of disagreements over Stalin's pact with France, an imperialist power; he also disagreed with the revised Communist philosophy which required him to teach that the enemies of exploited colonials were not the imperialist powers, but the growing fascist movement. Much vilified and persecuted by the communists the world over, hounded by the fascists in Hamburg and under surveillance by the British secret service, in 1935 he settled in London and began to earn a living as a journalist for Black newspapers worldwide.

Padmore resumed his friendship with C.L.R. James and forged working partnerships with I.T.A. WALLACE-JOHNSON, a Sierra Leone trade unionist then in London, as well as with Jomo Kenyatta who had attended the ITUCNW meeting, and the British Guiana-born RAS T. MAKONNEN. Under the leadership of James they formed the International African Friends of Abyssinia in 1935 to campaign against the Italian invasion of Abyssinia, one of the two remaining independent African countries. The campaign failed, and the organisation was transformed into the International African Service Bureau, which published *Africa and the World* (July – September 1937), banned in the Gold Coast in October 1937; *African Sentinel* (October 1937 – April 1938); *International African Opinion* (July 1938 – March 1939). The latter was edited by James; its motto was 'educate, co-operate, emancipate'. The Bureau's aim was to 'fight for the demands of Africans and other colonial peoples for democratic rights, civil liberties and self-determination'; Europeans could only become associate members. The Bureau held public meetings and demonstrations (e.g. on the 1937 strikes in Trinidad), wrote letters to the press, aided visiting delegations from the colonies and lobbied Members of Parliament over colonial issues. In 1937 the IASB created an overarching organisation of all Black groups in Britain, the Pan-African Federation.

During the pre-war period Padmore also worked with the Independent Labour Party, addressed its meetings and wrote for its journal, *New Leader*, as well as for other left-wing British publications. He spoke at any meeting interested in colonial issues and maintained a vast correspondence with activists the world over. In 1938 with ILP help, he mounted an exhibition to counter the falsehoods he saw displayed at the Empire Exhibition then being held in Glasgow. From the mid-1930s Padmore wrote almost weekly for Black newspapers around the world, including the Jamaican *Public Opinion*, the Gold Coast's *Ashanti Pioneer* and such US papers as the *Chicago Defender* and W.E.B. Du Bois' *Crisis*. His articles introduced readers to the Black world outside their own borders, informing US readers, for example, of contemporary events as well as the situation in South, East and West Africa, the metropoles and elsewhere in the colonised world.

Padmore was greatly assisted with both his research, his writing and the hosting of countless visitors by his partner, Dorothy Pizer. An ex-member of the London Communist Party, Dorothy earned a consistent income as a secretary. (She typed C.L.R. James' manuscript *World Revolution*.) Probably before leaving to settle in Ghana Padmore and Pizer were married.

Though during the Second World War political activities had to be somewhat curtailed, nevertheless Padmore and other Black groups in London organised protests against Prime Minister Churchill's declaration that the terms of the Atlantic Charter, which promised that 'sovereign rights and self-government' would be restored to peoples who had lost them, did not apply to the colonies. A *Manifesto on Africa in the Post-War World* was agreed by the London groups and sent 'for serious consideration' to the founding meeting of the United Nations in 1945. To strengthen the demands in the *Manifesto*, supportive meetings were called, including two 'Subject Peoples' Conferences organised by Padmore, which stressed the need for Afro-Asian solidarity and called for freedom for all colonised peoples.

The Pan-African Federation called a Pan-African Congress in 1945. Held in Manchester in October, the Congress, the sixth (not fifth, as usually stated) such gathering, attracted the colonial trade unionists then attending the first conference of the World Federation of Trade Unions, as well as Blacks resident or temporarily in the UK. Because of the problems of travel (the Second World War had just ended), the only African American present was W.E.B. Du Bois, who, in recognition of his having called the previous four Congresses, chaired all the sessions except the first, which was chaired by AMY ASHWOOD GARVEY. The Congress demanded, *inter alia*, 'complete and absolute independence' for West Africa; equality for all in South Africa; federation and self-government for the British West Indies; and that 'discrimination on account of race, creed or colour [in Great Britain] be made a criminal offence by law'.

The financial genius who made all this activism possible was Ras T. Makonnen. Post-war Padmore established the Pan-African News Agenecy at his home and continued writing for Black newpapers around the world, until the anti-communist hysteria led to his exclusion, despite his very public renunciation of Stalin in 1934! Padmore became the international secretary of the Pan-African Federation, which continued its involvement in local and international issues. He began to explore with the Nigerian political leader Nnamdi Azikiwe the possibilities for holding a Pan-African Congress in Africa; however, after the victory of his party in the Gold Coast elections in 1951, it was KWAME NKRUMAH who undertook to convene it.

Padmore became a founding member of the short-lived Asiatic-African United Front Committee as well as of the British Centre Against Imperialism which became the Movement Against Imperialism. The times were not auspicious, Padmore wrote to W.E.B. Du Bois in October 1949. The 'African nationalist and the anti-imperialist movements are branded as "communist" or as "Moscow agents" by the British, even the Labour Party. This has led to a split in the anti-imperialist movement'.

Barred from newspapers, Padmore worked on the book he claimed he had been asked to write by the delegates at the Pan-African Congress. A 'brief over-all survey of the Colonial Problem in British Africa, in the light of the new Economic Imperialism, euphemistically described as Colonial Development and Welfare', *Africa: Britain's Third Empire* was published in London in 1949. Divided into four parts, the book surveys the situation of Africans in the various colonies, analyses the nature of direct and indirect rule, reviews the Colonial Development and Welfare policies, and outlines 'how politically-minded Africans are meeting this challenge of the new Economic Imperialism' (p.12). Padmore accused the British government – using the politicians' own words – of planning to create a vast army in Africa in order to save British manpower, and of planning the even greater exploitation of African primary produce in order for 'Western Europe to achieve its balance of payments and to get world equilibrium [vis-à-vis] the two great World Powers, the United States and Russia ...' (p.10, quoting Ernest Bevin). Not surprisingly within a year of its publication the book was banned in most of the British colonies in Africa.

Padmore soon began working on another book, *Pan-Africanism or Communism?*, published in 1956, which he called a 'historical account of the struggles of Africans and peoples of African descent for Human Rights and Self-Determination in the modern world' (p.9). Padmore wrote the book partly to discredit the propaganda being spread by imperialists that all political activism in Africa, and the demands for independence, were communist-inspired. Padmore had no problems with a 'Marxist interpretation of history ... but refuse[d] to accept the pretentious claims of all doctrinaire Communism ...' (p.18). This belief led him into sometimes vituperative criticisms of communist anti-imperialist activists. Padmore also criticised the British government for failing 'to make good its promise of self-government within the Commonwealth, unless actually forced to do so by the colonial peoples'. Self-determination would, he argued, 'be the most effective bulwark against Communism' (p.20). He believed that there was a 'growing feeling among politically conscious Africans throughout the continent that their destiny is one, and that what happen[ed] in one part of Africa to Africans must affect Africans living in other parts'; this would ultimately lead to the 'creation of a United States of Africa' (p.22).

Padmore's small home was described in 1956 by his friend the African American novelist Richard Wright as his 'office and workroom through [which] have trooped almost all of the present day leaders of Black Africa. They come seeking information, encouragement, and help …'. Among these men in 1945 had been the then Francis Nkrumah, recommended to Padmore from the USA by C.L.R. James. Padmore enlisted the recently arrived Nkrumah's help with organising the Pan-African Congress. It was while acting in this capacity that Nkrumah changed his name to Kwame.

Thus began a partnership which was to last until Padmore's death. After his return home in 1947 Nkrumah maintained close links with Padmore in London, who became the propagandist of the 'Gold Coast Revolution' and advisor to the Gold Coast Convention People's Party's National Association of Socialist Student Organisations, a 'vanguard' group formed by Nkrumah. Padmore also continued to write, speak and lobby against imperialism both in the UK and abroad.

In constant touch with Nkrumah, Padmore paid his first visit to the Gold Coast in 1951; in 1957 he was a special guest at the Independence Celebrations and later that year he returned to take up the position offered by Nkrumah as Advisor on African Affairs. The presence of yet another non-Ghanaian close to Nkrumah caused some resentment which Padmore had to negotiate. He travelled to the Sudan, Ethiopia, Egypt, Libya, Tunisia, Morocco and Liberia to finalise arrangements for the Conference of Independent States to be held in April 1958 in independent Ghana.

Soon he was travelling again to enlist activists in the freedom struggles and trade unionists in both free states and colonies for the All African Peoples' Conference (AAPC) to be held in Accra in December. This was probably Padmore's crowning achievement: the culmination of a lifetime of dreams, plans and struggles, perhaps symbolised by his use of the icon of a Black man breaking his chains, that he had first used in his ITUCNW days, on AAPC literature. Some 300 delegates representing 28 countries attended the conference which elected Tom Mboya of Kenya as chairperson and Padmore as secretary-general. According to Makonnen's autobiography, while the 'official [meetings were] in the conference hall … there were unofficial meetings at the African Affairs Centre where you'd find the trade union element mixing with the ideological groups from various countries' (p.214).

The motto of the AAPC was 'Independence and Unity'; its aims included the 'acceleration of liberation; development of a feeling of community among the peoples of Africa; to work for the emergence of a United States of Africa'. It endorsed 'regional groupings' as a step towards achieving this. The resolutions included the demand for the immediate end to the 'political and economic exploitation of Africans by Imperialist Europeans'; 'full support to all fighters for freedom in Africa, to all those who resort to peaceful means … as well as to those who are compelled to retaliate against violence to attain national independence'; the ultimate objective of 'the evolution of a Commonwealth of Free African States'; condemnation of 'the pernicious system of racialism and discriminatory laws' and the imposition of economic sanctions on South Africa. Finally, the Conference warned that the imperialists were attempting, and would continue to attempt, to perpetuate their power through fostering tribalism and religious separatism.

Padmore was put in charge of the permanent secretariat set up by the AAPC in Accra; its main aims were to promote unity, accelerate liberation and 'mobilise world opinion against the denial of political and fundamental human rights to Africans'.

Padmore was also given the task of drafting a revision of the Ghanaian constitution and a socialist policy for the emerging new state. The policy, which aimed at 'economic independence on a socialist pattern', advocated, *inter alia*, the improvement and diversification of agriculture, and the possible introduction of cooperatives; the development of villages to provide social and cultural amenities; industrialisation, with financial input as well as technical and managerial assistance from the government, initially to 'save importations'; educational reforms to ensure that traditional subjects were taught from an African perspective and to introduce training in technical subjects; and the severe punishment of bribery and corruption, which were deemed crimes against society. Padmore concluded that:

> the colonialists, having been forced to concede the political power which auto-matically gave them control over the economic resources of our country, are concentrating upon the economic counterrevolution in an effort to restore their absolute control over us by economic means.

Resident at last in the country which he thought of – which he helped groom – as the model for African independence, Padmore was not to live to see the downfall of Nkrumah and the collapse of socialism in Ghana. Seriously ill, he was flown to London for treatment for recurring hepatitis, but died on 23 September 1959. He was given a state funeral in Accra and his ashes were interred in Christianborg Castle on 4 October 1959.

MS

Main publications not mentioned in the text

Padmore's articles are uncollected, as are his pamphlets.
How Britain Rules Africa, London, Wishart Books, 1936.
Africa and World Peace, London. Frank Cass, 1937.
The White Man's Duty [with Nancy Cunard], London, W.H. Allen, 1942.
How Russia Transformed Her Colonial Empire [with Dorothy Pizer], London, Dennis Dobson, 1946.
The Gold Coast Revolution, London, Dennis Dobson, 1953.

Further reading

Adi, Hakim and Marika Sherwood, *The 1945 Pan-African Congress Revisited*, London, New Beacon Books, 1995, which includes Padmore's account of the 1945 Pan-African Congress.
Arthur, John, *Freedom for Africa*, Accra, 1961.
Excerpts from Padmore's 'A Guide to Pan-African Socialism' are available in William H. Friedland and Carl G. Rosberg, *African Socialism*, Stanford, Stanford University Press, 1964.

The one unsatisfactory biography (unsatisfactory, not least because Hooker was known to be a CIA agent by most African American academics/activists, who consequently would not co-operate in his research) of Padmore is L.J. Hooker, *Black Revolutionary*, London, Pall Mall Press, 1967.

Paul Leroy Robeson

(1898 – 1976)

Paul Leroy Robeson, African American actor, singer and political activist, was born on 9 April 1898 in Princeton, New Jersey, USA. He was the youngest of five children and fourth son of the Reverend William Drew Robeson (1845–1918) a former runaway slave and Presbyterian minister, and Maria Louisa Bustill Robeson (1853–1904) a former school teacher.

In 1915, Paul Robeson won a scholarship to Rutgers College (now Rutgers University), New Jersey and was also educated at Columbia University Law School where he graduated in 1923. An outstanding athlete as well as scholar, Robeson was chosen for the All-American college football team as the finest player in his position. For a short time thereafter he played professional football and semi-professional basketball.

In 1921 he married his life-long partner, Eslanda Cordozo Goode, an analytical chemist in a hospital pathology laboratory. She would later manage Robeson's career, and even though their relationship was often stormy she was initially a major influence in his life and the author of an early biography *Paul Robeson, Negro* (1930).

Robeson began his acting career in 1920 appearing in *Simon the Cyrenian* in Harlem, New York and played his first professional part in 1922 in *Taboo*. It was in 1922 as a member of the cast of this play now renamed *Voodoo* that Robeson made his debut on the stage in Britain. In later years he recalled that it was during his performances in *Voodoo* at the Blackpool Opera House in 1922 that he first realised he had the talent to make a career as a singer. In 1923 he briefly worked at a law firm in New York, but his experiences of racism persuaded him that he might have more success as an actor than by attempting to practise as a lawyer.

In the USA he continued to develop his singing career and with Lawrence Brown, who was to become his accompanist for many years, he performed the first ever concert comprising entirely African American secular songs and spirituals in New York in 1925. Later that year he began his legendary recording career. The previous year he had made his first film *Body and Soul*, directed by Oscar Micheaux. During the next twenty-five years Robeson starred in ten films and twelve plays and musicals.

He returned to Britain in 1925 to star in the play *Emperor Jones*, and three years later first sang *Ol' Man River* on stage in the London production of *Showboat*.

During the late 1920s and 1930s Robeson and his family (his son Paul junior was born in 1928) made their home in London. Robeson initially believed that racism was less of a problem in Britain than in the USA. He toured the country several times making numerous stage and concert appearances, including his first and much acclaimed performance in *Othello* in 1930. He made numerous recordings and some of his most memorable films in Britain; these included *Song of Freedom* (1936) and *The Proud Valley* (1939).

In retrospect, Robeson believed that his time in Britain had a profound influence on his personal and political development. As a result of his many contacts with students and other African residents his serious interest in African cultures and languages developed. He said later that he 'discovered' Africa in London, where he became actively involved with organisations such as the Union of Students of African Descent, the League of Coloured Peoples, the International African Service Bureau, the Negro Welfare Association and the West African Students' Union that made him one of its patrons. It was during this period that Robeson declared 'I want to be African' and began his comparative study of African, African American and other folk cultures and began his writing on this subject. In 1934 he enrolled as a student of Linguistics and African languages at London University. He took a special interest in languages and is said to have mastered over twenty including Russian, Chinese and African languages such as Swahili, Efik and Yoruba. Robeson made contact with Indians, Africans and others active in the anti-colonial struggle and formed links in the workers' movement, and he began to exhibit a growing interest in socialism, the international communist movement and the Soviet Union, which he first visited in 1934.

From that time onwards he began to take an active interest in politics. He subsequently repudiated some of his films, such as *Sanders of the River* (1934), and his search for more acceptable acting roles led him to take the lead in C.L.R. JAMES' *Toussaint L'Ouverture* and to performances with the working-class Unity Theatre in London. He also began to use his great talents to support political causes such as the International Brigade in the Spanish Civil War. By the late 1930s Robeson had taken a clear political stand, which he explained in one of his most famous speeches made in London in 1937. 'The artist must take sides. He must elect to fight for freedom or for slavery. I have made my choice. I had no alternative.' His links with the miners of South Wales and other working people confirmed his belief in the oneness of humanity and influenced his choice of repertoire. Increasingly he included folk and political songs from around the world that he frequently sang in the original Russian, Chinese and other languages.

During the Second World War and throughout most of the 1940s Robeson remained in the USA. By then world-famous, he recorded his famous *Ballad for Americans* in 1940. In 1943–4 he starred in the long-running Broadway production of *Othello*. Despite temptations to abandon his political principles, Robeson maintained his principled refusal to perform before segregated audiences and in this period stepped up political activism. He was a founder and became chairman of the anti-colonial Council on African Affairs, perhaps the most important organisation in the USA working to disseminate knowledge about, and to establish support for, the liberation of Africa. Robeson was also co-chairman of the Progressive Party and a leading figure in the American Crusade to End Lynching. He also played a prominent part in the attempts to free from prison Earl Browder, the leader of the American

Communist Party. In addition Robeson performed in support of the Allied war effort and in 1945 took part in an extensive overseas tour to perform to US troops stationed in Europe.

During the Cold War era Robeson continued to defend the Soviet Union and to attack those aspects of US foreign policy that appalled him including the invasion of Korea in 1950. At the same time he vigorously opposed racism in the USA, and continued his support for anti-colonial and workers' struggles throughout the world and especially in Africa, and for the international peace movement. In 1951 he was one of those who presented the petition of the Civil Rights Congress to the UN, which charged the US government with genocide on the basis that 15 million Black Americans were subjected to conditions producing premature death, poverty and disease. Later in 1952 he was awarded the International Stalin Peace Prize 'for strengthening peace among people' and as one of those Americans who took a clear stand against the warmongering of the US government. All this led to increasing levels of FBI surveillance and attempts to stop him from speaking and performing. In 1949, following his remarks at the Congress of the World Partisans for Peace in Paris, where he said he thought it unthinkable that African Americans would go to war on behalf of those who oppressed them against a country like the Soviet Union which had raised 'our people to full human dignity', he was subjected to organised attacks on his concerts at Peekskill, New York. He was eventually to be arraigned before the notorious House Un-American Activities Committee and in 1950 the US State Department confiscated his passport on the grounds that his travel abroad would not be in the best interests of the USA and might bring 'diplomatic embarrassment' because he supported the anti-colonial struggles of the peoples of Africa.

Even during the period when he was unable to travel abroad and there were attempts to silence him, Robeson, who by this time was one of the most famous Americans in the world, refused to be cowed or betray his political principles. He continued to speak out for international peace, for colonial liberation, and against racism and political repression in the USA. In the 1950s denied entry to Canada he nonetheless sang at the famous Peace Arch concerts on the Canadian border and in 1955 sent a telephone message to the Bandung Conference of African and Asian states held in Indonesia. He also maintained his contact with friends and supporters in Britain who campaigned for the return of his passport. In Manchester, a National Paul Robeson Committee was established in 1954 and rapidly spread to other towns and cities. In 1956 a taped message from Robeson was played to a packed audience in Manchester. In 1957 he broadcast live via a telephone link to a vast gathering in St Pancras Town Hall and in the same year sang a programme in the same way for the miners' Eisteddfod at Porthcawl in Wales.

In 1958 Robeson published *Here I Stand*, his autobiography and political testament. In it he outlines his views on all the major political questions of the day, what his principles were and why he had stood by them. He explains his belief in the principles of scientific socialism and his conviction that socialist society represents a higher form of society than that based on private profit. He also writes of his 'discovery' of Africa and why he came to consider himself an African. The book was primarily directed at an African American audience and Robeson devotes a significant portion of it to advancing his view on what came to be known as the struggle for civil rights. In *Here I Stand* Robeson stated, in opposition to those who promoted a more gradualist approach to the demands for civil rights, that in his view 'the time is now'. Robeson argued that African American people should rise up in struggle for their citizenship rights and he spoke eloquently of 'the power of Negro action', stressing that African Americans could not wait for anybody else to give them their rights, they had to empower themselves, develop a common programme of action and effective leadership. Six years after the publication of the book Robeson was able to claim with some justification that many of the ideas about which he had written had been changed into reality; mass action and the demand for rights had been taken up by millions.

In 1958, following a worldwide campaign, his passport was finally returned. Robeson returned to Britain in 1958 as soon as he could travel. In the next few years he gave many memorable performances, including those at St Paul's Cathedral, where he was the first person of African descent to address a congregation, at the Eisteddfod at Ebbw Vale, as Othello at Stratford and his first television performance. He also appeared with some regularity at peace and disarmament rallies and at other political events throughout Britain. He also continued to tour throughout Europe, the Soviet Union and even in Australia and New Zealand. By the early 1960s Robeson's arduous life and the effects of the persecution he had suffered began to take their toll. In 1963 he began a long period of semi-retirement in the USA. Even in retirement Robeson continued to issue political statements and to receive numerous honours. In 1972 the US magazine *Ebony* proclaimed him one of the ten most important Black men in American history. He died of a stroke on 23 January 1976 in Philadelphia and was buried in Harlem, New York, after a funeral attended by over 5,000 people.

HA

Main publications

Here I Stand with Lloyd Brown, London, Cassell, 1998.
Paul Robeson Speaks – Writings, Speeches, Interviews 1918–74, edited with introduction and notes by Phillip Foner, London, Quartet Books, 1978.

Further reading

Paul Robeson—Artist and Citizen, edited and with an introduction by Jeffrey C. Stewart, Rutgers, NJ, Rutgers University Press, 1998.
Brown, Lloyd, *The Young Paul Robeson*, Oxford, Westview, 1997.
Duberman, Martin Bauml, *Paul Robeson*, London, Pan Books, 1991.

Walter Rodney
(1942 – 80)

Walter Rodney spent his brief life immersed in scholarship and politics. He was deeply committed to the spiritiual, political and economic liberation of Black peoples everywhere. He studied both Africa and the diaspora, producing some seminal books and a number of important articles. His political involvement in Guyana resulted in his death.

Walter was born into a politicised family: his father had participated in the British colony's anti-imperialist struggles through his active membership of the multi-racial People's Progressive Party. His family had a financial struggle to get him through primary school; a scholarship supported him through Queens College in Georgetown, British Guiana, and then through his first degree at the Mona (Jamaica) campus of the University of the West Indies (UWI), from where he graduated with first-class honours in history in 1963. He was also the University's champion debater and was active in student politics. On a UWI scholarship Rodney then went to Britain, where he gained his PhD at the School of Oriental and African Studies, University of London in 1966. While in London, Rodney participated in the political activities organised by both Caribbeans and Africans. This was a period of political ferment in Britain, where racism was institutionalised by the government, for example in the Immigration Act of 1962, which virtually barred immigrants from the colonies. There were huge protests before and after the passing of the Act, some led by Trinidad-born activist CLAUDIA JONES. Whether the two knew each other is not known but is very likely. Rodney was a part of the study circle around C.L.R. JAMES, who recalled that Rodney 'was socially a very quiet man ... he spoke about the impact of the slave trade on Africans'. It was at this time that he married a fellow Guianese also studying in London, Patricia Henry; she later completed a social work degree at UWI and then obtained post-graduate qualifications in public health at the University of Michigan.

Rodney's dissertation, 'A history of the Upper Guinea Coast 1545–1800', was published in 1970 (Oxford University Press) and caused a backlash from both conservative and liberal historians of slavery. The book describes Upper Guinea before the coming of the Europeans, and analyses the effects of European influences, direct and indirect, on the coastal societies. The trade in enslaved Africans was eventually controlled by mulattoes and other oligarchs who both sold and used slaves. These changes introduced by external forces resulted in the formation of a class society based on the control of labour and of land, and on the differential access to trade and consumer goods.

Undoubtedly attracted by the policies of JULIUS NYERERE, in 1966 Rodney accepted a post in the History Department of University College, Tanzania. Situated on 'The Hill', outside Dar-es-Salaam, Rodney learned to avoid the factionalism among the faculty, but participated in the ongoing debate about the role of the College in a socialist Tanzania. He argued that to overcome the entrenched colonial education system, a new, socialist ideological perspective should be introduced. Wanting to reduce the physical and psychological distance between the university and the people, Rodney began a practice he was to follow for the rest of his life. He gave history lectures to groups of students off campus, and to workers both in Dar and in the countryside. This was probably the first expression of his growing recognition that history analysed how 'a problem came into being'; but that he also wanted to find ways 'in which these problems can be resolved in actuality'.

In January 1968 Rodney and his wife returned to his Jamaican *alma mater* as a lecturer in history specifically to initiate a new course in African history. As he had done in Tanzania, he also gave open lectures on African history and was soon asked to give similar talks to off-campus groups, including the Rastafarians. Some of these talks were published in London by Bogle L'Ouverture Publications in 1969 as *The Groundings with my Brothers*. C.L.R. James said of it that it was 'one of the best [books] that I know'. In his talks Rodney indicted the 'two [Jamaican] reactionary trade unions, which are the most important social bases of the two reactionary political parties' (p.15). Speaking on Black power, he defined 'black people' as 'non-whites whose homelands are in Asia and Africa and in the Americas'. Whites exercised power over Black peoples and a:

> black man ruling a dependent State within the imperialist system has no power. He is simply an agent of the whites in the metropolis, with an army and a police force designed to maintain the imperialist way of things… . The present Black Power movement in the United States is a rejection of hopelessness … It recognises the absence of black power, but is confident of the potential of black power on this globe. MARCUS GARVEY was one of the first advocates of Black Power … MALCOLM X … became the greatest threat to White Power in the USA because he began to seek a broader basis for his efforts in Africa and Asia … Black Power is a call to black peoples to throw off white domination … In the West Indies it means … the assumption of power by the black masses in the islands [and] the cultural reconstruction of the society in the image of the blacks.
>
> (pp.18–21, 24, 28)

Following FRANTZ FANON's teachings, as well as the results of his own historical analyses, Rodney emphasised the need for self-liberation by rejecting the self-abasing attitudes fostered by colonialism and neo-colonialism. Knowledge of early African history, he believed, would free and mobilise Black peoples.

Rodney's activism proved too much for the government led by the Jamaican Labour Party. While he was attending the Congress of Black Writers in Montreal later in 1968, where he re-met his old London mentor, C.L.R. James, Rodney was banned from Jamaica. His banning led to riots and massive demonstrations. His wife and children were permitted to stay. He denounced the Jamaican government as:

> men who serve the interest of a foreign, white capitalist system and at home they uphold a social structure which ensures that the black man resides at the bottom of the social ladder … [The government] do not want anybody to challenge their myth about 'Out of Many, One People' … They will ban people from coming to the country like … Stokely Carmichael … [and] have banned … all publications by Malcolm X …
>
> (*Groundings*, pp.60, 63)

Rodney stressed that 'the black intellectual, the black academic must atttach himself to the activity of the black masses'.

Rodney now returned to Tanzania as associate professor of history and inaugurated a course on the African diaspora. He became a key figure in the debate then suffusing the country about the nature of socialist development. As Tanzania was the head-quarters of most of the African liberation movements, Rodney not only became involved with them but developed a Marxist school steeped in the reality of armed struggle as opposed to the existing abstract philosophies. But he was very careful not to lay down rules: he maintained that the strategies and tactics for revolution had to be forged in the struggle. To protest the ban by Caribbean governments on unofficial groups attending, Rodney did not participate in the sixth/seventh Pan-African Congress (this Congress is usually referred to as the sixth, but was in fact the seventh), held while he was in Dar-es-Salaam. In the speech he would have given, Rodney emphasised the collusion between the new African petit bourgeoisie and the neo-colonial powers, and reiterated that 'the exploitation of Africans can be terminated only through the construction of a Socialist society, and technology must be related to this goal…Pan-Africanism must be an internationalist, anti-imperialist and Socialist weapon'. Wole Soyinka, the Nigerian writer, who had hoped to meet Rodney and C.L.R. James at the Congress, was prevented from speaking, as were all 'groups like the New Jewel Movement, the anti-Mobutu, anti-Banda etc. movements. Only the obvious "legiti-mised" movements, those which posed no danger to anyone – anti-apartheid, anti-colonial … survived the purge'. (Soyinka, p.9)

But it was in London that Rodney's *How Europe Underdeveloped Africa* (Bogle L'Ouverture, 1972) was published. In this Rodney defines 'development' as the progress all peoples make throughout their existence in developing social structures, regulating both internal and external relationships and working towards economic and other improvements in their lives. 'Underdevelopment', contrary to much contemporary analysis, was the perversion of this natural and ongoing process of development, which resulted in development for Europe and underdevelopment for others, for example Africa. Beginning in the period of the export of enslaved Africans, West Africa underwent 'a loss of development opportunity' because innovation was stifled by the removal of young people and the importation of Western goods and technology. Under colonialism, a period during which the colonial administration functioned both as an economic exploiter and supporter of private exploiters, this process continued: Western technology had made huge advances, at least partly financed by the profits from slavery; African innovation was almost eradicated; African workers were underpaid, over-taxed and both under- and mis-educated. Furthermore, the colonial education system, which replaced the African systems, fostered the under-development of Africa's intellectual resources by limiting opportunities as well as the levels of education offered; it was no more than cultural imperialism.

In 1974 the University of Guyana invited Rodney to return home as Professor of African History. On his way he lectured extensively throughout the USA. On his arrival he found that the university had bowed to government pressure and had withdrawn the invitation. Nevertheless the Rodneys decided to stay at home. (Guyana had become independent in 1966; its Prime Minister was brought to power by a combination of US and British interference, through the removal of the Marxist leader Cheddi Jagan from office.) Prime Minister Forbes Burnham ensured that Rodney would be refused employment at any level in the education system. Soon his wife also lost her job and the family's (there were three children) economic situation became serious. As Rodney explained:

> the government uses its control over jobs to discipline and intimidate people ...
> [It] has become the dominant employer [so] economic victimisation is a very
> real threat in Guyana ... it is a real barrier to political mobilisation and expression.
> That has also affected my decision to stay ...
>
> ('Guyana's socialism', p.119)

Having to earn a living, and undoubtedly wishing to have his voice heard and to make contact with students and comrades, Rodney seized the many opportunities offered to lecture abroad at a number of universities and again met up with James. At home, Rodney continued his scholarly activities: despite the Guyanese 'archives being the most poorly kept archives in the world', Rodney managed to find enough material for two publications, *Guyanese Sugar Plantations in the Late Nineteenth Century* (Georgetown, 1979) and *A History of the Guyanese Working People, 1881–1905*, which was published posthumously by the Johns Hopkins University Press (1981). In this book Rodney traced the economic and technological advances which had taken place, which, *inter alia*, resulted in the elimination of small planters by foreign plantation companies. To replace those of African descent who refused to work on plantations as underpaid labour, Indians were imported to replace them. New industries, such as gold, diamond and timber extraction and rice farming were begun. These, coupled with a movement to urban areas, resulted in the formation of a very fragmented working class. Yet in November–December 1905 there was a series of strikes and riots in urban and rural areas by both Indian and African-descent workers, demanding higher wages and an improvement in their appalling living conditions. Supported by imported British troops the governor ordered those plantation managers who offered higher wages to withdraw the offer. Male rioters tried in the courts were flogged; women's heads were shaved. The power of the ruling class was re-established.

Believing that the Guyanese people were one, and that they had common histories of exploitation as well as a common stake in the future, Rodney put his beliefs into practice. He became a founder member of the Working People's Alliance, a multi-racial organisation, which drew together four groups, with both African and Indian leadership and membership. It aimed to break down the racist-oriented, divisive politics of Prime Minister Burnham and to undertake the task of 'political and ideological [socialist] education' of the people. Rodney, like Malcolm X, did not eschew the possibility of armed struggle if people could not win their freedom without it: but 'normally', he believed, 'armed struggle is the last form of struggle upon which people determine, because it is extremely costly. Some of our finest comrades have fallen …'. This freedom had to go beyond the attainment of political as well as economic independence, as frequently the newly independent petit bourgeoisie simply took over 'control of the state machinery and society in its own economic interest … [and] there are ties between the indigenous petit bourgeoisie and international capital'. ('Guyana's socialism', pp.112, 125)

Rodney became the WPA's most popular spokesperson, an effective mobiliser of the workers against exploitation and the leading critic of Forbes Burnham's government, which had put Guyana into a state of economic decline and increasing militarisation. A virtual reign of terror was instituted against the WPA, including the persecution of its leading members. Some members were killed in broad daylight while others were imprisoned on inadequate charges. C.L.R. James made public his concern for Rodney's safety.

Though having to disguise himself in order to defy the government's restrictions on his movements, Rodney managed to 'escape' from Guyana in order to attend the Zimbabwe independence celebrations in 1980. He refused the invitation of Prime Minister Mugabe to set up a research institute as he was committed to return to Guyana to continue the political struggle there.

Recognising the importance of teaching the young, Rodney began working on a series of children's stories. Sadly, only one was completed before his death: *Kofi Baadu: out of Africa* was published in Georgetown in 1980.

Walter Rodney was murdered on the evening of 13 June 1980 in Georgetown. Thousands attended his funeral. Memorial services were held around the world. His wife and children, to escape possible attempts by Rodney's political opponents to annihilate the whole family, fled to Barbados. James mourned the man he thought would have been instrumental in bringing together 'black and colonial people … Caribbeans and Africans and the United States … to understand one another and contribute to each other … to bind the people together'.

MS

Some of Rodney's works not cited in the text

World War II and the Tanzanian Economy, Ithaca, Cornell UP, 1976.
Articles in the *Journal of African History*: 6/3, 1965; 7/3, 1966; 8/2, 1967.
'The impact of the Atlantic slave trade on west Africa', in Roland Oliver (ed.), *The Middle Age of African History*, London, Oxford University Press, 1967.
'Africa in Europe and the Americas', in Richard Gray (ed.), *The Cambridge History of Africa*, vol. 4, Cambridge, 1975.

The text of the speech he had prepared for the Pan-African Congress, 'Pan-Africanism and Neo-Colonialism in Africa', is in *Black Liberator*, 2/3, June 1974–January 1975.

Further reading

Alpers, E.A., and P.-M. Fontaine (eds), *Walter Rodney, Revolutionary and Scholar: A Tribute*, UCLA, Center for Afro-American Studies, 1982.

Prescod, Colin, 'Guyana's socialism: an interview with Walter Rodney', *Race & Class*, 18/2, Autumn 1976.

Soyinka, Wole, 'The Man Who Was Absent', in *'And finally they killed him': speeches and poems at a memorial rally for Walter Rodney, University of Nigeria,* The Socialist Forum, nd.

'C.L.R. James on Walter Rodney', *Race Today*, 12/2, 1980.

Léopold Sédar Senghor
(1906 – 2001)

Léopold Sédar Senghor, poet, writer and politician, was one of the founders of the concept of Négritude, one of Africa's foremost poets and the first President of independent Senegal.

Senghor was born on 9 October 1906 in Joal, south of Dakar in what was then French West Africa. He was the fifth son of six children born to Basile Diogoye Senghor, a farmer and merchant, and his last wife Gnilane Bakhoum. Senghor was born into a prosperous Serer Catholic family, but he was born outside the four communes where Africans were entitled to French citizenship and some other privileges. In 1914 he began his education at the Catholic boarding school in N'Gasobil, and then from 1923 was a pupil at the College Liberman in Dakar. He passed the baccalaureate in 1927 and on the basis of his excellent academic results was granted a scholarship by the French government. In the following year he left for France to continue his studies at the Lycée Louis-le-Grand in Paris and from 1931 at the Sorbonne University where he studied literature. In 1933, with the help of the Senegalese politician Blaise Diagne, he was granted French citizenship and subsequently became the first African to pass the *agrégation de l'Université* in grammar, one of the highest examinations in France, which selects teachers for secondary schools and universities.

In 1931 Senghor met AIMÉ CÉSAIRE, at that time also a student in Paris. The two became friends and through Césaire Senghor came into contact with other students from the Caribbean and for the first time met African Americans. As well as studying French literature, he began to read the work of the African American writers and poets of the Harlem Renaissance and the 'New Negro' movement and was strongly influenced by them. Many of these writers, including Claude McKay, Langston Hughes and Alain Locke, were contributors to the journal *La Revue de Monde Noir*, which first appeared in Paris in 1931 and was published by two of Senghor's new friends, Paulette and Jane Nardal, who both originated from Martinique.

In 1934 Senghor became chairman of the student union founded by Senegalese students in Paris, L'Association des Étudiants Ouest-Africains. In the same year with Césaire he founded the journal *L'Étudiant Noir* in which they began for the first time to expound the concept of Négritude which Césaire defined as 'the manner of self-expression of the black character, the black world, black civilisation', and 'the search for universal black values'.

Négritude grew out of the discrimination and alienation experienced by African and Caribbean students and others in Paris at this time. Their awareness of racism and cultural difference consequently led to a questioning of their dual identity as both Black and French, a rejection of assimilation, the idea of the inferiority of African culture and a growing concern with Africa and a uniquely Black history and culture. Senghor was often called upon by his Caribbean friends to relate his own experiences of growing up in Africa and his own knowledge of African history and culture. It was in these conditions that he first began to write poetry that celebrated Africaness and being Black in what was seen as a hostile and racist society. During the 1930s he at first used the expression Nègre Nouveau, a direct translation of the term used in the USA, to describe his literary orientation. In 1936 he first employed the term Négritude, which he later defined as 'the ensemble of black Africa's cultural values' and 'the whole of economic and political, intellectual and moral, artistic and social values of not only the peoples of Africa but also of the black minorities of America, and indeed Asia and Oceania'.

In 1935 Senghor became a teacher of literature and grammar at a secondary school in Tours and then at another school in the Paris suburbs. As a result of his friendship with the future president Georges Pompidou, Senghor was drawn towards the socialism espoused by the Popular Front government in France. He became an activist in the teachers' union and also taught at a 'workers college' established by the French trade union movement. At the same time he began to study linguistics and African ethnography and was especially influenced by the work of Leo Frobenius and Maurice Delafosse, who seemed to substantiate his developing views on the uniqueness of African culture. In this period his career was closely monitored by the French government and in 1937 he was invited to carry out a study of education in Senegal, to speak to a meeting of the Franco-Senegalese Friendship Society in Dakar and at the International Congress on the Evolution of Colonial Peoples in Paris. He was subsequently offered, but declined to accept, the post of Inspector General of Education in French West Africa.

In 1939 at the outbreak of the Second World War, Senghor joined the French army, serving with two colonial infantry regiments. However, he was soon captured by the German army and spent eighteen months as a prisoner of war. After his release in 1942 he worked for a time with the French resistance movement before returning to the teaching profession. Even as a prisoner of war Senghor had continued writing and published several poems and articles in 1943 in the bulletin *L'Etudiant de la France d'Outre-Mer: Chronique des Foyer*. In 1944 he was appointed Chair of African languages at the École Colonial, the college training colonial officials in Paris.

Following the 1944 Brazzaville Conference, which set out the future relationship between France and its African colonies, French colonial subjects were entitled to send representatives to a Constituent Assembly in Paris, that was to draft a new constitution. Senghor provoked the criticism of many Africans for accepting an appointment to the Monnerville Commission, which prepared a report on future colonial representation in the Constituent Assembly. In 1945 Senghor and the Senegalese politician Lamine Guèye formed the Bloc Africain, linked themselves with the French Socialist Party (SFIO) and were both subsequently elected as deputies to the first and second Constituent Assemblies. Senghor was subsequently appointed to several of the Assemblies' special commissions.

The elected African representatives were generally opposed to the new constitution which emerged from the Second Constituent Assembly in 1946 and they met at Bamako to form the Rassemblement Démocratique Africaine (RDA), a mass anti-colonial party based in all the French African colonies that had links with the French Communist Party. But the SFIO, by then part of the French government, argued that the Bamako meeting would be dominated by communists, and persuaded Senghor and Guèye not to attend. Senghor was continuously re-elected to the French National Assembly during the next few years, but he soon became dissatisfied with the politics of Guèye and the SFIO and criticised them and the Bloc Africain in his new journal, *Condition Humaine*. In 1948 he formed his own party, the Bloc Démocratique Sénégalais (BDS), and joined the Indépendents d'Outre-Mer (IOM), a group of African deputies in the French National Assembly who were independent of both the SFIO and the RDA.

In 1945 Senghor's first collection of poems *Chants d' Ombre*, dealing with the theme of exile, was published and he was soon being recognised as a significant literary figure. In Paris in 1947, alongside the Senegalese intellectual Alioune Diop, he helped establish the cultural journal *Présence Africaine*, which promoted African culture and history in opposition to French cultural imperialism and the colonialist notion of assimilation. In 1948 Senghor published his *Anthology of the New Black and Malagasy Poetry in the French Language*, which in itself attempted to demonstrate the literary unity of the Black world. The *Anthology* contained an introductory essay by the famous French philosopher Jean-Paul Sartre, in which he defined Négritude as 'anti-racist racism'. African critics of Négritude were often more severe, accusing Senghor of 'irrationality', a 'mystification' of the actual problems facing Africans, and attacking his notion of a 'Negro Soul' and the fact that his poetry was written in the French language. By the late 1940s Senghor was seen by many as a faithful servant of the French government. He was given government appointments to UNESCO and the Assembly of the Council of Europe and in 1950 was nominated as a member of the UN Trusteeship Council. During the mid-1950s he was actually appointed a member of the French government and was denounced by FRANTZ FANON and others when, like many other African deputies, he even supported France's colonial war in Algeria.

In the 1951 elections to the French National Assembly, Senghor's BDS won both seats and he became the leader of the IOM. In 1953 the IOM proposed the formation of an African federal republic within the existing French Union, as France's empire was then known. The following year Senghor proposed the creation of two federations in French West Africa, with capitals at Dakar and Abidjan in the Ivory Coast. Senghor's proposals were opposed by the RDA and in 1956 he formed the Bloc Progressif Sénégalais (BPS), a coalition of parties which formed the Senegalese section of the Convention Africaine, a new inter-territorial party established by the IOM and based throughout the French African colonies in rivalry with the RDA. In 1957 the Convention even allied with Lamine Guèye's Mouvement Socialist Africain. Senghor, who in 1956 had been elected Mayor of Thies in Senegal, was opposed to what he viewed as the 'balkanisation' of French West Africa and the provisions of the *loi cadre* of 1956, the new law that gave more autonomy to individual colonies in their relationship with France. Nevertheless in the 1957 elections the BPS won the majority of seats and formed the government of Senegal. In 1958 Senghor became one of the leaders of the inter-territorial Parti du Regroupement Africain (PRA), firmly committed to a federation of all French West African states and a strong relationship with France and in the same year he again united with Lamine Guèye to form the Senegalese section of the PRA, the Union Progressiste Sénegalaise.

Senghor remained reluctant to break Senegal's links with France and was one of those African leaders asked by the French government to make recommendations about the future status of the West African colonies. At the time of the subsequent referendum on independence, in September 1958, he successfully campaigned for a 'no' vote. In December 1958 he played a leading role when politicians from Senegal, Soudan, Dahomey and Upper Volta met to discuss the formation of a West African Federation. The Federation of Mali was established the following March, with Senghor its first president. However by September 1959 Dahomey and Upper Volta had withdrawn from the federation and it subsequently collapsed, in August 1960, after political differences emerged between Senegal and Soudan. Senghor eventually became President of an independent Senegal in January 1961.

As President of Senegal, Senghor espoused what he called the 'African Mode of Socialism', which he combined with his earlier beliefs in Négritude. According to Senghor 'Negro-African society' was 'traditionally socialist' and therefore the key task was to build on this African foundation, 'keep the fervour of the black soul alive' while adding scientific planning and technology. In 1962 Senegal hosted the Colloquium on Policies of Development and African Approaches to Socialism, held in Dakar. Senghor did introduce some economic planning but his period in office is most notably connected with Senegal's continued closeness to France and other Francophone countries, and his increasingly repressive and paternalistic style of government. From 1963–76 Senghor's ruling Parti Socialiste was de facto the only legal political party. In 1976 the constitution was changed to allow three, and subsequently four, recognised and officially designated parties, and in 1978 changed again so that Senghor could name his own successor when he announced his retirement from the presidency in 1980. In foreign affairs Senghor initially aligned Senegal with the other former French colonies in the Brazzaville bloc of twelve states and in 1968 was one of the champions of Francophonie, a grouping of twenty-six states linked together by cultural and technological cooperation.

In 1984 Senghor became the first African to become one of the forty living 'immortal' members of the Académie Française, France's highest honour given to those who have made an enduring contribution to the French culture and statecraft. Senghor died in France on 20 December 2001.

HA

Main publication

The Collected Poetry, translated and with an introduction by Melvin Dixon, London, University Press of Virginia, 1991.

Further reading

Hymans, L.H., *Léopold Sédar Senghor: An Intellectual Biography*, Edinburgh, Edinburgh University Press, 1971.

Vaillant, J.G., *Black French, and African: A Life of Léopold Sédar Senghor*, Cambridge, MA, Harvard University Press, 1990.

Ladipo Felix Solanke
(c. 1884 – 1958)

Ladipo Felix Solanke, Nigerian nationalist and founder of the West African Students' Union, was born in the Yoruba town of Abeokuta in southern Nigeria. Little is known of his early family life. He was the second son of Charles Robert Paley Solanke, a farmer, and his wife Adeyola Ejiwunmi. His early education was in Abeokuta, he then attended St Andrew's Teacher Training Institution at Oyo and from 1917 began teaching at Leopold Educational Institute in Freetown, Sierra Leone. He then studied law in that country at the famous Fourah Bay College, at that time the only university level college in Britain's four West African colonies. After completing his first degree in 1921, Solanke travelled to England in 1922 to complete his legal studies at University College, London, from 1923–7. He subsequently qualified as a barrister at law and while he was a student was temporarily employed as a teacher of the Yoruba language at London University's School of Oriental Studies (today the School of Oriental and African Studies).

Solanke's experiences of poverty and racism in London led him to join the existing Pan-African student organisation in Britain, the Union of Students of African Descent, and to campaign vigorously against various racist articles in the British press. He was then inspired to organise other Nigerian students in Britain. With the assistance of AMY ASHWOOD GARVEY (the estranged first wife of MARCUS GARVEY) he founded the Nigerian Progress Union (NPU) in 1924, the first Nigerian organisation in Britain's history. The NPU was founded 'to promote the general welfare of Nigerians from an educational not a political point of view', but under Solanke's leadership the NPU concerned itself with political matters not only in Nigeria but also throughout the diaspora, as is evident from Solanke's 'Open Letter to the Negroes of the World', published in the African American paper *The Spokesman* in 1925.

It was his concern with such political matters as well as the problem of racism in Britain that led Solanke to establish a wider pan-West African organisation in Britain. In 1925 he and Dr Herbert Bankole-Bright, an African member of the Legislative Council of Sierra Leone and a leading member of the National Congress of British West Africa founded the West African Students' Union (WASU). Solanke became the organisation's first secretary-general and under his leadership WASU became the main social, cultural and political focus for West Africans, and many other Africans, in Britain for the next 25 years. It served as a training ground for many future political leaders and played an important role in agitating for an end to colonial rule in West Africa. WASU had a variety of aims, but most importantly wished to 'foster a spirit of national consciousness and racial pride amongst its members'. Its creation owed much to the rising level of anti-colonial consciousness in West Africa as well as the need to organise against racism and the colour bar in Britain.

Solanke became one of the main propagandists of WASU and a prolific writer on West African and especially Nigerian affairs. In 1927 he published *United West Africa at the Bar of the Family of Nations*, a demand for the recognition of equal political rights for Africans. Throughout his life he wrote many letters and articles demanding increasing self-government for Britain's West African colonies and for Nigeria in particular, and several essays on traditional Yoruba institutions and culture. Many of these appeared in the *Wasu*, the aptly named WASU journal. Solanke was the first person to make a radio broadcast for the BBC in the Yoruba language in the 1920s and he also made several of the first musical recordings in that language in the same decade.

In 1928, Solanke became acquainted with Marcus Garvey and was able to negotiate the use of Garvey's house as the WASU headquarters. Thereafter Solanke was at the forefront of attempts by WASU to establish a hostel for West Africans in London, not just as a 'home from home' and to solve the problem of discrimination, and also to prove that Africans could organise themselves on the basis of self-help and self-reliance. Between 1929–32 he embarked on a fund-raising tour of West Africa which provided at least some of the necessary funds for Africa House, the name given to the WASU hostel, the first such facility established by Africans in London. When Africa House was opened in Camden, London, in 1933, Solanke became its first warden. He and his wife continued to run the WASU hostel until the late-1940s when the organisation opened its third London hostel. While he was in West Africa, Solanke used the opportunity to consult both with traditional rulers and the new political elite and established over 20 branches of the WASU throughout the four colonies and in the Belgian Congo. These WASU branches later provided the nucleus for the anti-colonial youth movements in the Gold Coast and Nigeria, such as the Gold Coast Youth Conference and Nigerian Youth Movement, and helped to stimulate political activity throughout the region.

Solanke's activities on behalf of WASU and anti-colonial activity in West Africa often brought him into conflict with the Colonial Office and sometimes with other Black leaders and activists in Britain such as Dr HAROLD MOODY, the founder of the influential League of Coloured Peoples. These conflicts were particularly acute during the early-1930s when Moody became involved with the plans of the Colonial Office to open their own student hostel in London. Aggrey House, as it was known, was viewed by Solanke and WASU as an attempt by the Colonial Office to monitor Africans' anti-colonial activities and was vigorously condemned. In the course of these protests, Solanke, as the main leader of WASU, steered the Union into alliances with a variety of organisations including the communist-led League Against Imperialism and the National Council for Civil Liberties. During the Second World War, Solanke established closer relations between WASU and several leading members of the Fabian Colonial Bureau, including Arthur Creech Jones, the future Labour Party Colonial Secretary. As a direct result of these links, WASU established its own West African Parliamentary Committee that included five Labour Party members of parliament and enabled it to act as a more effective parliamentary pressure group channelling demands from a variety of individuals and organisations in West Africa.

Solanke was instrumental in developing WASU not just as a students' union and anti-colonial pressure group, but also as a bureau of information and a lobbying organisation for a variety of interests in Britain's four West African colonies. Under his leadership during the early-1940s the Union was in the vanguard of those demanding colonial reforms and 'Dominion Status' for the West African colonies and in 1942 was one of the first West African organisations to demand self-government in West Africa and attempt to put pressure not only on the British government but also on anti-colonial organisations in West Africa to advance and support this demand.

In 1944 Solanke began a second fund-raising tour of West Africa as part of plans to establish a new WASU hostel. It was during this visit that he was made a chief and given the title Atobatele of Ijeun (a district of Abeokuta). By the time that Solanke returned four years later, the WASU had become much more radical politically. He found that his brand of nationalist politics was considered old-fashioned and that there were attempts by new members and their supporters to remove him from his former position of power. He was replaced as warden of the new hostel, and although for some years in the early-1950s he managed to maintain one of the old hostels and to establish a rival WASU Unincorporated, he was effectively marginalised from influence and power in the organisation he had founded. Chief Ladipo Solanke died from cancer in London in 1958.

HA

Main publication

United West Africa (or Africa) at the Bar of the Family of Nations, 1927, republished by African Publication Society, London, 1969.

Further reading

Adi, Hakim, *West Africans in Britain 1900–1960 – Nationalism, Pan-Africanism and Communism*, London, Lawrence and Wishart, 1998.
Olusanya, Gabriel O., *The West African Students Union and the Politics of Decolonisation, 1925–1958*, Ibadan, Daystar, 1982.

Sékou Ahmed Touré
(1922 – 84)

Sékou Ahmed Touré, trade union leader, Pan-Africanist and first President of the Republic of Guinea, was born on 9 January 1922 in Farannah, near the source of the River Niger in what was then Afrique Occidental Française (French West Africa).

Sékou Touré was born into a family of poor peasant farmers but traced his ancestry from Samori, the great African leader who had carved out two empires and fought against the French in the western Sudan in the nineteenth century. He was educated at a local Koranic school and then at Kissidougou. In 1936 he went to the Ecole Georges Poiret in Conakry, but was expelled the following year for organising a student food strike. In the next two years he undertook a variety of jobs in order to pay for his continuing education, which he obtained mainly through correspondence courses.

In 1940 he began working for the Compagnie du Niger Français and then in 1941 passed an examination that allowed him to join the Post and Telecommunications Department. In 1945 he formed the first trade union in French Guinea, the Post and Telecommunications Workers' Union, and he became its general-secretary in 1946. In the same year he also helped to form the country's first trade union centre, the Federation of Workers' Unions of Guinea, and became its first general-secretary. This trade union centre was closely linked with the French Confédération Générale des Travailleurs (CGT), at that time associated with the communist movement in France and the World Federation of Trade Unions, and in March 1946 Touré attended the CGT congress in Paris. In the same year he was employed by the Treasury Department and was elected general-secretary of the Treasury Employees' Union. In 1946 he also became a founder member of the Rassemblement Démocratique Africain (RDA), the anti-colonial movement formed in Bamako in October of that year, which included representatives from all of France's West African colonies.

Sékou Touré lost his job in the Treasury Department because of his political activities and in 1947 was briefly imprisoned by the colonial authorities. Thereafter he was able to devote his time to the workers' movement and the struggle for independence from French colonial rule. In an interview he explained that:

> Trade Unionism is a faith, a calling, an engagement to transform fundamentally any given economic and social regime, always in the search for the beautiful and the just. To the degree that trade unionism is an apostleship, a choice, an engagement, it implies action against that which is contrary to the interests of the workers.

In 1948 he became secretary-general of the Coordinating Committee of the CGT in French West Africa and Togo, and in 1952 secretary-general of the Parti Démocratique de Guinée (PDG), the regional branch of the RDA which had soon developed a mass character based on the workers' movement. In 1953 he led a general strike which was openly anti-colonial in character, and managed to successfully utilise the strengths of the trade union movement for political goals, at the same time encouraging the unity of all African workers in opposition to 'tribalism' and any division between rural and urban workers. Trade union membership in Guinea increased rapidly, from 4,000 in 1953 to over 55,000 two years later. As a consequence Sékou Touré and other leaders in Guinea became famous throughout French West Africa. In 1953 he was elected to the territorial assembly but in 1954 he lost in the election to the French National Assembly in Paris, after open vote-rigging by the colonial administration. In the same year he became a member of the Coordinating Committee of the RDA, in 1955 he became Mayor of Conakry and in January 1956 he was finally elected the deputy for Guinea to the French National Assembly in Paris.

But Touré also became dissatisfied with the links between Guinea's trade unions and the communist-led CGT. In 1956 he formed the Confédération Générale de Travail Africaine (CGTA) and broke with the CGT and the World Federation of Trade Unions, although the following year there was a rapprochement between the CGT and the CGTA, which created the Union Générale des Travailleurs d'Afrique Noire (UGTAN) with Sékou Touré as its first secretary-general and later president. The formation of the UGTAN which aimed to unite and organise the workers of Black Africa to 'coordinate their trade union activities in the struggle against the colonial regime and all other forms of exploitation ... and to affirm the personality of African trade unionism' has been seen as a symbol of the growing demand for independence from France as well as a significant pan-African movement in its own right.

In 1956 the French authorities enacted the *loi cadre* that established universal suffrage and internal autonomy in French West Africa, and created an Executive Council in each territory with an elected vice-president. In the elections of March 1957 Sékou Touré was elected Vice-President of Guinea and entitled to form a government under the overall control of the French Governor. He began a programme of Africanisation and industrialisation, and limited the power of the chiefs by establishing village councils and peasant cooperatives.

In 1957 he became a member of the Grand Council of French West Africa, but as he appeared willing to cooperate with France many more radical nationalists began to criticise him for not demanding independence. In 1957 he was elected Vice-President of the RDA and began to advocate that France's African colonies should form a federation through which they could determine their future relationship with France, rather than establishing a relationship as individual states. However, in the next few years when the colonies were offered either a limited autonomy within a new 'French Community' or complete independence from France, Sékou Touré, unlike most other leaders, called for complete independence. Before the referendum in September 1958 he stated, 'We prefer poverty in freedom to riches in slavery', and was subsequently expelled from the RDA. However, the people of Guinea voted overwhelmingly for independence and the country became a republic in October 1958 with Sékou Touré as its first President.

The French abruptly pulled out of Guinea taking with them capital, equipment and many skilled personnel, and for many years afterwards the two countries had no formal links. But Sékou Touré was able to gain economic support from newly independent Ghana and from the Soviet Union, which both offered loans, as well as from many eastern European countries, the USA and China. Touré also began to develop a neutral non-aligned foreign policy and established close relations with China, the Soviet Union and many eastern European countries as well as with the USA, West Germany and other 'Western' countries. However, in 1961 his government expelled the Soviet ambassador from Guinea following unrest in the country in which several countries appeared to be implicated. He publicly stated that Guinea would accept support from any country but 'refuses to be drawn into choosing sides in a power struggle between two blocs'.

Like Ghana's KWAME NKRUMAH, he also had Pan-African aims and in December 1958 established an agreement to form a union between Guinea and Ghana. Touré saw this agreement as developing a unity that would be translated 'into a common co-operation and action in all fields to realise rapidly a United States of Africa'. In May 1959 the two leaders signed the Conakry Declaration opening the union to all African countries. Sudan and Senegal briefly joined and in 1960 Mali too and there were plans for further economic and political cooperation in the future. It was stated that the main objective was 'to help our African brothers subjected to domination with a view to ending their state of dependence, widening and consolidating with them a Union of Independent African states'. In 1959 Nkrumah, Touré and President William Tubman of Liberia signed the Sanniquellie Declaration setting out principles for a proposed 'Community of Independent African States', but in the next few years disagreement broke out between African leaders about how Pan-African unity might be achieved. In 1961 Touré attended the Summit Conference in Casablanca and became associated with the 'Casablanca bloc' of states, Ghana, Mali, Morocco, the UAR, Algeria and Libya, which was seen, despite its diverse membership, as the more radical grouping and was opposed by the more moderate 'Monrovia bloc'. Sékou Touré made several efforts to establish unity between the two blocs and met with several other African leaders during 1962. His efforts along with those of others led to the historic meeting in Addis Ababa in 1963 that founded the Organisation of African Unity.

Touré was also a staunch supporter of PATRICE LUMUMBA during the crisis in the Congo. In a speech to the UN General Assembly in 1960 he bitterly attacked the UN and its Secretary-General for their policies towards the Congo and encouraged Lumumba to call for the assistance of the 'socialist camp' to forcibly end Katanga's secession. He was also a close friend and supporter of Nkrumah and welcomed him to Guinea, where he remained until his death, when he was forced into exile following the coup in Ghana in 1966.

Within Guinea, Sékou Touré initially attempted to develop what he termed a 'communaucratie', an economic and political system that necessitated a large degree of central government control, exercised by a single party, the PDG, and even involving the use of forced labour. But following French withdrawal, economic development in Guinea was slow and there was some relaxation of state control in the early-1960s and rapprochement with France in the 1970s. However, Guinea was increasingly seen as an impoverished, repressive and corrupt one-party state, with many of its population living in exile. Sékou Touré came to be seen as an authoritarian leader and his regime responsible for large-scale arrests and even the execution of those who opposed government policies. Even in the realm of foreign policy his earlier radical Pan-Africanism gave way to alliances with some of Africa's most reactionary leaders and he later became known as a 'moderate' Islamic leader, even championing the claims of Morocco and King Hassan over the Western Saharan Sahrawi Arab Democratic Republic.

By the early-1980s Sékou Touré set out to attract 'Western' and Arab capital investment in Guinea, as a means to exploit the country's rich resources of bauxite, diamonds, iron and oil. In 1982 he visited the USA in order to encourage business support and in the same year led the delegation sent by the Islamic Conference Organisation to attempt to mediate in the Iran–Iraq war. In 1984 he played a significant role in securing Egypt's re-admission to the Islamic Conference and was still seen as a leading African statesman at the time of his death.

Sékou Touré, one of the longest serving African political leaders, died of heart failure in an American hospital on 26 March 1984 from where his body was returned to Conakry for burial.

HA

Further reading

Jackson, R., and C. Rosberg, *Personal Rule in Black Africa*, Berkeley, University of California Press, 1982.

Segal, R., *African Profiles*, Harmondsworth, Penguin, 1962.

I.T.A. Wallace-Johnson
(1894 – 1965)

Isaac Theophilus Akunna Wallace-Johnson, Pan-Africanist, trade union leader, politician and journalist, was born on 6 February at Wilberforce Village, Freetown in Sierra Leone, at that time a British colony. He was born into a poor Krio family, the descendants of nineteenth-century liberated African slaves and Maroons; his father was a farmer and his mother a market trader; and he was educated locally at the Centenary Tabernacle School and the United Methodist Collegiate School in Freetown. After leaving school he was variously employed until in 1913 he joined the Sierra Leone customs department. He soon became a workers' leader and in 1914 helped to organise a strike for better conditions and higher wages, for which he was dismissed from his post. He was later reinstated, began his career as a journalist and during the First World War worked as a clerk in the British army. He was then stationed in various parts of Africa until being demobilised in 1920. He was again employed in a variety of jobs until he became a seaman, travelled to ports throughout Africa and became a member of the British National Seamen's Union. According to his own account it was during this period that he first came into contact with communism and the British Communist Party, and he may possibly have been a distributor of communist literature amongst seamen. In 1929 he was working as a clerk in the Gold Coast and made some journalistic contributions to the *Daily Times* of Lagos.

In 1930 he moved to Nigeria and, with Frank Macaulay, established the African Workers' Union, one of the first Nigerian labour organisations. In the same year he attended the founding meeting of the International Trade Union Committee of Negro Workers (ITUCNW), held under the auspices of the Red International of Labour Unions or Profintern in Hamburg, Germany, as the representative of the Sierra Leone Railway Workers' Union. He was subsequently elected to serve on the presidium of the ITUCNW and became a member of the editorial board of its publication *Negro Worker*. In 1931 he visited Moscow, attended the International Labour Defence Congress and for some 18 months was a student at the University of the Toilers of the East in the Soviet Union.

In 1933 Wallace-Johnson returned to West Africa and worked as editor of the conservative *Nigerian Daily Telegraph*. When he was deported from Nigeria for his anti-colonial political activities he went to the Gold Coast and continued his work as a political activist, union organiser and journalist, writing for the *Gold Coast Spectator* and other publications. In 1935 he helped establish the Gold Coast section of the West African Youth League, which spread Marxist and anti-imperialist ideas through its many branches and agitated against colonial rule. Wallace-Johnson's intention was to establish an organisation throughout West Africa including the French and Portuguese colonies. During this period he had also established links with communist-led organisations in Britain, including the Negro Welfare Association (NWA) and the League Against Imperialism (LAI), and through them was able to bring political grievances to the attention of anti-colonial activists in Britain and even before Parliament. He also agitated to gain support for the African American defendants in the famous Scottsboro case in the USA during the 1930s and for Ethiopia's rights following the Italian invasion in 1935. He supported protests against repressive colonial legislation in the Gold Coast and throughout West Africa in this period and was referred to by the Gold Coast Attorney-General as a 'most dangerous agitator and demagogue'.

In 1936 he was arrested for sedition following the publication of a famous article in Nnamdi Azikiwe's *African Morning Post* entitled 'Has the African a God', that attacked European imperialism and its so-called 'civilising mission'. After being fined £50, Wallace-Johnson travelled to Britain to appeal before the court of the Privy Council and to seek the opportunity to further the aims of the WAYL through contacts in London and in Paris. In Britain he helped to found and became the general-secretary of the Pan-Africanist International African Service Bureau (IASB), the organisation which in 1937 grew out of the International African Friends of Abyssinia founded by GEORGE PADMORE and others in 1935. During this period in Britain he played a leading role in establishing and editing two publications connected with the IASB. The earliest, 'a news bulletin', was known as *Africa and the World* but in the autumn of 1937 the *African Sentinel* was also published as 'a journal devoted to the interest of Africans and peoples of African descent, all over the world', and several editions were published until Wallace-Johnson's return to Sierra Leone in 1938. While he was in Britain Wallace-Johnson maintained his links with the NWA and the LAI but his other links with organised communism are unclear, and he later claimed that he broke his ties with the British Communist Party in 1938.

In that year Wallace-Johnson returned to Sierra Leone and established the West African Civil Liberties and National Defence League and the Sierra Leone section of the West African Youth League (WAYL). He became the secretary-general of the WAYL and the editor of its paper, the *African Standard*. He challenged the existing and more conservative political leaders in Sierra Leone and roused mass support for the WAYL's four candidates, who in 1938 were all elected to Freetown City Council. The WAYL was one of the first mass political organisations in West Africa and aimed at economic and political reform but not the end of colonial rule. Even so, Wallace-Johnson's political activities, especially the organisation of trade unions in Sierra Leone, were viewed with alarm by the colonial authorities. He helped organise eight unions and when in 1939 two of those unions affiliated to the WAYL went on strike, colonial officials decided to act. In the same year the *African Standard* was implicated in inciting mutiny amongst African soldiers and police, and the colonial government passed no fewer than six Bills on 'sedition, undesirable literature and trade union activity' to counter Wallace-Johnson's activities and influence. Later that year he was arrested and charged with criminal libel for a publication in the *African Standard* that alleged that an African had died while being flogged on the orders of the colonial District Commissioner. As a consequence of this arrest and his other political activities, Wallace-Johnson was detained under the emergency Colonial Defence Regulations during the Second World War. He was initially held at an internment camp for 'enemy aliens', and then placed in solitary confinement until being interned on Sherbro Island in Sierra Leone until 1944. Even Wallace-Johnson's wedding to Edith Downes in 1942 was initially banned by order of the Governor of Sierra Leone. It was while he was imprisoned that he wrote *Prison in the Muse*, a series of poems criticising prison conditions, which later led to an official investigation and some eventual improvements.

In 1945 Wallace-Johnson went to London to represent the Sierra Leone TUC at the founding conference of the World Federation of Trade Unions (WFTU). During the conference Wallace-Johnson emerged as one of the leading personalities. He spoke out against imperialism, proposed a 'Charter of Labour for the Colonies', on behalf of all the colonial delegates, and demanded self-determination for all colonies. At the Paris Congress of the WFTU he was elected to the organisation's executive committee. Returning to London, he was one of the main speakers at the second Subject Peoples Conference held in London in October 1945 and again reiterated the fighting unity of the colonial peoples and their demand for self-determination. 'This unity among the coloured races the vast majority of whom are workers and peasants', he told the conference, 'may yet lay the foundation for the wider unity among all workers and the exploited and oppressed'. In 1944 the WAYL had been one of the founding organisations of the Pan-African Federation, the coalition of organisations that convened the historic Manchester Pan-African Congress. Wallace-Johnson played a leading role in the organisation of the 1945 Congress and was elected chairman of its resolutions committee. Following the Congress, with KWAME NKRUMAH, he was one of the main organisers of the London-based West African National Secretariat (WANS) and was elected its first chairman. The anti-imperialist WANS acted as a coordinating and information bureau and aimed to build West African unity in order to realise 'United West African National Independence'. Whilst he was in London, Wallace-Johnson was also a regular contributor to the Independent Labour Party's *The New Leader* and spoke at several meetings organised by the PAF and other organisations.

When Wallace-Johnson returned to Sierra Leone in the late-1940s he remained active in politics and political journalism. However, he found that his political aims and orientation were soon overtaken by those, such as the Sierra Leone People's Party, that demanded independence and had a wider popular base throughout Sierra Leone. In 1951 he became a leading member of the National Council of the Colony of Sierra Leone (NCCSL), an amalgamation of several political organisations including the WAYL, but led by H.E. Bankole-Bright, a conservative member of the Krio elite, and a former opponent of Wallace-Johnson. In that same year Wallace-Johnson was elected a member of the colony's Legislative Council and became an active member of the opposition to the Sierra Leone People's Party. In 1952 he left the NCCSL but remained a member of the Legislative Council.

In 1954 Wallace-Johnson became one of the founders of the United Progressive Party (UPP) and, following a growth of popular support, he was re-elected to the House of Representatives. In 1957 he was expelled from the UPP and then founded the Radical Democratic Party. In 1960 he was one of the delegates to the London talks for Sierra Leone's independence. When the All Peoples Congress (APC) was founded in 1960, demanding an election before independence and in opposition to the United National Front of Milton Margai, Wallace-Johnson was one of its first MPs. Following violence between the two rival political organisations in 1961 on the eve of independence, Wallace-Johnson was arrested and detained along with Siaka Stevens the leader of the Congress and thirteen other APC leaders. From that time on, although recognised as an elder statesman, he took little part in active politics. He died in a car accident in Ghana on 10 May 1965 while attending the Afro-Asian Solidarity Conference. More than 40,000 people filed past the body before his state funeral in Freetown, Sierra Leone on 16 May 1965.

HA

Further reading

Spitzer, L. and La Ray Denzer, 'I.T.A. Wallace-Johnson and the West African Youth League', *International Journal of African Historical Studies*, VI, 3, pp.413–52 and VI, 4, pp.565–601, 1973.

Eric Williams
(1911 – 81)

Eric Williams, who took the Caribbean colonies of Trinidad and Tobago into independence, had a life-long interest in the unification of the whole Caribbean area. Much of his historical writing also encompassed the whole area, which is probably still a unique approach. His major contribution to pan-Africanist history is his seminal, path-breaking economic analysis of slavery and its abolition. He also sought to establish links with Africa and was the first Caribbean leader to hold discussions with African leaders on issues of mutual concern.

Williams, the son of a Roman Catholic post office worker in Port-of-Spain, was supported by government scholarships throughout his high school education at the colony of Trinidad's elite Queen's Royal College, where he was a pupil of C.L.R. JAMES. As there were virtually no other opportunities for a high school educated Black person in the colony where all white collar work of the middle rank and above was reserved for Whites, Williams worked as a teacher and studied to take the Island Scholarship examination which would enable him to study at a university in Britain. In 1932, having won a Scholarship, he left for Oxford.

James had arrived in Britain in the same year and the two men renewed their acquaintance. Probably through James Williams soon met the Pan-Africanists with whom James was involved – men like PADMORE, MAKONNEN, and Kenyatta. However, the available evidence does not indicate a close relationship.

Williams obtained a Double First in Modern History for his first degree. He was awarded the PhD degree for his dissertation on 'The Economic Aspect of the Abolition of the British West Indian Slave Trade and Slavery'. The work, a strikingly original study, was based on suggestions of James, who had been researching French imperialism for his book *The Black Jacobins*. Williams refuted the claims of contemporary historians that it was due to pressure from philanthropists that Britain ended its involvement in the trade in enslaved Africans and emancipated her slaves in the Caribbean. It was 'mature industrial capitalism that destroy[ed] the slave system', he argued. Furthermore, he demonstrated that 'Negro slavery and the slave trade provid[ed] the capital which financed the Industrial Revolution in England'. The PhD was published as *Capitalism and Slavery*, in the USA in 1944, but not in Britain until 1964! It is still the source of detailed controversy.

While in Britain Williams married Trinidadian Elsie Riberio; they had two children, but the marriage ended in divorce. His second wife was his secretary Joyce Mayou;

the couple had one daughter. This marriage also ended in divorce; his third wife was Dr Mayleen Mook Sang of Guyana.

Probably because Oxford was unwilling to offer him a position, Williams accepted an invitation to teach social and political science at Howard University, Washington DC. The following year, 1940, he was awarded a Julius Rosenwald Fellowship to study social and economic conditions in the non-Anglophone West Indies. This resulted in *The Negro in the Caribbean,* uniquely encompassing the whole area, published in the USA in 1942. Describing it in his foreword as a 'brilliantly written book', Padmore published it in London in 1945, carefully noting that Williams had 'never been a member of the International African Service Bureau, and does not necessarily endorse its aims and objects'. The booklet, an economic history, concluded that the Caribbean lies under the 'government of sugar, for sugar, by sugar'; mono-culture and the lack of industrialisation resulted in poverty throughout the area, which was 'geographically and economically an American lake' (p.65).

The Anglo-American Caribbean Commission (AACC) was set up under joint US/UK auspices to 'maintain stability in the Caribbean' during the Second World War (and, some would argue, to increase US influence in the region), which the USA especially felt was necessary for its own safety. After some expression of dismay that there were no West Indian members, in 1945 the AACC appointed Williams as Secretary of its Washington-based Caribbean Research Council. By 1948 he was deputy-chair of the Council and had moved to Port-of-Spain.

From many perspectives the Trinidad to which Williams returned was different from the colony he had left. There had been violent trade union upheavals in 1937, which resulted in some amelioration of conditions, and an increase in nationalist activity. Britain and the USA had signed the Lend Lease Agreement at the beginning of the Second World War, which exchanged forty mothballed US naval vessels for ninety-nine-year leases on territory in a number of Caribbean islands, but particularly Trinidad, on which the Americans built military/naval bases. West Indians had not been consulted. This brought US dollars into the economy and, at least for a period, relatively well-paid employment for many. 'Small-islanders' rushed to Trinidad to participate in the bonanza. The culture of the USA began to replace that of the UK. In 1946 the UK had granted the franchise to all adults over twenty-one; more political parties were formed. However, except for a few educated elite and the organised sugar workers, the descendants of the indentured labourers from India, who formed roughly half the population, continued to live in the rural areas and did not participate in urban politics.

Back in his home town, Williams began to make contacts with the local intellectuals and to lecture in public at what came to be known as the University of Woodford Square. (Woodford is the main square in central Port-of-Spain.) This was a unique experiment in public education, where Williams addressed historical and contemporary issues in a language understandable by even the uneducated. His aim was to educate people so that the demand for independence would not only become more politically practicable, but also free people's minds from the effects of colonialism.

When the AACC decided to disband in 1955, Williams was ready to enter the political arena. Based on the Teachers' Economic and Cultural Association Limited he formed the People's National Movement (PNM) in 1956. (The teachers remained amongst Williams' main supporters.) The PNM issued a 'People's Charter', which stated that it stood for 'a comprehensive social security programme for the general welfare of all the people of Trinidad and Tobago'. The PNM's aims included immediate self-government in internal affairs; a 'British Caribbean Federation with Dominion Status in not more than five years'; international standards for all workers and the reorganisation of the economy to make the fullest use of the resources of the islands. Unexpectedly, the PNM won the elections, making Williams the first Chief Minister; a step towards independence. By 1959 Williams had achieved internal self-government.

Concerned with the fragmentation, underdevelopment, external domination and lack of cohesion of the Caribbean, Williams was a natural proponent of the Federation of the (Anglophone) West Indies, which came into being in 1958. But he soon came to view the Federation as weak and inimical as it concentrated almost exclusively on administration. He also felt that the Federation was not backing his demand for compensation from the USA for the free use for twenty years of the territory at Chaguaramas, and for their immediate withdrawal of the US military from Trinidad. While the reasons for the breakup of the Federation are disputed, it would appear that Williams' proposals for a federal centre which was more powerful than its constituent members led to distrust and the withdrawal of Jamaica in 1961. This broke up the Federation, and Williams now turned his attention to demanding independence for Trinidad and Tobago alone, which was granted in1962.

Though with no experience of government, management, or of political parties, Williams attracted considerable support among political activists and among the people. His achievements include the provision of free primary education to most children. He also obtained substantial US funding, as part-payment for the use of Chaguaramas, for the College of Arts and Science at the St Augustine (Trinidad) campus of the University of the West Indies. He attracted foreign investment to develop the oil industry. Political parties and the free expression of various political perspectives was allowed. However, the economic power structure remained unchanged: the economy remained mainly in the hands of Whites. Long-urbanised and generally better educated (than Indo-Trinidadians) Afro-Trinidadians replaced Whites in professions and the upper levels of the civil service.

However, Williams neither allowed democracy to flourish within the party he ruled so strongly (if not dictatorially), nor did he prevent corruption or ethnic nationalism taking a hold. Little attempt was made to engage the long-established trade unions or their leaders. The rise of the Black Power movement, coupled with increasing poverty and the propagation of leftist philosophies resulted in a Black Power uprising in 1970. Resorting to a mixture of repression and conciliation, and subsequently aided by the oil boom, Williams was able to improve the education and road systems and spend money on welfare and public utilities. Living standards rose; patronage and corruption increased.

Soon after the achievement of independence, Williams began to reach out to the non-English-speaking Caribbean, hoping to create an inter-Caribbean transport system. He also planned and launched the Caribbean Free Trade Area for the Anglophone countries in 1967, which six years later became CARICOM, the Caribbean Economic Community. Meanwhile, though opposed to Castro's communist policies, he headed the movement to reinstate Cuba to the Organisation of American States, and established diplomatic relations with that state in 1973.

By his own account, due to his interest in the African states' thirty-four votes at the United Nations, Williams undertook a tour to East, West and North Africa in 1964. He thus became the first West Indian premier to forge links with Africa. He met with the leaders of eleven countries, discussed common problems in developing countries and negotiated for Caribbean representation at the headquarters of the OAU, which he visited. While in Addis Ababa he was given an audience by Emperor Haile Selassie, who agreed to visit Trinidad the following year. In Kenya the government asked him 'for assistance with stenographers, secondary school teachers, lawyers for the Ministry of Justice, doctors of medicine [and for places] for Kenyan students at the College of Agriculture of the University of the West Indies'. (*Inward Hunger*, p.292) In Sierra Leone, as no elected African head of state had ever visited the Caribbean, he invited Premier Sir Milton Margai to be the first. He also announced that Sierra Leone and Trinidad would adopt a joint policy at the forthcoming World Trade Conference. He obtained promises from all the West African premiers to establish diplomatic relations: a Jamaican embassy for West Africa would be sited in Lagos. A Trinidad embassy for East Africa, based in Addis Ababa, would represent Trinidad, Jamaica and Barbados. Williams pledged Trinidad's support at the forthcoming Commonwealth Prime Ministers' Conference to the proposal that Britain should withhold independence from Southern Rhodesia until a democratic constitution was established there.

He spoke at many universities during his tour, 'interpreting West Indians and the West Indies to my African audiences', and also addressing the issue of intellectual decolonisation. He also proposed the establishment of Afro-Caribbean studies and the 'special study of the slave trade relating to African depopulation and the population of the Caribbean', and on the influence these slaves exercised in the Caribbean and Brazil. At the University of Addis Ababa Williams lectured on the role of African universities in the development of African unity, and urged that the OAU should set up a 'committee for academic co-ordination and exchange'. He praised Ghana's efforts in producing text books on African history, which 'will aid the move from colonial status to nationhood'. (*West Africa*, 7/3, 1964; 11/4, 1964; 16/5, 1964)

On his way home Williams stopped to speak at two Canadian universities and then at Howard in Washington DC, where he again addressed the issues of intellectual decolonisation and the part African studies were playing in this field.

Williams never gave up scholarship, which, he said, is a 'sheer necessity in the gross materialism induced by the previous history of colonialism, to seek distraction from the day to day pressures, if only to maintain [my] sanity'. (*British Historians*, p.v) While working for the AACC, he had drafted what became the *History of the People of Trinidad and Tobago* (1962). He had also begun collecting documents for a planned five-volume documentary history of the Caribbean, but pressure of work reduced it to one only, *1492–1655: From Spanish Discovery to the British Conquest of Jamaica* (1963). The following year saw the publication of his *British Historians and the West Indies*, which sought to 'emancipate his compatriots whom historical writings … sought to depreciate and to imprison for all time in the inferior status to which these writings sought to condemn them' (p.iv). Thus Williams sought a more peaceful route to that advocated by FRANTZ FANON to escape from what both saw as the devastating effects of a 'colonised mentality'. Williams' autobiography, *Inward Hunger*, was published in 1969 and his final book, *From Columbus to Castro: the History of the Caribbean 1492–1969*, in 1970. He also published articles in learned and more popular journals, as well as a number of pamphlets.

Eric Williams died during his fifth term of office as Prime Minister on 29 March 1981.

MS

Further reading

Eric Williams: Images of his Life, a special edition of *Caribbean Issues*, March 1998.
Boodhoo, Ken I. (ed.), *Eric Williams: The Man and the Leader*, Lanham, University Press of America, 1986.

Henry Sylvester Williams
(1869 – 1911)

Henry Sylvester Williams convened the first Pan-African Conference in July 1900 in London. It was the first international gathering of people of African origins and descent and established the phrase and the notion of Pan-Africanism.

Williams was the first son of immigrant parents from Barbados settled in Trinidad. His father Henry was a wheelwright, and thus as a tradesman one of the 'respectable' lower middle class. But as a Black man Williams would have lived a segregated life in the British colony which was completely under British and local planter domination. Young Henry attended the Arouca government primary school and qualified as a teacher at Tranquillity Normal School. This meant little more than having his elementary school certificate and minimal additional training in the 'basics'.

Williams taught in country schools around Trinidad until 1890 when he left for the USA to gain qualifications unobtainable in Trinidad, where even high school education was the preserve of the rich. How he got to the USA (it would have been impossible to save the passage money from his meagre wages) is unknown. Equally unknown are his places of sojourn and activities in North America. The only concrete information is that he studied law at Dalhousie University in Halifax, Nova Scotia for the academic year 1893–4. At that time there were no entrance qualifications for Dalhousie. We have to surmise that he participated in some of the many political meetings taking place at this time in the USA – meetings to protest lynchings, to advocate unity and various forms of action in the face of the retrenchment of the promises of Reconstruction.

Arriving in London in 1896, Williams enrolled at King's College as an evening student taking Latin. The following year he was admitted to Gray's Inn to prepare for legal qualifications. As the entrance examinations for Gray's Inn included Latin, again we have to surmise that he might have taken some college courses which included Latin while in the USA.

Williams earned his living as an official lecturer for the Temperance Society. In 1898 he married Agnes, daughter of Capt. Francis Powell of Gillingham, Kent, despite the captain's objections to his colour. The couple were to have five children.

Williams lectured on colonial issues on many platforms around Britain and in Ireland. He was, for example, one of the hundred or so lecturers speaking at the series on 'Empire' sponsored by the South Place Ethical Society in 1895–8. There he criticised Britain's administration of Trinidad and asked for representative government, free and compulsory education and higher wages. In 1899 he succeeded through contacts among the Liberals in London in addressing a meeting at the House of Commons, where he again appealed for representative government for Trinidad.

After contacting Black people – apparently mainly university students – around the country, in 1898 Williams founded the African Association, whose membership was restricted to those of African descent. Others could become associate members. The Association immediately set about organising public meetings, which all criticised British policies towards the 'natives' in various parts of the Empire. A 'Memorial on the Distress in the West Indies' was despatched to the Secretary of State for the Colonies, advocating changes in the land tenure system and the raising of the standard of education, and criticising the agricultural monopolies which impoverished the small farmers. This was soon followed by another Memorandum on the proposed constitution for the new colony of Rhodesia: the Association asked the government to 'safeguard the vital interests, customary laws and welfare of her Majesty's native subjects …'.

The Association also planned on calling a Pan-African Conference. Among those who supported the idea of a conference were Booker T. Washington, president of the Tuskegee College, USA; Professor W.S. Scarborough, president of Wilberforce University, USA and Judge David Straker of Detroit, who was of Barbados origins; the Rev. Majola Agbebi, founder of the first independent church in West Africa and the nationalist Bishop James Johnson of Nigeria; Bishop James Holly of Haiti, an African American who advocated emigration from the USA to Haiti; and Dadabhai Naoroji, Indian-born Liberal MP, who became one of the financial supporters of the Conference. Williams would have met the two African churchmen during their stay in the UK; the African Association had presented Bishop Johnson with an engraved memorial on his departure just before the Conference. We have to presume that while all Black men would have heard of Booker T. Washington, Williams might have met Scarborough and Straker, both politically active, during his years in the USA.

The aims of the Conference were:

> to bring into closer touch with each other the Peoples of African descent throughout the world; to inaugurate plans to bring about more friendly relations between Caucasian and African races; to start a movement to secure to all African races living in civilized countries their full rights and to promote their business interests.

Attended by representatives from Africa, the Caribbean, the USA and by Black people residing in Britain, the issues discussed ranged broadly: the lack of equal rights in the USA and in the British colonies, where, for example, trade unions were forbidden and the franchise, if it existed at all, was grossly limited. While there were some possibilities for higher education in the USA, there were none in the colonies and only the lowest positions in the civil service were open to qualified Blacks. The exploitation of native peoples by the colonising commercial companies in Africa were condemned. It was argued that the aim of the British capitalists in South Africa appeared to be the enslavement of Africans, who elsewhere were treated little better than serfs.

The existing conditions and upcoming settlement of the war in South Africa were discussed. The Conference sent a petition to Queen Victoria regarding conditions in southern Africa. Colonial Secretary Joseph Chamberlain, an arch-imperialist, replied in the name of the Queen that the government would not 'overlook the interests and welfare of the native races'. However, the British government, then involved in dispossessing the Boer settlers in South Africa of the lands they had taken from the Africans, had no such intentions.

The speakers naturally also turned their attention to the prevailing philosophies of social Darwinism (that is, the immutable hierarchy of races with Africans at the bottom of the pyramid) and the eugenics movement, which believed that the children of mixed race unions were 'mongrels' and inherited only the characteristics of the 'lower' of the parents. Human civilisation had begun in Africa, speakers asserted. Africans were not brutes – even when measured by Western standards, they had achieved success as scientists, artists and writers.

The speakers, who represented the whole of the Black world, included two African American women: Washington teacher Anna Cooper, who was to become the first Black woman to earn a doctoral degree at the Sorbonne, and another teacher, Anna Jones, from Kansas.

A final statement 'To the Nations of the World' was drafted by a committee which included W.E.B. Du Bois. It defined 'the problem of the twentieth century as the problem of the colour line' and demanded, *inter alia*, the 'cessation of racial discrimination'; responsible government for British colonies, and the ending of the oppression of 'American Negroes'.

The Conference set up a new organisation, the Pan-African Association (PAA), which aimed to:

1) secure civil and political rights for Africans and their descendants throughout the world
2) encourage friendly relations between Caucasians and Africans
3) encourage educational, industrial and commercial enterprise among Africans
4) influence legislation which concerned Black peoples
5) ameliorate the condition of 'oppressed negroes' in Africa, America, the British Empire and other parts of the world.

African Methodist Episcopal Zion Bishop Alexander Walters was elected president; Williams was elected general secretary; and Dr R.J. Colenso (son of the famous pro-African Bishop Colenso of Natal) was named general treasurer. The executive committee, which included representatives for the USA and Africa, also included two Black Londoners, John R. Archer (who would become the first elected mayor of a London borough in 1913) and Samuel Coleridge-Taylor, the composer. Branches were to be set up in the home countries of the Conference delegates. It was planned to hold general meetings every second year.

After attending the Anti-Slavery Conference in Paris later that year, Williams left for the West Indies to publicise the Pan-African Association. In Jamaica and Trinidad hundreds joined and many branches were formed. En route back to London he visited colleagues in the USA and addressed the Afro-American Council on the 'Union of the Two Negro Races'. Unfortunately no report of this intriguingly titled speech appears to exist. On his arrival he was confronted with the immediate need to resuscitate the Assocation, which had been declared defunct during his absence by some of the London-based officers.

In October 1901 Williams published the first issue of a monthly journal, *The Pan-African*, only the first issue of which has survived, though it is believed that Williams managed to publish six. Under the motto 'Liberty and Light', in this first issue Williams stated that the journal would act as the 'mouthpiece of the millions of Africans and their descendants' as without adequate representation in their governments, they could not make their voices heard. As 'members of the race are clubbed together, indicating so many helpless subjects fit for philanthropic sympathy' the journal would endeavour to present alternative perspectives. The journal carried short news items, copies of correspondence on a variety of issues with the British government, information on the war in South Africa and a transcript of the speech given by Acting Colonial Secretary Sydney Olivier at the founding of a Pan-African branch in Kingston, Jamaica in March that year. The short life of the journal reflected that of the PAA, which, supported mainly by students and other African and Caribbean transients, collapsed some time in 1902–3.

The following year, 1902, Williams published the text of two of his lectures as *The British Negro: A Factor in the Empire*, in which he emphasised the 'valuable service rendered by African and West Indian troops in the Boer [and other] wars'. He also stressed that West Indians had to pay tax, 'but had no voice in government'. He hoped 'that throughout the British Colonies a man's colour will form no hindrance to advancement … At present colour prejudice operates …'.

Having been called to the Bar in June 1902, Williams left for South Africa, where there was not one African lawyer. Despite numerous obstructions, he was admitted to the Cape Town Bar in October 1903, but he was boycotted by White lawyers. He quickly became involved in local politics: he was appointed to the board of the Cape Coloured community's Wooding's School, and elected president of the SA Citizens' Committee, which advocated equal civil and political rights for all South Africans and worked with the African Peoples' Organisation (APO) president Dr A. Abdurahman.

Probably because of the boycott which reduced his earning power, Williams returned to London and his family in 1905. He joined the National Liberal Club and the Fabian Society, which appointed him to its African Industrial Committee, probably established at Williams' instigation in July 1905. The Committee aimed to investigate 'the problems of the relations between black and white labour', especially in South Africa. Fully using his contacts in Fabian and Liberal circles, Williams addressed numerous public meetings throughout Britain, speaking on colonial issues. Seeking to emulate Dadabhai Naoroji, who had supported his activities, Williams now aimed to become Britain's first MP of African descent, but failed to win a nomination. However, in 1906, with the support of the Workers' Union, he won a seat as a Progressive on the London borough of Marylebone's Council. His attendance at the Council was irregular; his recorded contributions include support for improvements in public housing, and critcism of plans to increase the salaries of borough officials and of the suggestion to import Irish labourers for Marylebone projects.

Working from his law office at Essex Court, Williams was soon increasingly involved with Africans, African issues and African delegations to London. For example, in late 1905 he corresponded with the government regarding new legislation in the Transvaal which deprived Africans of titles to land. In 1906 he helped the deputation from the town of Cape Coast (Gold Coast) protesting against the imposition of direct taxation and a town council which was only partially elected. The following year he acted as intermediary between the Basuto chiefs and the British government. The chiefs had come to London to seek permission to buy land in their own country – the Boer/British Orange Free State, and compensation for cattle and horses taken from them by the British during the Boer War. For a while Williams served as the official representative of the APO. His aid to Liberian President Barclay, who was in London hoping to resolve the outstanding loan from British bankers, and boundary and trade disputes, resulted in an invitation to visit Liberia for its jubilee celebrations in January 1908. During his visit Williams addressed the National Bar Association. Britain's Consul Wallis used this address and misinformation regarding Williams' activities in South Africa to warn the Foreign Office that Williams was a danger 'to British interests in Africa and the Empire's tropical possessions generally'.

It is likely that Williams, as a Black barrister, encountered problems in earning a living in London. Equally possible is that as a critic of government, obstacles were put in his way. Whatever the reasons, Williams with his wife and four children, returned to Trinidad in 1908. He was admitted to the Bar and soon built a successful practice in Port-of-Spain and San Fernando. He continued speaking out on political issues, but because of intermittent ill health lived a quiet life. He died on 26 March 1911 of a kidney ailment.

Mrs Williams, who shortly after the funeral gave birth to their fifth child, lived in straitened circumstances: for example, she had to take in boarders. One of these was H.A. Nurse, whose son Malcolm, known later as GEORGE PADMORE, was to carry on the Pan-African tradition engendered by Henry Sylvester Williams.

MS

Further reading

Hooker, J.R., *Henry Sylvester Williams*, London, Rex Collings, 1975.
Mathurin, Owen Charles, *Henry Sylvester Williams and the Origins of the Pan-African Movement, 1869 – 1911*, Westport, Greenwood Press, 1976.
Sherwood, Marika, *Henry Sylvester Williams* (forthcoming).

Index

Abdurahman, Dr A 193
Aborigines' Rights Protection Society
    (ARPS) *see* Gold Coast ARPS
Adams, Grantley 120
Africa: Britain's Third Empire 155
Africa and the World 119, 153, 182
African Association (UK) 191
African Interpreter 143
African Liberation Committee 9
African Morning Post 187
African National Congress (ANC) 9,
    94, 129, 130, 132, 149
African Origin of Civilisation, The 41
African Peoples' Organisation (APO,
    South Africa) 193, 194
African Progress Union (UK) 3, 84
African Society (UK) 3
African Students' Association (USA)
    143
African Standard 182
African Times 87
African Times and Orient Review 2, 3, 4,
    76, 82
African Workers' Union (Nigeria) 181
Afro-American Council 193
Afro-American Liberty League 77
Afro-Asian Bloc 140
Afro-Asian Peoples' Solidarity
    Organisation (UK) 9
Afro-Shiraz Party (Zanzibar) 149, 150
Afro-Women's Centre (London) 74
Agbebi, Majola 14, 191

Aggrey House (London) 175
Algeria 65, 66, 68, 140, 141, 179
Ali, Dusé Mohamed 76, 82
All Peoples Congress (Sierra Leone)
    184
American Anti-Slavery Society 44
American Colonization Society 11, 13
American Committee on Africa 106
American Council for African
    Education (ACAE) 30
American Negro Academy 4, 48
Amin, Idi 151
Anglo-American Caribbean Committee
    186
Angola 140
*Anthology of New Black and Malagasy
    Poetry in French* 171
Anti-Slavery Society (UK) 3, 61
Archer, John 192
Arusha Declaration (Tanzania) 150
Asiatic-African United Front
    Committee (UK) 155
Association for the Advancement of
    Coloured People (UK) 74
Association des Etudiants Ouest-
    Africains (France) 169
Association des Etudiants du
    Rassemblement Démocratique
    Africain (France) 40
Association Générale des Etudiants
    Africains en Paris 40
At the Rendezvous of History 98

Atlantic Charter 135–6, 154
Azikiwe, Namdi 30, 58, 62, 117, 155, 182

Baghdad Pact 140
Baldwin, James 22
Bankole Bright, Herbert 174, 183
Basuto chiefs 194
Beauvoir, Simone de 68
Beyond the Boundary 97
Black Africa 42
Black Jacobins, The 96, 185
Black Man 79, 80
Black Power (Trinidad) 187
Black Skins White Masks 64
Black Star Line 69, 79
Blackman, Peter 135
Blake 37
Blake, William 26
Bloc Africain (Paris) 170
Bloc Démocratique Sénégalais 171
Bloc Progressif Sénégalais 171
Blyden, Edward 83
Botha, President P.W. 131, 132
Botsio, Kojo 126
Boukman 109, 110
Boumedienne 8, 10, 68
British Centre Against Imperialism 155
British Historians and the West Indies 188
British Negro 193
Browder, Earl 160
Brown, John 46, 112
Brown, Lawrence 159
Bruce, John E. 3, 4
Bunche, Ralph 62
Burnham, Forbes 166, 167
Burundi 149

Cahier d'un Retour au Pays Natal 21
Cairo 126
Cameroon 79, 140
Campaign Against Racial Discrimination (CARD, UK) 107

Campbell, Robert 37
Capitalism and Slavery 185
CARICOM 188
carnival (London) 103
Carpentier, Alejo 97
Césaire, Aimé 65, 97, 169
Chama cha Mapinduzi (CCM, Tanzania) 150, 151
Chants d'Ombre 171
Charter for Coloured Peoples (UK) 136
China 103, 145, 150
Christianity, Islam and the Negro Race 12
CIA 115
Civil Rights Act (USA) 107, 108
Civilisation or Barbarism: An Authentic Anthropology 42
Clarke, Dr Cecil Belfield 135
Clarkson, Thomas 54
Coleridge-Taylor, Samuel 2, 192
Colour and Democracy 50
Coloured Peoples' Organisation (SA) 130
Colenso, Dr R.J. 192
Comet 5
Comité Révolutionaire d'Unité et d'Action 8
Committee of African Organisations (CAO, UK) 102, 127
Committee of Afro-Asian Caribbean Organisations (UK) 102
Communist Parties: Egypt 140; France 171, 177; Great Britain (CPGB) 101, 103, 144, 181, 182; South Africa 129; USA (CPUSA) 100, 143, 152, 161
Conakry Declaration 179
Confédération Générale de Travail Africaine (CGTA, Guinea) 178
Conferences: Africa – New Perspectives (New York, 1944) 91; Afro-Asian Conference (Algeria, 1965) 9; Afro-Asian Conference (Conakry) 66; All African Peoples Conference (Accra,

1958) 17, 66, 92, 93, 114, 149, 156; All African Peoples Conference (Cairo) 17; All African Peoples Conference (Tunis) 66; Bandung Conference (Indonesia, 1955) 140, 161; Belgian–Congolese Round Table Conference (Brussels, 1960) 114; Casablanca Conference of Progressive African States 1961 9, 17, 179; Colonial Conference (USA 1945) 72; Conference of Africans in British West Africa (Accra, 1920) 84; Conference of Independent African States (Accra, 1958) 9, 156; Conference of Independent African States (Addis Ababa, 1960) 66, 145; Congress of African Historians (Dar-es-Salaam, 1965) 148; Congress of African Students (Paris) 127; Congress of Black Writers (Paris, 1956) 22, 41, 65; Congress of Black Writers (Rome, 1959) 24, 41; Cultural Congress (Havana) 22; First Congress of All African Writers (Dakar, 1976) 98; International Congress on the Evolution of Colonial Peoples (Paris, 1937) 170; League Against Imperialism (1929) 152; Maritzburg Conference (South Africa, 1961) 130; Non-Aligned Movement (Belgrade, 1961) 140; Pan-African Conference (1900) 4, 48, 191–2;
Pan-African Conference (1919) 49;
Pan-African Conference (1921) 50;
Pan-African Conference (1923) 50;
Pan-African Conference (1927) 50;
Pan-African Conference (1945) 50, 70, 73, 119, 136, 143, 144, 154, 183;
Pan-African Conference (1974) 98, 122, 165; Subject Peoples Conference (London, 1945) 154, 183; Tenth World Conference

Against the Hydrogen Bomb (Japan, 1964) 103; Tricontinental (Cuba, 1966) 18; Universal Races Congress (London, 1911) 48
Conference of British Missionary Societies 136
Congo 14, 79, 91, 121, 126, 127, 141, 145, 150
Congo, My Country 113
Congress Alliance (SA) 130
Congress of Racial Equality (CORE, USA) 107
Congress View 91
Constantine, Learie 95
Cooper, Anna 192
Council on African Affairs (CAA, USA) 30, 51, 71, 72, 91, 92, 93, 143, 160
Council to Promote Understanding between White and Coloured People (UK, 1929) 134
Council of Solidarity of Afro-Asian Peoples (UK) 17
Convention People's Party (CPP, Ghana) 144, 156
Crisis, The 49, 50
Crummell, Alexander 12, 49
Cuba 9, 107, 188
Cultural Unity of Black Africa 41
Cummings-John, Constance 93
Cummings-John, Ethnan 29, 32

Da Rocha, Moses 4
Dafora, Asadata 30
Dahomey 79, 172
Damas, Léon 21, 23
Davis, Benjamin 73
Decision on Africa 93
Delafosse, Maurice 170
Delany, Catherine Richards 34
Delany, Martin 12, 45
Dessalines 110, 112
Diagne, Blaise 49, 169
Diop, Alioune 23, 171
Diop, Birago 23

Discourse sur le Colonialisme 24
Domingo, W.A. 77
Douglass, Frederick 34
Du Bois, W.E.B. 34, 41, 77, 78, 92, 94, 103, 119, 154, 155, 192
Dusk of Dawn 50

Egypt 8, 156
Egypt's Liberation: The Philosophy of Revolution 140
Encyclopaedia Africana 93, 94
Equiano, Olaudah 26
Ethiopia 118, 120, 130, 182, 188
Ethiopia Unbound 83
L'Etudiant Noir, 21, 22

Fabian Colonial Bureau (UK) 60, 61, 62, 175
Fabian Society 193
Faisal, Prince 125
Fanon, Frantz 22, 23, 34, 35, 98, 164, 171, 189
Fanti Confederation (Gold Coast) 88
Faruq, King 139
Federation of the West Indies 187
Federation of Workers' Unions of Guinea 177
Ferris, William 3
Festival of Negro Arts, Dakar 24
Ford, James 153
Frederick Douglass' Paper 45
Free Officers (Egypt) 138, 139
Freedomways 92
Frelimo (Mozambique) 149
Frobenius, Leo 170
From Columbus to Castro 189
Front Libération Nationale (FLN, Algeria) 8, 9, 65, 68, 140

Garrison, William Lloyd 45
Garvey, Amy Ashwood 76, 77, 95, 154, 174
Garvey, Amy Jacques 79
Garvey, Marcus 3, 14, 49, 69, 70, 74, 95, 103, 123, 164, 175

Gold Coast/Ghana 73, 87, 88, 93, 94, 98, 106, 115, 121, 125, 141, 145, 148, 156, 175, 179, 181, 184, 188, 194
Gold Coast Aborigines' Rights Protection Society (GCARPS) 71, 82, 118, 120
Gold Coast Chronicle 82
Gold Coast Echo 82
Gold Coast Native Institutions 83
Gouvernement Provisoire de la République Algérienne 8, 9
Groundings with my Brothers, The 164
Guèye, Lamine 170, 171, 172
Guinea 9, 93, 141, 145
Gumede, Josiah 3
Guyana 166
Guyanese Sugar Plantations in the Late 19th Century 166

Harlem Renaissance 21, 69
Harris, Wilson 97
Hayes, Roland 3
Hayford, Adelaide Casely 31
Hayford, J.E. Casely 2, 14
Here I Stand 161
History of the Guyanese Working People 166
History of Negro Revolt 96
History of the People of Trinidad and Tobago 188
Holly, Revd J. 36, 191
Horton, James 29, 83
House Committee on Un-American Activities 93, 161
How Europe Underdeveloped Africa 165
Hughes, Langston 169
Hunt, James 87
Hunton, Alphaeus 30, 73, 101, 104, 126
Hunton, Dorothy 90, 93

Independent Labour Party (UK) 95, 154, 183
Indépendents d'Outre-Mer (Paris) 171

India 106

Interesting Narrative of the Life of Olaudah Equiano, The 54

International African Friends of Abyssinia (IAFA, UK) 71, 95, 118, 153

International African Opinion 96, 119, 153

International African Service Bureau (IASB, UK) 29, 71, 95, 118, 153, 160, 182

International Monetary Fund (IMF) 151

International Trade Union Committee of Negro Workers (ITUCNW) 152, 153, 181

Inward Hunger 188, 189

Israel 9, 139, 140, 141

Islamic Conference Organisation 180

Jagan, Cheddi 166

Jamaica 79, 164, 165, 187, 194

James, C.L.R. 22, 71, 77, 80, 118, 119, 135, 150, 152, 153, 154, 156, 160, 164, 165, 167, 185

James, Selma 97, 99

Johnson, Revd James 191

Jones, Anna 192

Jones, Arthur Creech 175

Jones, Claudia 74, 93, 126, 127, 163

Kazume, Sheikh Abeid 149, 150

Kasavubu 115

Katanga 115, 116

Kaunda, Kenneth 94, 148

Kennedy, John F. 107

Kenya 79, 91, 93, 188

Kenyatta, Jomo 60, 71, 91, 95, 117, 118, 120, 122, 126, 149, 153, 185

Key, The 135

King, Revd Martin Luther 102, 103

Klerk, F.W. de 132

Koinange, Mbiyu 149

Korea 161

Kunene, Raymond 104

League Against Imperialism (LAI) 152, 153, 175, 182

League of Coloured People (UK) 29, 30, 60, 62, 96, 134–7, 160

League of Nations 78, 80

Leclerc, General Charles 111

Letters on the Political Conditions of the Gold Coast 88

Leys, Norman 62

Liberator 44

Liberia 11, 12, 13, 50, 73, 74, 78, 144, 156, 194

Liberian Herald 11

Libya 8, 156, 179

Libyan Institute (USA) 117

Life of Captain Cipriani, The 95

Life and Struggle of Negro Workers 153

Life and Times of Frederick Douglass 45

Liverpool 120, 137

Locke, Alan 169

London Corresponding Society 55

Love, Dr Robert 76

Lumumba, Patrice 25, 66, 67, 128, 141, 145, 179

Luthuli, Albert 106

Macaulay, Frank 181

Makonnen, Ras T. 60, 71, 73, 125, 153, 154, 156, 185

Malcolm X 107, 164, 167

Mali 141, 145

Manchester 119, 120

Mandela, Winnie 130

Manley, Norman 103, 120

Manning, Sam 70, 71, 74

March on Washington 102, 107

Mariners, Renegades and Castaways 96

McKay, Claude 169

Mboya, Tom 148, 149, 156

Mecca 125

Medical Geography of the West Coast of Africa 86

Menelik, Emperor 120

Micheaux, Oscar 159

Milliard, Dr Peter 119

Minty Alley 95
Mobutu 115
Moise 110
Monolulu, Prince 118
Montgomery bus boycott 105
Moody, Harold 29, 96, 175
Moore, Richard B. 4
Moore, Tufuhin G.E. 118
Morocco 8, 156, 179
Moscow 103, 152
Mpolo, Maurice 115
Mouvement National Congolais
    (MNC) 114
Mouvement pour la Démocratie en
    Algérie 10
Mouvement pour Triomphe des
    Liberées Démocratiques (Algeria) 8
Mouvement Socialist Africain 171
Movement Against Imperialism (UK)
    155
Movimento Popular de Libertação de
    Angola (MPLA) 9, 16
Mozambique 149
Mugabe, Robert 167
Muhammad, Elijah 124, 125
Murumbi, Joseph 149
My Bondage and My Freedom 45

Naoroji, Dadabhai 191, 193
Napoleon Bonaparte 111, 112
Nardal, Paulette and Jane 169
*Narrative of the Life of Frederick
    Douglass* 45
Nasser 149
Nation of Islam 124
National Association for the
    Advancement of Colored People
    (NAACP, UK) 49, 50, 108, 135
National Congress of British West
    Africa (NCBWA) 71, 79, 82, 84,
    174
National Council of Civil Liberties
    (NCCL, UK) 61, 175
National Council of the Colony of
    Sierra Leone 183

National Council of Nigeria and the
    Cameroons (NCNC) 5, 62
National Negro Congress (NNC, USA)
    90, 91
National Party (Egypt) 138
Native African Union of America 4
Négritude 21, 169, 170
Negro 13
Negro in the Caribbean, The 186
Negro Welfare Association (UK) 135,
    160, 182
Negro Worker 153 181
Negro World 4, 77, 79
Nehru, Jawaharlal 140
Neto, Agostinho 16
New Africa (UK) 144
New Africa (USA) 91
Niagara Movement (USA) 49
Nigeria 79, 91, 98, 106, 125, 175
Nigerian Daily Telegraph 5
Nigerian Progress Union (UK) 70, 174
Nkomo, Joshua 102, 148
Nkrumah, Kwame 9, 14, 51, 66, 71,
    73, 84, 92, 93, 94, 96, 106, 114,
    116, 118, 119, 120, 121, 122, 125,
    140, 149, 155, 156, 179, 183
Nkrumah and the Ghana Revolution 96
Nobel Peace Prize 107, 132
Nollekens, Joseph 26
Non-Aligned Movement 9, 17, 140
North Star, The 34, 45
Nyasaland 79
Nyerere, Julius 97, 126, 164

Obote, Milton 126
*Official Report of the Niger Valley
    Exploring Party* 37
Oge 109
Okito, Jozeph 115
Oliver, Sydney 193
Organisation of African Unity (OAU)
    9, 10, 17, 121, 126, 130, 141, 143,
    145, 147, 151, 179, 188
Organization of Afro-American Unity
    (OAAU) 125–6, 127, 128

Organization of American States 188
Orizu, Nwafor 30
Osborne, Herman 72
Oxford Union Debate 127

Padmore, George 14, 29, 60, 62, 71, 73, 80, 93, 95, 96, 117, 118, 119, 120, 121, 126, 143, 149, 182, 185, 186, 194
Palestine 141
Panaf Service (UK) 120
Pan-Africa 117, 121
Pan-Africa or Communism? 155
Pan-African 2, 193
Pan-African Association (UK) 192
Pan-African Federation (UK) 118, 119, 120, 143, 154, 155, 183
Pan-African Freedom Movement of East and Central Africa (PAFMECA) 130, 149
Pan-African News Agency 154
Pan-Africanist Congress of Azania 9
Pankhurst, Sylvia 121
Parti Démocratique Guinée 178, 179
Parti de Peuple Algérien 7
Parti du Regroupement Africain (PRA) 171
Parti Socialiste (Senegal) 172
Partido Africano para a Independência da Guiné e Cabo-Verde (PAIGC) 16, 17, 18, 19
Paul Robeson, Negro 159
Peace Information Center (New York) 51
Peace Pledge Union (UK) 59
People's National Movement (PNM Trinidad) 187
Phelps Stokes Fund 58
Philadelphia Negro 48
Phylon 50
Pizer, Dorothy 96, 154
Pompidou, Georges 170
Powell, Adam Clayton 71
Pre-colonial Black Africa 41
Présence Africaine 21, 22, 23, 40, 41, 127, 171

Prince, Mary 26
Principia of Ethnology: The Origin of Races and Colour 38
Profintern (Red International of Labour Unions) 152
Progressive Party (USA) 160
Prosser, Gabriel 112

Rabemananjara, Jacques 23
Radical Democratic Party (Sierra Leone) 184
Ramsay, James 54
Randolph, A. Philip 106
Rassemblement Démocratique Africain (RDA) 177, 178
Rassemblement National Démocratique (RND) 41, 171
Revolutionary Command Council (Egypt) 139
Revue de Monde Noir, La 169
Reynolds, Joshua 26
Rhodesia 149, 188
Rigaud 110
Rivonia Trial (SA) 131
Robben Island prison 131
Robeson, Eslanda Goode 100, 126, 159
Robeson, Paul 30, 70, 71, 91, 92, 93, 96, 100, 103, 118, 126
Roosevelt, Eleanor 31, 72
Rustin, Bayard 106
Rwanda 149

Sankoh, Laminah 119
Sarbah, Mensah 14
Sartre, Jean-Paul 68
Scarborough, Professor W.S. 191
Scholes, Theophilus 117
Scottish Council on African Questions 147
Sekyi, Kobina 3, 4, 120
Senegal 79, 172, 179
Senghor, Léopold Sédar 20, 21, 22, 23, 41, 144
Sharpe, Granville 27, 54, 55

Sharpeville massacre 9, 130
Sierra Leone 12, 13, 55, 79, 144, 188
Sierra Leone People's Party 31, 32, 183
Sierra Leone Weekly News 14
Sierra Leone Women's Movement 31, 32
Socialist Workers Party (USA) 96, 125
Sociology of the Yoruba, The 59
Solanke, Ladipo 29, 59, 60, 71, 73, 80,
    84
Souls of Black Folk, The 48
South Africa 9, 10, 79, 91, 102, 106,
    131, 140, 150, 193
South African Indian Congress 130
South Commission 151
Southern Africa Development
    Community (SADC) 151
Southern Christian Leadership
    Conference (SCLC, USA) 106, 107
Soyinka, Wole 165
Spotlight on Africa 91
Spanish Civil War 160
Stevens, Hope 72
Stock, Dinah 121
Stop South Africa's Crimes 92
Straker, Judge David 191
Stride Towards Freedom 106
Student Non-violent Co-ordinating
    Committee (SNCC) 107, 108
Sudan 172, 179
Suez Canal 140
Suez Crisis (1956) 140
Sukarno, President 140
Suppression of the African Slave Trade 48
SWAPO 9
Syria 141

Tambo, Oliver 130
Tanganyika African National Union
    (TANU) 98, 147–8, 149, 150
Tanzania 98, 164, 165
Tete-Ansa, W. 4
*Thoughts and Sentiments on the Evil and
    Wicked Traffic and Commerce of the
    Human Species, Humbly Submitted to
    the Inhabitants of Great Britain* 26

Touré, Sékou 126, 130, 145
Toward the African Revolution 66
Towards Colonial Freedom 144
Tragédie du Roi Christophe, La 24
Transvaal 194
Treason Trials (SA) 130
Tribute to the Negro, A 87
Trinidad 97, 186, 192
Tropiques 23
Trotsky, Leon 96
*Truth about the West African Land
    Question, The* 83
Tshombe, Moise 115
Tubman, President William 130, 179
Tunisia 140, 156
Tutu, Archbishop Desmond 132

Uganda 79, 97, 140, 149, 151
Umma Party (Zanzibar) 149
Une Saison au Congo 25
UNESCO 41
Unkhonto we Sizwe 130
Union Minière (Katanga) 115
Union of Students of African Descent
    (London) 174
United Arab Republic (UAR) 9, 139,
    141, 179
United Gold Coast Convention
    (UGCC) 144
United Liberation Front of Guinea and
    Cape Verde 17
United Nations (UN) 19, 51, 66, 91, 92,
    93, 115, 116, 120, 121, 126, 131,
    136, 141, 145, 148, 151, 154, 161,
    171, 179
United Negro Improvement Association
    (UNIA) 49, 69, 76–80, 123, 143
United Progressive Party (Sierra Leone)
    183
*United West Africa at the Bar of the
    Family of Nations* 175
Unity Theatre (London) 160
Upper Volta 172
USSR 103, 115, 140, 145, 150, 160,
    161, 162, 179

Vietnam 108, 128, 145, 150
Vindication of the Negro Race, A 12
Voting Rights Act (USA) 108
Voix de l'Afrique Noire, La 40

Wafd 138
Wallace-Johnson, I.T.A. 29, 30, 62, 153
Walters, Bishop Alexander 192
Washington, Booker T. 3, 14, 49, 76, 82, 191
Welfare of Coloured People in the UK Advisory Committee 137
West Africa 59
West African Countries and Peoples 87
West African National Secretariat (WANS) 84, 143
West African Pilot 5, 63
West African Reporter 14
West African Review 60
West African Students' Union (WASU, UK) 29, 59, 60, 71, 84, 96, 135, 143, 160, 174–6
West African Youth League (WAYL) 30, 181, 182
West Indian Gazette 74, 102
West Indies National Council (WINC, USA) 72

Western Saharan Sahrawi Arab Democratic Republic 180
Wilkerson, Doxey 73, 91
Williams, Eric 95, 97, 119
Williams, Henry Sylvester 2, 98, 152
Winston, Henry 103
Wood, Samuel R. 71
Working People's Alliance (Guyana) 167
World and Africa, The 50
World Federation of Trade Unions (WFTU) 136, 177, 178, 183
World Revolution 96, 154
Wretched of the Earth, The 67, 68
Wright, Richard 23, 156

Yemen 141
Yergan, Max 91, 92, 116
Young Egypt Party 138

Zaire 149
Zambia 94
Zanzibar 149
Zimbabwe 167
Zimbabwe African National Union (ZANU) 9
Zimbabwe African People's Union (ZAPU) 9